Black Feathers

Black Feathers

A Pocket Racer Sails
The Singlehanded TransPac

Robert & Jeanne Crawford

iUniverse, Inc.
New York   Bloomington

Black Feathers
A Pocket Racer Sails The Singlehanded TransPac

Front Cover Photo courtesy of Latitude 38 *Magazine/LaDonna Bubak*
Back Cover Photo courtesy of Winston Crawford

iUniverse books may be ordered through booksellers or by contacting:

iUniverse
1663 Liberty Drive
Bloomington, IN 47403
www.iuniverse.com
1-800-Authors (1-800-288-4677)

Because of the dynamic nature of the Internet, any Web addresses or links contained in this book may have changed since publication and may no longer be valid.

ISBN: 978-1-4401-9196-1 (sc)
ISBN: 978-1-4401-9197-8 (ebk)

Printed in the United States of America

iUniverse rev. date: 01/22/2010

Dedication

My wife, Jeanne, and I are pleased and honored to dedicate this book to my parents, Bud and Jeanne Crawford, the most inspiring supporters of my 1994 TransPac experience. Without their enthusiasm and encouragement, I would never have made it to the starting line of that race. In spite of the fact they both died several years before *Black Feathers* sailed the TransPac, Jeanne and I came to realize their enduring spirits had also provided the inspiration for the 2008 race.

Acknowledgements

To the many sailors of the Singlehanded Sailing Society who continue to openly and honestly provide any information about sailing alone that the enthusiastic learner is willing to accept.

To John Hill, an old salt and fellow TransPacer, who generously gave of his time and expertise to help *Black Feathers* through her evolution from a daysailer to a pocket racer. What is all the more amazing is that he did this thinking the whole time that Robert was a bit crazy.

To Nicolas Odlum—his calm supporting manner made Robert feel he had a true advocate at his harbor, South Beach, where Nicolas worked as they prepared *Black Feathers*. We always valued his thoughts and manner.

To Dr. Charlie McKelvey and Dr. Phil Grossman, as well as Winston Crawford, for the web blogs they provided that allowed countless numbers of friends and enthusiasts, some as far away as Australia, to experience the race each day as *Black Feathers* made her way to Kauai.

To Winston Crawford, for his many cherished photographs and numerous hours spent manipulating those photos, and others, so they could be published in this book.

To our editors, Bryan Gardner, Joan Henderson, Judy Molloy, and Neil and Doris Selman for their dedication to our project. Their patience and expertise are most appreciated.

Purpose

This book was written with this hope and purpose:
To inspire the common sailor
to hold fast their dreams of going to sea
in a small but seaworthy craft of their choosing, and
to provide some advice as to how it can be done.

This book tells the story of how a basic small sailboat, a Cal 20, evolved from a daysailer to a pocket TransPac racer. It reflects one skipper's experience with one boat. Our hope is that it will provide some useful information and ideas to stimulate thought, further investigation—and adventure.

Although this book was written as an account of one sailor's adventure and intended to provide a guide to small boat preparation for the Singlehanded TransPac Race, it should be noted the Singlehanded Sailing Society was not involved in its writing and takes no responsibility for the subject matter or interpretations. The authors remain solely responsible for the content of this publication. Author Robert Crawford reminds each skipper it is their continuing responsibility to evaluate all opinions and suggestions offered as to the appropriateness for their particular vessel and personal capabilities.

Table of Contents

The solo sailor always refers to "we."
The "we" is the sailor
AND his boat.
The solo sailor sails alone,
But in the company of his vessel.
They depend on each other.
They become a crew of two.
Hence the "we."

Prologue

By 11 p.m. we were experiencing our first significant taste of heavy weather. Our desired course: To head directly toward Kauai at about 240°, but this caused the boat to slam too hard into the waves so I let her fall off to the south. Still screaming along at just a little over 7 knots, with two reefs in our mainsail, the 25 - 30 knot wind left us cold and wet. Water regularly came over the bow, spraying the dome and cockpit. Unfortunately, a small but significant stream of this water also made its way under the dome hatch and sprayed the inside of the tiny cabin. For the first time in the race things were getting wet and I was unable to prevent it.

Although heading more southerly than I wanted, I felt the best and safest plan would be to simply hold my course and hang on. It was like "sailing before the storm," although we certainly were not dealing with a storm. I mentally ran through the various heavy weather tactics one plans for, concluding that as long as the boat was under control, not over-stressed and the Monitor Windvane steered well, we'd carry on. I didn't want to do anything to reduce our speed as long as we maintained control. My reasoning here—in a race speed is obviously critical, but also when you are running with the waves astern, you want to sail fast enough that they don't break into your cockpit.

Because it had become wet, dark and nasty in the cockpit, I stayed all closed up in the cabin. I distributed some of the inside weight around to keep the heeling angle of the boat reasonably comfortable. For my own state of mind, and in case anything unforeseen happened, I had the life raft and abandon ship bag ready to go. The amount of emergency stuff in the ditch bag made it awkward and heavy, so I culled out all but the absolute essentials. With this done, little remained for me to do but try to enjoy the ride and attempt to control the wetness.

The night passed with the boat whizzing along and spray regularly engulfing the boat. With towels stuffed into every suspicious area around the hatch cover, the spray on the inside gradually subsided and the situation became stable.

As the night gave way to yet another overcast dawn, I felt things getting colder in spite of our more southerly position. I spent the morning beneath the dome in my folding chair as it gave my knees a chance to relax in a normal sitting posture. The dome, well situated, allowed me to enjoy the view and follow the boat's progress as I watched the AIS plotting any oncoming vessels. So there I sat with my head in the dome, my body supported by the chair and handrails—the miles passing by. During the chilly, overcast morning, I observed most of the wetness I now experienced appeared to be due to condensation rather than the intrusive spray of the night before. The roughness of the waves seemed reduced although the wind strength remained unchanged. All in all it seemed like a promising day as we continued to make great time with a jib and double-reefed main.

As the day progressed, the boat did well and we made good mileage. Although I thought it might make things a lot rougher, I wanted to get more westerly so I adjusted our course from its slightly too-southerly route to a straight shot for Kauai. *Black Feathers* held her speed even though she endured more slaps against her hull and the now regular spray across her bow and over the dome. I, however, experienced a smoother ride than anticipated. Each time I looked aft, I couldn't help but be thankful for such a reliable and durable windvane that held its course impeccably. There is nothing like a good self-steering device.

By evening, things imitated the night before. This would be another "night of survival." Nothing to do but sit there, monitor things, try to control the wetness and hang on—too rough to read, too wet to practice my concertina and too uncertain to sleep. The life raft and ditch bag were again moved into position for quick access. Sitting there, I could feel frustration creeping over me. Things weren't going as I had hoped, and as I became more and more fatigued, my spirits began to sag. The boat was a mess. Supplies were everywhere. Little room remained for me. I was getting weary, and most of all, everything was becoming wet. This wasn't pretty. I felt I had planned better. Where did I go wrong?

Fortunately, the frustration did not turn to despair. As I sat there, a bit like a pouting child, I came to realize it made no difference if "it wasn't pretty." So what if things got wet? If all I had to complain about was that everything got wet, it didn't mean the situation had to be deemed insurmountable. All things would eventually dry—and long before we arrived in Hawaii. As long as the boat remained secure and we were moving through the water with things working, I had nothing to complain about or apologize for. In fact, unless I told anyone how wet things got, no one would ever know. What a revelation! Within minutes my attitude turned around and my sense of confidence returned. This renewed confidence allowed me to sit back and accept the situation, embracing just how pleased I felt being there, even as uncomfortable as it was.

The Singlehanded TransPac Race (SHTP) consists of numerous solo sailors like myself who have, at least for a while, put their regular lives aside to partake of an adventure. What is the attraction? And why do so many racers return to do it again—and again?

Although it came to life in the summer of 1978, the SHTP was conceived in 1977 after the successful completion of the first Singlehanded Farallones Race.

Cold, barren and inhospitable are terms often used to describe the rocks known as the Farallone Islands that sit some 30 miles outside the Golden Gate Bridge. The largest of this group is the Southeast Farallone Island, home to an impressive array of seabirds, the Great White Sharks and about eight research scientists. On a clear day from the hills of San Francisco, you can usually see this island with its serenely rotating lighthouse beacon, but in a small boat on an average day, the land mass doesn't start coming into view until you are about six or seven miles away.

The island emerges from the horizon, first as a small knoll, but given time develops into a craggy outcropping of weathered rock. You begin rounding the island along the windward side and quickly begin to believe the wind and current are conspiring to bring you uncomfortably close to the unforgiving rocky shoreline.

The ride out to the island has been a long upwind battle, and you hope your present tack will be far enough offshore to carry you beyond the island, where you can then do a final gybe that will put you on a tack to carry you back to the Golden Gate. A sense of accomplishment and relief fills your mind as you complete the rounding and head for home. It's all downwind from here and can become as lively a ride as you dare to make it.

Those first Farallones singlehanders faced wild and blustery conditions forcing most of the racers to drop out. For the 14 finishers, however, it proved to be a thrilling ride and a challenge they would look forward to tackling again. The race was considered such a great success by the sailing community that even the naysayers offered congratulations to the gutsy and tenacious finishers, as well as to the race's bold sponsor, George Sigler.

In 1974, George Sigler and Charlie Gore, ex-naval aviators with a passionate commitment to promoting survival at sea, sailed a 16' inflatable Zodiac, rigged with a small sail, from San Francisco to Hawaii. The 56-day odyssey being a test of their concepts of what was necessary for survival at sea. For nourishment, they took no water and only six pounds of candy. They survived on their solar still for water, and the judicious rationing of their carbohydrate diet.

Following their daring experiment, they opened a survival-at-sea business in Oakland, California known as Survival and Safety Design to serve the ocean cruising and racing community.

George had previously organized some local singlehanded races and sponsored them through the newly-organized Singlehanded Sailing Society (he served as the first SSS commodore).

With the first Farallones race firmly anchored as an ongoing Society event, it seemed natural to follow it the next year with the first SHTP.

The theme of the first Singlehanded Sailing Society seminars I attended in 1991 seemed to be directed toward how to make the boat you had seaworthy, safe and efficient for singlehanding. That atmosphere nurtures enthusiasm and creative thinking which ultimately results in seaworthy boats handled by effective, prudent singlehanders. However, over the years I sensed a change among the singlehanders in what they deemed an adequate boat for safe offshore singlehanding. In the past few years there have been some truly amazing developments in boat and sail design, navigation, weather tracking, communications and electronics in general. For some potential singlehanders, the financial commitment required to fulfill what they saw as the Society's necessary requirements for safe singlehanding began to quickly move beyond their reach. This troubled me, and led me to follow a different course as I looked for my next TransPac boat, and made plans for her preparation.

My wife, Jeanne, and I have attempted to take you through our experience with the 2008 Singlehanded TransPac Race. Our hope is that our adventure will allow the event to come to life in your mind and provide some insightful thoughts should you endeavor to make a similar journey. The third portion of the book addresses the more technical aspects of small boat preparation presented in simple guide format.

Out The Gate

PART I

Black Feathers—A Pocket Racer Sails The Singlehanded TransPac

Chapter 1

The Singlehanded TransPac Race

Amid fears by the press and many local sailors that a potential disaster was in the making, the first Singlehanded TransPac Race set sail from San Francisco to Kauai in May of 1978. No disaster occurred and the race was deemed a great success.

The Singlehanded TransPac Race celebrated their 30th year anniversary in 2008. At this writing, approximately 296 racers have sailed out of San Francisco, by themselves, on this race since 1978. Among the boats have been some of the hottest vessels created for demolishing sailing records, but also included have been a number of boats fashioned for the common man with his simple dream of sailing alone to Hawaii. The racers are generally ordinary men and women taking on a very out-of-the-ordinary endeavor. Although a few sail the race with the specific goal of setting a record, most do not. Instead, they sail the race to achieve a sense of personal accomplishment that may mean very little to others but is of extreme importance to the sailor.

The Singlehanded TransPac is a biennial event occurring on even numbered years. The objective is simply to sail your boat as fast as you can from San Francisco to beautiful Hanalei Bay in Kauai, a distance of approximately 2,200 miles. You must be alone and you cannot use your engine. In fact, prior to departure the Race Committee seals your engine shaft. The boats must be seaworthy vessels ranging from 20′ to 60′ in length and can be either monohulls or multihulls. You must arrive in Hanalei Bay by the 21st day of the race unless there is that rare extension due to a lack of wind. Most boats that have done the race have been in the mid-30 to mid-40 foot range.

The fastest crossing was accomplished in 1998 by Steve Fossett in his 60′ trimaran, *Lakota*. He finished in 7d 22h. Peter Hogg's 40′ trimaran, *Aotea*, took Line Honors in 1994 with a crossing of 8d 20h, a new record at the time. Among monohulls, Ray Thayer, in his 60′ Brewer, *Wild Thing*, did the fastest crossing in 1996. His time of 10d 22h broke the record Stan Honey set in the 1994 race of 11d 10h in his Cal 40, *Illusion*. Stan Honey's performance still stands as the fastest corrected time of all Singlehanded TransPac contestants. Corrected time is the actual time altered by the boat's handicap.

Although not the most popular group of boats for the race, the small boats have held their own in the TransPac. Over the years, boats of 25' or less have won the TransPac's coveted trophy as the overall winner on corrected time once, but three times they have been second, once third, and three times fourth. The best performance of a small boat based on corrected time has to go to Doug Graham in 1996, when on his Pacific Dolphin 24, *Big Dot;* he sailed into Hanalei Bay in an elapsed time of 16d 19h. With his handicap of 278, his corrected time is the ninth fastest in Singlehanded TransPac history.

The elapsed finishing times for boats of 25' or less are as follows (includes the 2008 finishers): (Boats are listed in order of size—smallest to largest)

Cal 20	-	19d 21h
Wilderness 21 (2)	-	18d 7 h and 18d 16h
Santana 22	-	17d 14h
Dana 24	-	19d 5h
Pacific Dolphin 24	-	16d 19h
Moore 24 (8)	-	14d 4h to 17d 7h
Capri 25	-	16d 12h
Golden Gate 25	-	18d 7 h
Olson 25	-	16d 1h
Merit 25 (3)	-	15d 13h to 18d 2h
Freedom 25	-	20d 19h

These small compact pocket racers have shown they can be effective competitors in the Singlehanded TransPac. They will arrive after many of the other contenders, but the larger, faster racers cannot rest too comfortably until these potential spoilers sail into Hanalei Bay.

Chapter 2
Some Personal Sailing Experience

Boats have always been a big part of my life, but sailing has not. My first sailing experience came when I bought a 16' daysailer at the age of 30 and took it out on a lake near Dallas, Texas. As it turned out, it was a good starter boat for it had some durable and well-positioned hardware, plus the mast and boom were rather hefty for such a small craft. The mainsail could be reefed and this proved invaluable once I moved my family from Dallas to the San Francisco Bay Area and had to deal with the windy Bay conditions.

Most of my early boating was done on lakes and such landlocked bodies of water do not so easily allow for dreaming of that big voyaging adventure. Once I found myself in the Bay Area, I saw the Golden Gate not as a gateway to the Bay but as my gateway to the ocean, and once "out the Gate," it is easy to visualize a voyage to anywhere. Once you visualize your dream, it is only life's material issues that must be overcome.

From the 16' daysailer, I moved up to an Ericson 32, *Now or Never,* for me the perfect name and sentiment. Much of the labor to prepare this boat for cruising or a TransPac had already been done. I took possession of *Now or Never* in September of 1991 and attended my first Singlehanded Sailing Society (SSS) meeting the next month. Beginning in October of the year before the race, the SSS puts on a series of informative lectures/ seminars pertaining to the TransPac experience and requirements. They cover one or more sailing topics a month from October through June of the following year. It was a great way to get started with *Now or Never.*

Very much uncertain of what to expect from this group of singlehanded sailors, I had significant feelings of insecurity. I questioned the appropriateness of my even being at this first seminar, not only because of my limited sailing experience, but also due to my uncertainties with my newly-acquired sailboat. Was she seaworthy in the eyes of this group? Would she prove appropriate for singlehanding? Could I develop my skills to the level needed to participate in this society's events? Walking into a strange group of sailors with these feelings is not comforting!

But such fears were unfounded for I quickly realized that this group was out to promote singlehanded sailing done in a safe manner. They didn't try to impress you by intimidation. Instead, I found a wealth of information available to all who were interested, and that a variety of singlehanded races were scheduled to allow you to test out things and expand your horizons.

Seven months after purchasing the boat, I headed out the Gate for the first time to do the Singlehanded Farallones Race, and to this day I have never been so nervous about an event. But being nervous can be a good thing. It motivates you to plan things out and prepare yourself and your boat. The race went well and I found one quickly grows in ability and confidence with each event undertaken.

—◆—

It would turn into be a beautiful day that 27th day of July, the start of the 1992 TransPac, but it began with a chilly, overcast marine layer covering the Bay as the clock ticked down to the gun. That morning, I walked the docks and spoke with several of the skippers as they gathered with family and friends for their final goodbyes. Everyone could feel the excitement in the air. Each skipper had fulfilled the Race Committee requirements. Given the fact all the skippers were officially "ready" for the race, I observed an interesting contrast—some were confident and serene, while others were frantically scurrying around completing last-minute tasks. All were pleased to have you come aboard to view their boats. I stood on the race deck, watching the flags go up and jumped when the gun went off as the racers maneuvered for their favored spot to cross the starting line. As their boats headed toward the Gate and their adventure got underway, I realized I would be among the starters of the 1994 TransPac.

The next two years passed quickly as I gained much experience in handling my boat offshore. For self-steering I opted for a Monitor Windvane and enjoyed a great weekend with my dad mounting it onto the stern of *Now or Never*. The LongPac Race in August 1993 served as my required TransPac qualifier. The TransPac requires each skipper to sail a solo voyage or race of at least 400 nautical miles (nm) extending a minimum of 100 miles offshore. This qualifier does not allow use of an engine, and must be done in the boat that is to be sailed on the TransPac. The LongPac (Great Pacific Longitudinal Race) serves as the TransPac qualifier for many racers from the Bay Area.

Before I knew it, the 1994 TransPac was upon us. That year proved wonderful for me because I sailed the TransPac; and as well, it turned out to be a great year for the TransPac Race because of exceptional accomplishments by various skippers who participated.

Peter Hogg of the multihull, *Aotea*, set the multihull record. Stan Honey of the Cal 40, *Illusion*, set the monohull record that still stands as the fastest corrected time record. Also Reed Overshiner in his International Folkboat, *Reliance*, turned in a stellar performance and still holds the record of the third fastest corrected time. The windy conditions that year enabled those expert racers to perform to their true potential, turning in some outstanding results.

Adding to the 1994 TransPac adventure, I experienced a great bonus by sailing *Now or Never* back to San Francisco. We participated in many races with the SSS over the next few years. My son, Winston, often sailed with me to the Farallones, and my daughter, Kendra, at age 16, joined me on the 1997 LongPac Race. I am pleased to report that after four and a half days stuck on a boat with her dad, she was still speaking to me when we sailed back into port. In 1999, a close friend, Wayne Crutcher, and I doublehanded *Now or Never* to Kauai. Life's other commitments seemed to be compromising my sailing, so in late 1999 I reluctantly sold the boat. Sad to see her go, I felt very pleased with what we had accomplished together.

Far less than a year after I sold *Now or Never*, I came to terms with the fact I NEEDED another boat. The need for a boat seems to be more a need of a project with a possible future goal. The many parts of the project include the fun of sailing and the development of those skills, the challenge of fixing up a boat and dealing with the many possible technologies involved—and always the dream of such adventures as the TransPac. For me, it doesn't get any better than that.

In 2000, I began splitting my time between my newly-acquired mountain home in Mi Wuk Village near Yosemite, and the San Francisco Bay Area where I worked, so any boat I would consider buying had to be one that would not occupy too much time. My budget was nominal—it was not minimal. The criteria I set for my next boat would be: 1) It would cost less than $7,000. 2) It would be in the low 20s in length (a boat needs to be at least 20' to sail with the SSS). 3) The maintenance and harbor fees would be low enough that I wouldn't feel guilty using it on an irregular basis. 4) Of course, it would be seaworthy.

Such small boats are usually not handled by brokers so I found myself driving throughout the Bay Area to check out boats that were for sale by owners. In November of 2000, I came upon an ad in *Latitude 38* for a 1961 Cal 20, hull #14. The purchase price: $1,000.

A survey had been done two years before I purchased the boat, and although she then carried no name, the survey listed two names she had previously sported—*Insecto Calliente* and *Victory*, neither of which held meaning for me. I needed a name for her and I did not have to wait very long for it to come to me. It arrived by way of a dream. In the dream, my eyes fell upon a beautiful woman with long black shiny hair. As I approached her, her shiny tresses actually proved to be black feathers. This made her image not only beautiful, but also mystical. From that day forward my little Cal 20 would be called *Black Feathers*.

Over the next few years the longer races of the SSS became training grounds. These races went out the Golden Gate, and either the 25 miles or so south to Half Moon Bay or the approximate 30 miles west to the Farallones. These races, along with the consistently strong winds within the Bay, allow a skipper to gain ample experience with all points of sailing under reefed and unreefed conditions. On a typical summer day on the Bay you can expect consistent 15 - 20 knot winds with many days of 30 - 35 knots. If you practice in these conditions, you will be well prepared and your boat readied for a Singlehanded TransPac.

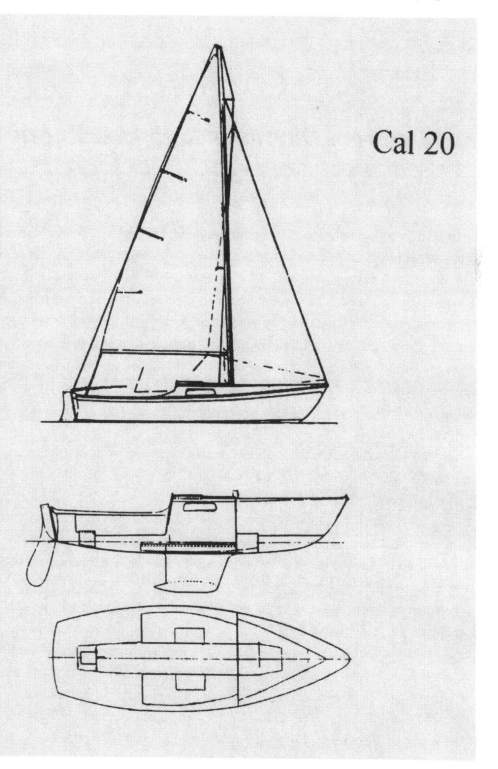

Cal 20

Chapter 3

From Daysailer to Pocket Racer

It can be a bit intimidating to take a common boat and begin planning all the changes and additions necessary to transform her from a daysailer to an offshore pocket racer. It takes a lot of time and money. Many of life's routines will be indefinitely altered. Although you sail alone, the time and money spent on this project may not be yours alone. Your support system must be enthusiastic. If you are honest with yourself, you will accept you cannot be totally confident that all this effort and expense will result in success. Many a racer has begun the LongPac and/or TransPac and found a need to withdraw for any number of reasons—some racers qualify but may never cross the start line. So you must be good at dealing with doubt; doubt about yourself, and doubt about the boat. Part of the adventure is addressing these doubts.

Lastly you must realize there will be many naysayers who will belittle or discourage your efforts. Most often you will be unaware of their remarks. Generally, I care nothing about naysayers, for they will think and say what they like. I do realize, however, that if they are influential, they can affect you by altering the rules of the race. An example of this can be the effective elimination of small boats from a race by shortening the finish time. I have not seen this occur in the SSS TransPac, but it has happened in another popular offshore race in the Bay Area.

As daunting as the task may seem, there is a real joy in taking on the project, particularly if you enjoy thinking about your boat and musing about the various options available to you. As we alter the intended use of our boats, we realize new demands are being placed on them that will require changes in the boats and/or the addition of new equipment. (For a full discussion of the process, equipment purchased and sources used in my preparation for the 2007 LongPac and 2008 TransPac, please see the segment of this book entitled Part III: Thoughts on Small Boat Preparation for the Singlehanded TransPac.)

When we simply sail our boats on protected waters, we must follow basic Coast Guard requirements. When we sail a singlehanded race with the SSS, they too have a list of requirements going beyond that of the Coast Guard. A singlehanded race extending into coastal waters expands on this list, and a race offshore to Hawaii will expand the requirement list even further.

This progression of requirements provides a helpful outline of how to proceed in setting up your boat. Although the setting up of your boat CAN be done quickly, it normally tends to take a few years. This time is well spent, however, because you gain experience by sailing in different events. It allows you to develop your individual techniques, as well as see if you really want to proceed in your project of developing an offshore racer. For *Black Feathers*, it was a rather slow progression for the first couple of years, and then it became a more determined effort for the three years leading up to the 2008 TransPac. The tasks are generally things you can accomplish yourself if willing, so labor costs can be kept to a minimum. Keep in mind, "minimum" in this case does not alleviate the "maximum" outlay of cash.

Black Feathers was purchased in late 2000 for $1,000, the going price of a Cal 20 at the time. When she crossed the starting line of the 2008 TransPac, she had some $25,000 worth of changes and adornments. Most of these improvements were necessary, but certainly not all. All added equipment was bought new, including some additional back-up equipment. I purchased, rather than rented, the life raft and satellite (SAT) phone. In other words, I wanted to spend the time and money to equip *Black Feathers* as appropriately as possible. Had I borrowed some equipment, that being an emergency rescue beacon, life raft and satellite phone, plus purchased some used sails and the self-steering device, etc, I might have reduced that $25,000 to $17,000, but that's a guess.

The annual Farallones race and the biennial LongPac race (the TransPac qualifier) provide fertile training grounds for both you and your boat. The conditions and duration of these races allow the skipper to try out ideas to evaluate their effectiveness. During a Singlehanded Farallones race I broke my boom through my improper use of preventers. In another Farallones race I lost the use of the rudder because the supporting hardware broke. During yet another Farallones race I became so cold and wet I could hardly function. From such trials and tribulations you learn and make adjustments for the future. And with each problem solved, you gain confidence.

The LongPac race of 2007 proved invaluable. *Black Feathers* functioned well, but events within the race demonstrated the need for some additional equipment and sailing strategies.

Some 30 boats crossed the starting line in a mild breeze and headed out for the Golden Gate and beyond. Most were singlehanded, this serving as their TransPac qualifier. A few doubledhanders were out for an adventure. Our quest: Cross the longitude of 126° 40', (200 miles due west of San Francisco), then turn around and enjoy the usual long downwind run home. At least 420 miles would be sailed by the end of the race.

Working our way toward the Farallones, the mild breeze of the start quickly built to a rough upwind battle with lumpy seas. It gave me pleasure—crossing tacks with the larger boats reminding them this little Cal 20 was holding her own as a contender. By late evening, in the area of the Farallones, the strong winds lessened and the seas flattened. A thick fog descended on the fleet and an eerie stagnation left *Black Feathers* drifting, muffled silence replacing the blustry conditions of just a short time before.

Sitting in the cockpit blinded by fog, I hoped my mere presence in the chilly night air might encourage a return of the wind and improve my ability to see. *Black Feathers* had no radar to pierce the fog, but she did have a Collision Avoidance Radar Detector (CARD), a device designed to detect the radar of other vessels and warn of their presence. In addition, hopefully our radar reflector would prove effective, thus allowing us to be noticed by other vessels with radar.

After a couple of anxious hours of this unwanted peaceful stillness, the CARD alarm broke the silence. Its alarm begins with a single beep when it first detects the emission of a radar wave, and then emits a beep for each subsequent wave it detects. A single light flashes on the face of the instrument for each wave received. Upon hearing the first beep, I immediately went into the cabin to check the CARD. At first, nothing appeared on the screen, but when it beeped again, I saw a single light indicating the direction from which it came. The fog outside allowed but a few hundred feet of visibility at best and I could see nothing. The CARD becomes your eyes penetrating the fog and darkness, but it can become your tormentor as well. As a target vessel approaches, the radar emissions grow stronger, and with that happening the number of flashing lights increases, as well as the beeps of the alarm. As the vessel closes in, the CARD becomes overwhelmed by emissions, lights flash from all directions and the piercing sound of the alarm increases dramatically in volume.

The intermittent single beep accompanied by a single flashing light had increased to a full line of lights pointing to the target vessel, but I could still see nothing through the fog. I stood paralyzed in the cockpit of this motionless sailboat, being battered by the pulsating alarm and staring into an abyss of blackness and fog.

I had delayed too long in retrieving my small engine from its storage bin and installing it in the engine well. I rationalized it probably didn't matter anyway because by the time I could have identified the invader and determined which way to turn, there would have been no time to respond. And likewise, if *Black Feathers* had not appeared on the approaching ship's radar, the ship would have had no response time in which to avoid a collision.

Desperate to do something, I reached for my searchlight, shining it into the fog. All lights flashed on the CARD's panel. The alarm added to my frustration so I threw the switch to silence it. A blessing, but the silence did nothing to minimize the problem. As I directed my heat radiating, 400,000 candlepower beam into the fog, I concluded it was about as ineffective as shining your high beams while driving into heavy falling snow.

While moving the light beam through the fog, I heard the low rumbling sound of an engine. Although I believed it now too late to avoid disaster, I turned the beam up onto my listless, white sails and held the light steady. Possibly, the ship might see my sails, but could it turn in time?

Humbled by the knowledge my fate rested in the hands of others, I stood there holding the upward-turned light, listening to the ominous rumble of the approaching vessel. Straining to observe anything coming from the direction of the sound, I felt relieved and elated to see the faint green glow of a passing light. It had to have been within 100 yards of *Black Feathers*. A single red or green light indicates the side of the vessel. Seeing both red and green lights heading for you is your ultimate fear. I have no idea if my waving of the searchlight alerted the ship to my presence, or if the ship, never aware of my presence, simply passed me in the foggy, black night—or perhaps less dramatic, my radar reflector told the ship I was in their path and they simply changed direction.

The mental trauma you endure when anything bad happens stimulates your thought process. I have relived that night a hundred times, hearing the alarm, seeing the flashing lights, feeling the searchlight in my hand, and hearing the low rumble of the engine over and over again. But the worst to relive: My sense of hopelessness.

To avoid a repeat of that night, I needed a plan to address such alarming conditions—the ability to get the boat moving quickly when experiencing a lack of wind along with poor visibility. (This is the greatest disadvantage of having an engine stowed away.) Likewise, I needed a way to effectively communicate with any ship in the area. The thick fog of the first night of that race, and the terrifying night that ensued, demonstrated the need for an Automatic Identification System (AIS) to monitor the commercial ships.

It was also during this LongPac race that I became conscious of the need for more effective communication with my family. This race did not require the boats to have a single sideband (SSB) long-range radio or a satellite (SAT) phone. I had neither, and my VHF radio proved generally too short-ranged to be effective in communicating with the other racers, so there was no way for the Race Committee or my wife, Jeanne, to follow my progress. This placed a great deal of stress on Jeanne. Several racers dropped out of the race due to fog, rough seas and extreme seasickness, but no report came in on *Black Feathers*. This lack of knowing creates stress. The first words I spoke to her as I pulled up to the dock after the race were, "We have to improve our communication!"

After the LongPac, we had one year to complete the final preparation for the 2008 TransPac. By this point, little remained to be done—basically I needed to install a solar panel, an AIS with a dedicated GPS, and a SAT phone antenna. Then I would need to do some sailing to gain experience in using all the newly-installed equipment. Too often we get so involved in our boat preparation, we do not go sailing. The TransPac isn't boat preparation—it's sailing!

The SSS holds a series of monthly TransPac seminars as a lead up to the race. I have attended many of these over the years and always come away with enriched thoughts. Also, these seminars allow the potential racers to meet one another and exchange ideas. Past TransPacers and Race Committee members are willing to share any bits of wisdom they have garnered.

During the yearlong run up to the TransPac, Jeanne took on several event-planning responsibilities for the TransPac. This gave me some added insight into how complex it can be to put on an event of this magnitude. Although she often became greatly enmeshed in her tasks, I felt her efforts added greatly to our overall TransPac experience.

The last couple of months before the start were filled with various deadlines and the making of final plans. When you start buying food and filling water tanks you know race day is nearing.

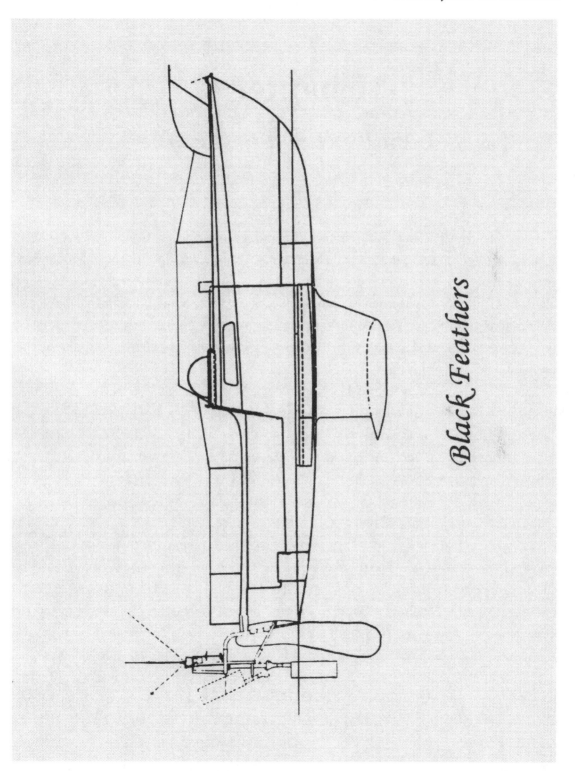

Black Feathers

Chapter 4

Coming Down to the Gun

Although the TransPac race still remained three days away, when Jeanne and I awoke the morning of July 9th, we realized we were entering a pre-race period where just about every move we made was a scheduled event. We got up at 7 a.m. and were on the road by 9. The ride from Mi Wuk Village to San Francisco takes about three hours if the traffic cooperates. A clear sunny morning, the ride to San Francisco gave us time to reflect on what had taken place over the past months to get us here—and what lay ahead. Anxious anticipation denoted the feeling of the day.

Our plan: To arrive at South Beach Harbor at Pier 40 in San Francisco around noon and load the boat with all the food, and any supplies and equipment not already onboard. I decided against taking the time to fully organize the placement of things within the boat while at South Beach. Such organization seemed an appropriate task to undertake during the next couple of days while at the Corinthian Yacht Club. Jeanne drove the car across the Golden Gate to Tiburon where the race would start and also where we had rented a condo for the three remaining nights before the start of the race.

As it always takes longer to do last-minute tasks than you expect, I was not surprised to find myself motoring out of the marina a bit late. Although I didn't do the final organizing of the gear, I did make sure things were secure. I didn't want gear being tossed about the boat unnecessarily. The first half of the motoring proved quite delightful. Things generally become choppy, windy and cold, and possibly wet as you approach the middle of the Bay on a summer afternoon. And that's just what happened. By the time I got on the lee side of Angel Island, where things calmed down, I once again appreciated this was a sailing race and not a motoring race. Sailboats sail so much smoother than they motor on choppy water. When we arrived within the Corinthian harbor, I called the harbormaster on the VHF and was pleased to find he had selected a very fine, comfortable slip for *Black Feathers*, one that would be convenient to sail from when the race began. Jeanne had already arrived in Tiburon, checked into our condo, and patiently awaited our arrival at dockside. Hard to believe, we were actually here—and reasonably ready to depart!

All the boats were required to arrive at the Corinthian by the afternoon of the next day, July 10th. We had come a day early to allow Jeanne time to finalize the last-minute preparations for the Aloha Banquet. In spite of our early arrival, some of the other racers were already in their slips and several more appeared as *Black Feathers* was being put to bed for the night. Excitement filled the air as Jeanne and I left the Corinthian to head off to our condo for some relaxation and final preparations. I hoped for a few solid nights of sleep before the start, but that seemed unlikely to happen. In my mind, the race had already begun!

Summer mornings in Tiburon are often overcast with a marine layer of light fog and clouds blanketing the coastal hills and marinas. This is what we found that Thursday morning, as we left the beautiful condo to drive the short distance to the Tiburon Peninsula. The Peninsula juts out into San Francisco Bay with the Corinthian Yacht Club perched near its tip. I knew it would be an interesting day. By late afternoon all the skippers were required to be at the Club with their boats, and that evening would be the send-off Aloha Banquet.

As is generally the case at marinas on a summer morning, things seemed calm, sounds a bit muffled and no sense of urgency evident. Our tasks this day involved Jeanne meeting with the Corinthian's event coordinator to ready things for the evening's dinner, while I did the final packing of the boat.

Today would be the first time that absolutely everything needed to go on the race would be placed aboard *Black Feathers*. To the items already onboard, we added the required 30-day supply of food. This was significant both in bulk and weight. Even though everything had been weighed and accounted for weeks ahead of time, I had concerns about the weight of each item. Jeanne and I had spent a great deal of time planning the food, tailoring it as close as possible to my needs and desires, focusing only on necessary items. All the food fit in four carry-on type bags, one for each week, with each bag weighing in at approximately 30 pounds. Before I left South Beach Harbor for the Corinthian, I filled the inflatable water tank, as well as eight individual one-gallon plastic milk containers—all with water. This, along with 48 cans of Kern juice drinks, brought us in compliance with the 21-gallon water requirement. The 48 cans of juice drinks were divided evenly among the four bags of food.

As it is very important that the weight be evenly distributed, we had drawn diagrams of where everything would be placed in each area of the boat. The areas available for storage consisted of: 1) V-Berth, 2) Cabin: right side, left side, and middle, 3) Left side aft of cabin with access only from the cabin, 4) Right side aft of the cabin with cabin access, but also accessible through a lazarette (compartment) open to the cockpit, and 5) The central area under the cockpit. This held the 13-gallon inflatable water tank.

Clearly we would need to make some changes to our diagrams. The morning sky was beginning to clear as I shuffled things around the cabin of *Black Feathers,* often stepping off to check how changes impacted the boat's waterline and list.

Black Feathers—Fully Loaded

By mid-afternoon all the skippers had arrived. An electrifying and contagious buzz set in around the docks. Most skippers had met before at previous seminars, races, or at marinas where the out-of-town boats had resided across the Bay for a few days prior to today's gathering. A few of the skippers I had not yet met, although I had come to know them somewhat from reading their biographical notes and observing their online photos on the SSS website. I found it interesting and indeed a pleasure to actually meet them in person and have the opportunity to check out their boats. A 60' boat looks rather normal in a picture, but when you actually stand next to it, you get a whole new perspective. The other skippers probably felt the same when they saw *Black Feathers* and could appreciate her diminutive size.

The Aloha Banquet serves as both a time of closure as well as a time of introduction. It has a true therapeutic value. It signifies closure because much of the work of the racers is over. The skippers have all completed the qualifying portion of the race—now they are chomping at the bit for the race to begin. Their task ahead is to "just do it." The 2008 Race Committee, bless their souls, had completed a tremendous amount of work to get the race to this point. They planned and coordinated an incredible list of activities and items under the direction of the race chairperson, Synthia Petroka. Race Committee members serve as arbitrators, as well as planners, and in doing so create an "esprit de corps."

Much remained for both racers and the Race Committee to accomplish. All involved were on-hand and everyone felt anxious about what lay ahead.

Jeanne and I returned to the condo in the late afternoon to relax and prepare for dinner. Such a dinner would generally be a somewhat dressy affair, but knowing past TransPac skippers, I knew to expect just about any type of attire. As Crawford is a Scottish name and Jeanne and I both enjoy Celtic events and garb, we decided to go Scottish. I wore my Crawford tartan kilt with a formal Prince Charlie jacket and she, a Renaissance-style dress and bodice with a Crawford tartan sash. I had spoken to another skipper, Alan Hebert of *Ankle Biter,* and he too planned to wear his kilt. Alan, aside from his sailing interests, participates in many of the Scottish Highland Games as an athlete, so he is always willing to don a kilt given the opportunity and the occasion.

The Aloha Banquet is an event open to anyone who wishes to attend. You are likely to see past TransPac skippers, interested SSS members, family and friends of the present skippers, and many from the sailing community who have shared their expertise during the pre-race seminars. We invited two special friends to attend with their wives. One, Wayne Crutcher, my long-time sailing buddy who had doublehanded to Hawaii with me in my previous boat, *Now or Never*, and whom I have raced against in many SSS races since. Our other guest, John Hill, a more recent friend, had competed in the 1980 TransPac and helped me during the last year and a half preparing *Black Feathers* for this TransPac. John used a self-steering device of his own design and construction on four round-trips to Hawaii. We tried to determine if we could use it with *Black Feathers*. Ultimately, I chose to go another route with the steering, but I will be forever grateful to this 80+-year-old, pony-tailed, salty sailor for his electrical expertise and general advice, but mostly I treasure his friendship.

The Corinthian reflects a yacht club of traditional elegance. The excitement of those attending deemed the dinner a great success. It was inspiring to be in a facility with a history of significant sailing events and competitive sailors. Jeanne worked with the event coordinator on the menu and felt quite pleased to see what a fine job they had done. She now had only one more dinner to coordinate—that being the Awards Ceremony at the Princeville Resort in Kauai. Between now and then, we SIMPLY had to do the race!

A repeat of the previous day, the morning of the day before the race started cool and overcast. Today's tasks: Attend the skippers meeting, have a final inspection of the boat, get the engine shaft sealed and spend some meaningful private time with Jeanne. Each important, but the private time was the most critical.

Walking along the docks and greeting the skippers as they woke up and milled around, you could see that for this race, there was a general sense of calm in the air.

Only one boat appeared to be having a problem, that being Thomas Kirschbaum's boat, *Feral*. *Feral* is a 26' International Folkboat—a great boat for this race. *Feral* was experiencing engine problems and several of the skippers were helping Tom try to remedy the ailment. It struck me how calm Tom dealt with this matter. Evidently he was not depending on his engine to charge his batteries, and the lack of an engine appeared to present no dilemma for a race that disallowed the use of an engine, except for charging batteries. An interesting tidbit—over the years a number of TransPac skippers have opted to do the race sans an engine.

The skippers' meeting would be the last time Synthia would have all the skippers together prior to the race. At this meeting each skipper received a manual spelling out such details as the communication protocol, and what to do and expect as we approached the finish line; as well as Bay Area, Kauai and onboard contact numbers for the Race Committee and skippers, plus relevant Coast Guard numbers. We also gathered for the 2008 TransPac group photo taken by *Latitude 38*, the popular sailing magazine for the San Francisco Bay Area. *Latitude 38* has been an ardent supporter of the TransPac since its inception.

Final inspections and the sealing of each boat's propeller shaft, to ensure any use during the race would be detected, took up the rest of the afternoon. As each boat finished in Hanalei Bay, a Race Committee member would board the boat and confirm the seal remained unbroken. If the seal were broken, the skipper would be required to meet with the committee to explain the circumstances that warranted breaking the seal. The committee would then determine if a disqualification would be appropriate.

As the afternoon turned to evening, Jeanne and I returned to our condo. *Black Feathers* was loaded, inspected—and ready to go.

One last task remained, which involved the SAT phone. Reliable and effective communication is critical to this race, so I needed to make sure I collected and properly entered all the phone numbers into the SAT phone. Programming the numbers into the phone could prevent the nasty situation of having to dial long numbers under adverse conditions (e.g. from a life raft). Also included with the various pertinent numbers were two numbers for the U.S. Coast Guard, one for asking questions—the other for requesting emergency assistance. These USCG numbers applied to the mainland areas, as well as Hawaii.

This done, Jeanne and I settled in for some much needed relaxation and quiet time. We knew the next morning would be busy receiving family and friends at the boat and these last few hours should be for ourselves.

As much as you hope for a comforting solid night's sleep, it just doesn't happen the night before a TransPac race. Too many things are running through your mind. Too many questions are unanswered—the challenges to be met lay ahead in mystery.

Chapter 5
The Adventure Begins

What a relief to finally get up and take control of the beginning day. All was ready at the boat, but not at the condo. The mundane tasks of loading the car and checking out of the condo demanded our attention even though our minds wanted to be elsewhere. These chores did, however, fall in line in an orderly manner and by 8:30 a.m. we were driving toward the Corinthian, 10 minutes away. Our guests would begin arriving shortly after 9 a.m. and we wanted to be ready for them.

The forecast for the morning—comfortably cool. Fog covered the Marin hills but lifted over the Gate so my fears of a foggy start faded. When we arrived at the Corinthian Yacht Club, there were several skippers roaming the docks and small groups of visitors gathered here and there. The next couple of hours, family and friends of the skippers would walk the docks meeting the other skippers boarding their boats to check them out.

Jeanne and I were honored by the number of friends who drove down from the mountains to share the start with us—some making arrangements to spend the weekend in the Bay Area, while others made the long trek home immediately following the start of the race. Over the past couple of years, they had heard much about *Black Feathers* and this was the perfect time to see her, most for the very first time. Walking the docks before the race, you could see a boat like *Dogbark*, a sleek 60' ocean racer, and marvel at how one person could handle that much boat, especially at sea for several days. Then, on another finger of the dock, you would see *Sparky* (22') and *Black Feathers* (20') and wonder why one person would want to handle a boat of that size at sea. There were many contrasts within the fleet, not only of size, but type, comfort level and cost. However, there was one obvious constant: Each of these boats represented a significant amount of sweat and tears in preparation, and the hopes and dreams of a race worth the effort. The Singlehanded TransPac is a race definitely worth the effort—it is an adventure—it is the fulfillment of a dream.

There would be three starting times in 10-minute intervals beginning just after noon. The first start would consist of the large monohulls (40' to 60') and the fast sport monohulls (27' to 30'). The second start would include the medium-sized monohulls (31' to 40') and the small monohulls (20' to 28'). The last start featured the only multihull in the race, a sleek 54' trimaran. Twenty-two boats in all would cross the line that day—July 12, 2008—headed for Kauai.

San Francisco Bay can present its own challenges to an ocean racer. The flood tide can be so strong that it will not let you through the Gate until the tide changes. This is what happened in 1994 when it took me over four hours to go the two miles or so to get under the Gate. Trying to escape the Bay's grip that day, exhausted most of the skippers. The Bay can also give you no wind so you drift endlessly or more likely, so much wind you get whipped ragged before you escape to the more normal winds of the open ocean. You never know for sure what to expect in spite of the latest weather reports. Moments before our racers were to be towed out of the harbor, they could be seen reviewing their computers for the latest weather in hopes of selecting the best sail combination for as speedy a departure as possible. Most of the racers had computers and e-mail capabilities onboard. The smaller boats did not. I had no desire to put my faith in a sophisticated computer-based weather and communications system on *Black Feathers*. The chances of it getting wet were simply too great. I would do without these technical devices, and simply rely on some basic weather information from Jeanne twice a day when I called her on the SAT phone.

Shortly after 11 a.m. the time had finally come for me to cast off the dock lines and join my fellow racers who had either sailed out under their own power, or been towed out by the committee boat—remember, all engines were sealed at this point. With a strain in my voice, I expressed my appreciation to our friends who had come so far to see me off and offer support to Jeanne. After a warm embrace from my daughter, my son and his wife, I turned to my wife, Jeanne. It is not easy to keep your emotions in check when you see your loved ones trying to say goodbye. Neither you nor they know what lies ahead. They can only hope you are well prepared and will make appropriate judgments as challenges present themselves. They can only look at you and hope that in a few weeks they will, once again, be able to hold out their arms and have you come to them. So it was, as Jeanne and I held each other, and we were for a short moment as one, alone, on the dock. I turned toward *Black Feathers*, stepped aboard, and my daughter and son pushed *Black Feathers* away from the dock and I slowly sailed away. Before I got too far away, I remembered to flash a happy smile and give a warmhearted wave, in spite of the momentary emptiness that resided in my heart. I was off.

Sailing from The Corinthian

The starting line ran between an outlying buoy and the race deck of the Corinthian. A light but steady breeze and a slack tide made it easy to tack around in the area between the Corinthian on the Tiburon Peninsula and Angel Island. This area is known as Raccoon Straights, and during a strong tide can either be of great benefit or a frustrating impediment. This day, during this slack tide, it proved neither. Shortly after we started, the slack tide began to turn to a slight ebb tide so I anticipated an easy ride out to the Gate and through the ship channel on the way out to the Farallones. My objective for the afternoon and evening—get as far west as possible. To do this I needed *Black Feathers* to point well into the wind.

Sometime between leaving the Corinthian dock and the firing of the warning gun for the final countdown to the start, each skipper must hail the Race Committee on their VHF to identify themselves and receive an acknowledgment. This ritual would seem but a mere administrative formality, but it has become a joy for most skippers racing with the SSS.

I had not yet called the Race Committee so I picked up the handheld VHF and pressed the button. "TransPac Race Committee, TransPac Race Committee, this is *Black Feathers*, Sail #14, checking in for the Small Boat division, come in please."

To this, the Race Committee replied, "*Black Feathers*, we have you checked in. Have a good race, Robert."

My final reply of "Thank you, Shama," left me thinking of the many times during the last 17 years I had heard Shama Kota's graceful voice. Her rich English accent, always so appropriately elegant, commands attention and respect. Hers has been the voice that has responded to my call in nearly every meaningful race I have entered. It just wouldn't have been the same had she not answered my call for the start of my 2008 TransPac adventure.

I enjoyed listening to her voice as she spoke with each of the skippers. Her words were clear, controlled, and always graciously presented. Surely each skipper in the fleet enjoyed her voice and manner as much as I did.

During our last TransPac seminar, Stan Honey offered his hard-earned sage advice regarding weather and wind strategies pertaining to different parts of the race. Having raced in many international races, Stan is a highly sought-after navigator and strategist. With these impressive credentials, each TransPac skipper hung on his every word. The one message we all took home as a pearl of wisdom: To get beyond the Farallones as quickly as possible in order to get out to the consistent wind, as that wind is less likely to die out during the night and early morning. This meant we wanted to go west and not be tempted to ease off to the south. (For a discussion of the weather and how it impacts race strategy, see Chapter 31, Planning the Race and Return.)

Black Feathers enjoyed the 45 minutes or so of tacking back and forth in Raccoon Straights with the other boats. In most cases, it would be the last time I would see them until we reached Hanalei. I particularly enjoyed crossing tacks with *Dogbark*, the 60-footer, and *Hecla*, the 54' trimaran. But most of all I favored seeing *Sparky*, the 22-footer and *Carroll E*, the beautiful Dana 24, for these along with *Feral*, were my main competitors. I knew the fleet was divided up between fast and slow boats, but within those groups there certainly would be some great competition and the slow boats should put on a good show. Also, the higher handicaps of the slower boats meant that varying amounts of time would be taken off their actual time. With this "corrected time" factor, the faster boats knew they had to perform well to overcome the handicap of the slower boats.

During this pre-race time, sincere waves and well wishes were being exchanged between the racers as we crossed tacks. We all wanted to do well, but we also wanted the others to make a good showing and have a safe trip. As the minutes ran down to my start I sailed closer and closer to the line to test the wind and see how the boat would respond during a tack. I was pleased I had enough time to test these things. Sometimes that is not the case.

The race deck could easily be seen from the water, but the people were too small to be identified. In spite of this, every time *Black Feathers* sailed toward the race deck my eyes would strain to see Jeanne and my kids. With just a few minutes to go, I headed toward the line one last time. A large yellow banner cascaded down like a waterfall. It was Jeanne's way of wishing me off and it caught me by surprise. She had used this colorful signal the year before on my qualifying race so I could see where she was, but I didn't know she planned to wave it this time. It was like a last kiss before I had to swing about to cross the line and get my official start. Full of emotion, I heard the gun for our division start. We crossed the line pointing toward the Gate. I looked back a few times as I headed out, but with each look the race deck of the Corinthian grew smaller and smaller so I decided to look back no more. As I crossed the Bay, the wind picked up considerably holding steady in the mid-20 knot range. Our adventure had definitely begun and before me lay the Golden Gate and beyond.

The word "beyond" is a wonderful word. It implies boundless, adventurous—and something I love to do—go sailing "beyond" the harbor, "beyond" the Gate and "beyond" the Farallones. Those were the things I dreamt about, and today I was sailing "beyond."

The day remained overcast as I cleared the Gate, then Point Bonita with its welcoming lighthouse, and headed for the ship channel. You could benefit by what little ebb existed by staying within the deeper water of the ship channel. With no commercial traffic to contend with, the fleet fell pretty much in line as it headed west. As we slowly stretched out, I felt a calmness descending over *Black Feathers* and me. We were all but alone now. Jeanne, my kids, and friends were probably in their cars heading home. I wondered what they were thinking. If they crossed the Golden Gate, they would surely look west and strain their eyes trying to see where I might be, but this tiny speck of white could not be seen from that distance. There was too much ocean and I was but a dot upon it.

The fresh breeze inside the Bay diminished considerably as I headed out toward the Farallones, but the overcast day began to clear making the open ocean most inviting.

The afternoon provided some beautiful, although calm, sailing. The wind, coming out of the west, prevented me from heading where I wanted to go, so I found myself going too far south or too far north, depending on the tack. The seas were smooth and it seemed almost eerie gliding along so peacefully in an area where I am used to being tossed about. With the wind so light the Monitor Windvane couldn't steer effectively, so I used the autopilot. Also, since the autopilot didn't have a paddle in the water like the Monitor, we experienced less drag.

When things are smooth, you often notice marine life, which goes undetected in rough seas. Several whales were in the area and if I didn't see them, I could at least hear and smell their husky breath as they broke the surface. A vision of a sudden romance between a whale and *Black Feathers* is not a happy thought and I felt relief that no such encounters occurred.

A common occurrence off the California coast—you can suddenly find yourself sailing through large numbers of jellyfish. This day they were purple, about a foot and a half across with bushy tentacles that streamed 4' - 6' behind them. The first race day ended on a very peaceful and relaxed note.

Smooth Sailing

With a haziness developing and everything under control, I took this opportunity to practice some Irish tunes on my concertina while sitting in the cockpit. I never expected that to happen in this usually rough and cold area. With such a pleasant but light-winded day I told Jeanne later that evening, "It's not a good day to go out to the Farallones and back, but it's a great day to go out to the Farallones and beyond."

As the sun dropped over the horizon the wind picked up a bit and we glided across the smooth water at about 3 knots—not fast sailing but beautiful and comfortable. All clouds had cleared leaving a sky full of stars and moonlight glistening off the water. A slight chill filled the air, but not cold enough to rob me of my great pleasure of sitting in the cockpit, letting the Monitor steer while I simply gazed out over the water.

The disruption of the water in our wake created a glittering bio-phosphorescence that is mesmerizing to watch. You can't help but wonder the purpose of such a phenomena or whether the temporarily glowing microscopic organisms have any control over the event. No matter what the reasoning, a magical moment results.

I could see the masthead lights of about 10 other race boats scattered about—all trying to make their way through the light wind to the stronger synoptic breeze usually positioned further offshore. Although everyone would have preferred a stronger start for this first day of the race, at least we were on our way, with no reported equipment failures and little risk of seasickness. We had to wait it out. We could only hope the calm conditions wouldn't last too long. The slower boats do have more of a concern with the slow days. If we lost too many days to a lack of wind, we might not arrive in Hanalei by the 21st day. Faster boats could give up some days to light winds or poor sailing and still finish on time, so as patient as I tried to be, thoughts of time lost to light wind were ever-present in the back of my mind.

At 7 p.m. it was time for our first scheduled check-in and I eagerly awaited the opportunity to speak with Jeanne.

Racers could choose from two check-in protocols. 1) If you were checking-in over the SSB radio, you would tune into the communication boat (one of the racers) and wait your turn at roll call. The format: To identify your boat, and give your position, speed, course and distance to the finish (DTF). Once all racers had responded, the communications boat would announce the information that had previously been received by the Race Committee from those racers calling in by SAT phone. 2) For those racers using a SAT phone, they would simply call their shore-side contact, in my case, Jeanne, and then their contact would e-mail the Race Committee their current position. SAT phone users would call in at 0700 (7 a.m.)

Pacific Daylight Time (PDT) and 1900 (7 p.m.) PDT, thus allowing the Race Committee time to relay the information to the communication boat that would then contact all SSB reporting boats at 0900 (9 a.m.) PDT and 2100 (9 p.m.) PDT. After the Race Committee had all updates in-hand, the information would be posted on the SSS website.

At 1900 hours, I placed my first check-in call to Jeanne, and was thrilled to hear her voice. She had spent some time with our friends on the race deck at the Corinthian after the start, gone to lunch with some of the women, and then headed home. For both of us, having the hectic schedule of all the pre-race activities behind us, allowed for a routine to begin. It comforted me knowing with the SAT phone I could call her as easily as with a cell phone, but with much greater reliability.

Chapter 6
The Windy Reach

When you are singlehanding, sleep becomes a major concern. The way you deal with it depends greatly on where you are at any given time. By late night, the excitement of the first day had ebbed and the need for some sleep became evident. Since we were positioned in an area of high commercial traffic by that time, the likelihood of meeting several ships during the night became very real. To help me detect other ships, I had the CARD and AIS running—each equipped with an alarm. To simply let myself sleep for an undetermined amount of time relying blindly on the efficiency of the CARD and AIS seemed reckless. I had done so in the 1994 TransPac but I didn't feel confident doing it now. A ship takes about 15 minutes to come over the horizon and cross your path, so every time I went to sleep I set my timer for 15 minutes. I would faithfully follow this routine for about four days. During the daylight hours it seemed appropriate to take naps of up to 30 minutes because the odds of being visually detected by commercial traffic greatly improved. To alert other vessels of my presence, I had my radar reflector, and at night always ran my strobe light located at the masthead. When I detected a vessel at night, I would also turn on my navigation running lights. I didn't keep them on all the time at night because I wanted to minimize battery consumption. Since my running lights were located only about 4' off the water, other vessels probably could not see them from any appreciable distance.

So it was. My sleep consisted of multiple 15-minute naps. This is not the best quality sleep mode, but it worked quite well and I never felt exhausted. Once far enough out into the open ocean (at least 250 miles), I relaxed these sleep restrictions until about two days before arriving in Kauai. Then I resumed the 15-minute nap cycle.

The second race day started with no wind and a glassy sea surface, but mercifully gave way to some light wind for parts of the day. *Black Feathers* glided along at 3 - 4 knots. The adverse direction of the wind created a great deal of mental anguish, with me pondering the advantages versus the disadvantages of choosing a course too far to the north or south of our desired course. To make it to Hanalei on time I needed to average about 4 knots, which would give me close to the 100 miles a day I hoped for. Every hour of a lesser speed meant I'd have to make it up later. I tried not to dwell on that reality.

As the day progressed, slight swells developed under an overcast sky. We were moving, and in somewhat the right direction. The marine life of the first day continued and the number of whales around the boat amazed me. At one point I saw a white mass, somewhat slender, about 18' long, swim past just slightly under the surface. Although I can't be sure, I will always want to think it was a white whale—are we thinking Moby Dick here? As had been the case so far in the race, the water remained an uninviting dirty green color.

By evening of the second day, the wind died and I watched *Black Feathers* glide to a halt on the glassy smooth sea. As any boat trapped by a lack of wind, she would point in any and all directions having no wind to hold her on any definitive course. Then the rocking would begin, and with each motion, the slack mainsail would slap from side to side. This proved to be an ideal time to activate the preventers. Although designed to prevent an accidental gybe when going downwind, during this time of no wind, the preventers take on another important but much less thought-of function—that of holding the boom constant so it doesn't just drift around the cockpit due to the uncontrolled motion and lack of wind. Even with the preventers holding the boom stable, the slack mainsail slaps back and forth. By 10 p.m. I'd had enough of this banging and took the main down. I left the jib up, however, so I would be better able to detect a freshening wind.

Throughout the night I kept my 15-minute watch schedule hoping for improved conditions that never occurred. At 0700 when I called Jeanne, *Black Feathers* and I sat discouraged and frustrated on a flat, dead calm sea.

At times during the day, slight ripples would grace the water and my anticipation of wind would rise only to be dashed as the glassy surface returned, causing any movement of *Black Feathers* to stop. I would stare at the water's surface, this time further away from the boat, hoping to detect ripples. This went on for hours. There were definitely other things I could have done to occupy my time—in particular practice my concertina, which I love to do, but when you are in a race, you feel obligated to give it your full attention even when there is little you can do. My thoughts would drift to the other racers, particularly the slower boats. What is *Carroll E* doing that I should be doing? What about *Feral*? Is she as trapped as *Black Feathers*? This high pressure area that most of the fleet was stuck in was killing our time, but I realized such thoughts were like thoughts of guilt—they served little useful purpose and needed to be pushed aside. The flip side of all this: We were on a majestic sea that remained calm and very peaceful. While nature rested, we should too. She is not a lady to remain unchanged and when she decided to become lively, we needed to be ready.

Glassy Smooth Sea

As the day progressed, the wind did pick up. It never got to be much but it got things moving and the concerns about which tack to be on replaced concerns about the lack of wind. My pre-race strategy involved sailing a course similar to the average of previous small TransPac boats that had done well given a wide range of conditions. I had drawn this projected course out for Jeanne and placed approximate points where I might be each day. Although real-time conditions always impact such a plan, it seemed better than having no plan at all.

I had no weather fax capabilities onboard. Jeanne would be providing weather fax information from our home computer, communicating 48- and 72-hour projected weather conditions through a graph format I had developed, but for the immediate situation I really only knew what to expect with the weather by observing my surroundings. Another important consideration in using weather forecasts in determining your strategy is whether your boat is fast enough to do anything meaningful with the provided information. If you can only plan on getting 5 - 7 knots of speed, you will not get much value out of knowing where you should be if that distance is not within your reach. In other words the weather can change faster than you can change your location.

My pre-race thoughts were to stay slightly south of the rhumb line. A rhumb line path will generally be your shortest effective route to Hanalei, but you must worry about the Pacific High dropping down on you. To be safe, I had planned to take a slight southerly dip from the rhumb line during the first third of the race, and then, once in the trade winds, head straight for Kauai.

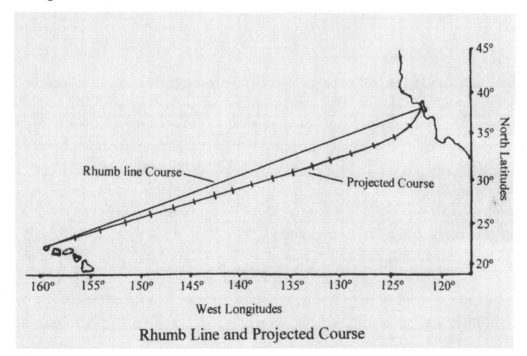

Rhumb Line and Projected Course

At the end of the third day of the race, I was virtually where I had planned to be in relation to the rhumb line, but almost two days behind schedule. Long ago I determined a sailor must develop his or her sense of patience so when considering the realities of my position and time, I would repeat my mantra of, "Keep it in mind, but don't dwell on it."

I didn't realize it then, but the morning of the fourth day proved to be the end of the frustration and stagnation we had experienced since passing the Bonita Lighthouse near the Golden Gate Bridge. Mother Nature stood poised to cut us free and finally let us RACE to Hawaii. The day started out overcast, like all had been except the first day, and remained so. The gray-green seas had swells of a foot or two, but we glided along quite comfortably making about 4 knots with wind in the 10-12 knot range. Even sailing hard on the wind, I saw little spray because of the fairly smooth water, and the boat remained dry.

With all but the lightest of winds, the Monitor had done the steering leaving me with plenty of time to read and practice my concertina. My hope with the music: To sail to Hanalei fast enough that a couple of the other skippers would still be there and we could play some Irish tunes at Tree Time. Tree Time is a daily 5 p.m. gathering of the TransPac skippers with their families and friends on the shore of Hanalei Bay. Everyone brings food and beverages to share and the discussion focuses on the current TransPac and other sailing adventures. Before the race, I gave copies of about 20 tunes to Alan Hebert aboard *Ankle Biter*, and Barbara Euser of *Islander,* with the hope we could play tunes together at Tree Time. They both play penny whistles.

You begin to fall into a routine after about three days at sea. A welcome thing for it means you are doing things automatically. Matters of personal hygiene, equipment inspections, checking chafe on lines and sails, checking for looseness of anything and everything, or the proper tightness of the Monitor's self-steering lines become natural functions. Also a quick look around the deck and cockpit might reveal something missing or something extra like fish that get washed onboard. A careful look at your rig might find a slack shroud or sloppy line holding your radar reflector. You never know for sure what you might find so you have to keep your mind open and your eyes peeled.

A very pleasant happening came on the morning of July 15th. I saw a sail behind me on the horizon. Gradually it overtook me and as it came abeam, we spoke over the VHF. A Pacific Cup boat, it had left the day before on its race from San Francisco to Oahu. The boat, *Rain Drop*, was being doublehanded by a couple of past Cal 20 sailors. They expressed a great deal of interest and enthusiasm in my efforts with *Black Feathers*, and I most appreciated their words of encouragement. For the first time, I realized people other than my immediate family and friends might have a real interest in how *Black Feathers* and I would do in this race. My spirits, not particularly down before I spoke with *Rain Drop*, were noticeably up afterwards. It also pleased me to discover that my position in the ocean couldn't be too far off a desired course if I was meeting other racers on their way to Hawaii. As it turned out, *Rain Drop*, not only won the Pacific Cup doublehanded division, but also took overall honors on corrected time.

A second PacCup boat also passed me later in the day. This fully crewed boat called itself *No Ka Oi*. As she slowly pulled abeam of *Black Feathers*, we spoke over the VHF, and again I appreciated the encouragement they offered. For a couple of hours I could look out and see their sails, and with that came a sense of camaraderie, but finally the grayness of the day and the increasing distance between us made them disappear from the horizon.

By evening, the steady 15-knot wind made it pleasurable to finally feel the need to put a reef in the main. There are two times when I consider putting in a reef. The first is whenever the thought enters my mind. Such thoughts of reefing don't occur without a reason and usually it is because the boat is heeling to a point it is uncomfortable, or there seems to be too much weather helm on the tiller making it more difficult to steer. When either of these incidents occurs, I generally reef. Cal 20s are not designed to be sailed with too much heel. If you get more than 15 degrees of heel, you are impeding your performance. The second reason I reef is when there is a moderately fresh breeze, 15 knots or greater, and it is getting dark. For me, things seem a bit spooky at night when out on the open ocean, so I choose to do whatever seems prudent to be safe and reasonably comfortable. I would rather shake a reef out when it becomes unnecessary, than to struggle in the dark and wet to put one in.

There hadn't been any sun since the first day of the race so it became a concern as to how well the batteries were recharging. I use as little battery power as possible with *Black Feathers*, but still there are navigation lights and autopilot requirements. Since there are no cabin lights I always use a small headlight at night, but this runs on its own batteries. As it turns out, the batteries were charging quite adequately during those overcast conditions. The battery monitor indicated that any power lost was fully recharged by the solar panel. This is what I expected, but I felt relief to have it prove to be so. We sailed all night with a fresh breeze and one reef in the main. When I awoke during the night, I would glance back at the Monitor and see it doing its continual dance with the tiller keeping us on course. You can't help but marvel at this piece of mechanics that acts as your slave and sets you free. I am somewhat hesitant to say it, but truth be told, there develops in the singlehander a sincere admiration and affection for the self-steering device, and some have been known to give it a name and address it with endearment.

The beginning of the fifth day of the race brought us continual good winds.

I shook the reef out of the main. The boat, doing fine, moved along at 5 - 5 1/2 knots. We recorded a noon-to-noon distance of 110 nautical miles so we started meeting our daily mileage goal. If we could achieve 125 nautical miles (nm) per day, we should arrive in Hanalei Bay in a timely fashion and might even pose a threat to several boats on corrected time.

With the boat moving well, I started thinking about the talk I had yesterday with the past Cal 20 sailors aboard *Rain Drop*. They hailed from Portland and spoke of a rather large Cal 20 fleet in their area that was enthusiastically following my TransPac progress. Their comments surprised and flattered me. The ability to follow the progress of these races on the Internet certainly broadens the potential audience. I did, however, feel a bit more pressure to do well, not only for myself, but also for the boat. I would hate to think that a poor performance on my part could reflect badly on *Black Feathers* or similar boats. The more I thought about it, the more I valued that sense of responsibility believing it might help me get through some of the challenging times of the race that might develop. It didn't take me long to find out.

By 11 p.m. we were experiencing our first significant taste of heavy weather. Our desired course: To head directly toward Kauai at about 240°, but this caused the boat to slam too hard into the waves, so I let her fall off to the south. Still screaming along at just a little over 7 knots, with two reefs in the mainsail, the 25 - 30 knot wind left us cold and wet. Water regularly came over the bow, spraying the dome and cockpit. Unfortunately, a small but significant stream of this water also made its way under the dome hatch and sprayed the inside of the tiny cabin. For the first time in the race things were getting wet and I was unable to prevent it.

Although heading more southerly than I wanted, I felt the best and safest plan would be to simply hold my course and hang on. It was like "sailing before the storm," although we certainly were not dealing with a storm. I mentally ran through the various heavy weather tactics one plans for, concluding that as long as the boat was under control, not over-stressed, and the Monitor steered well, we'd carry on. I didn't want to do anything to reduce our speed as long as we maintained control. My reasoning here—in a race speed is obviously critical, but also when you are running with the waves astern, you want to sail fast enough that they don't break into your cockpit.

If we ended up too far south, it would mean we would be sailing more miles than necessary. Because it had become wet, dark and nasty in the cockpit, I stayed all closed up in the cabin. I distributed some of the inside weight around to keep the heeling angle of the boat reasonably comfortable. For my own state of mind, and in case anything unforeseen happened, I had the life raft and ditch bag (abandon ship bag) ready to go. The amount of emergency stuff in the ditch bag made it awkward and heavy, so I culled out all but the absolute essentials. Things of immediate concern were: 1) Emergency Position Indicator Rescue Beacon (EPIRB), 2) SAT phone, 3) some flares, 4) VHF radio, 5) water and 6) watermaker. With this done, little remained for me to do but try to enjoy the ride and attempt to control the wetness.

The night passed with the boat whizzing along and spray regularly engulfing the boat. With towels stuffed into every suspicious area around the hatch cover, the spray on the inside gradually subsided and the situation became stable. As I lie in my berth trying to relax and get any sleep I could, an observation amazed me. That being—I could not tell which direction (forward or backward) the boat was headed. While lying in my berth the boat would rock from right to left—that motion being obvious to me, but I became oblivious to the direction of travel. Being pitch black outside, I could detect no visible clues. If I didn't think which direction was forward in the cabin, I could not detect the direction of travel from the movement. This observation, tantalizing to think about and play with in my mind, helped the night pass.

As the night gave way to yet another overcast dawn, I felt things getting colder in spite of our more southerly position. I spent the morning of July 17th beneath the dome in my folding chair as it gave my knees a chance to relax in a normal sitting posture. The dome, well situated, allowed me to enjoy the view and follow the boat's progress as I watched the AIS plotting any oncoming vessels. The lightweight folding chair below the dome proved just the right height to allow me to look all the way around the boat. I could look down to my right at the compass to check the heading, and look forward at the AIS screen to see my latitude/longitude (lat/lon) location, course, speed, and the plotting of any oncoming ships.

Once the sun went down each night, I would don my small LED headlight. Being as it is so lightweight, it posed no encumbrance—I could sleep comfortably with it on. To my pleasant surprise, I found while in the cabin, I rarely had to use it except when trying to read something because the AIS provided a warm, comfortable glow from its plot screen. With the AIS always on, there was no need for a cabin light and its dampened glow did not adversely affect my night vision as some cabin lights will do. I had not counted on this fortunate side effect and this made me all the more pleased with the AIS.

So there I sat with my head in the dome, my body supported by the chair and hand rails—the miles passing by. During the chilly, overcast morning, I observed most of the wetness I experienced now appeared to be due to condensation rather than the intrusive spray of the night before. The roughness of the waves seemed reduced although the wind strength remained unchanged. All in all it seemed like a promising day as we continued to make great time with a jib and double-reefed main.

Sitting in the dome with the boat all closed up obviously shuts out the outside noise pretty effectively, but it doesn't let your senses relax too much because it accentuates the inside noises, which are significant. These interior noises can be alarming in themselves.

The slightest click sounds like a crack, the slap of a wave against the hull is like a personal assault, and then there is the perception of speed. When you are below and particularly when you are closed up within the cabin, the sounds make you feel as if you are going much faster than you are, and often it sounds like things are getting out of control. Many times I would go below because of the cold out in the cockpit, only to become alarmed and stick my head out of the cabin to check on what was taking place. Finding all well, I would return to the cabin only to repeat the process. Sounds do strange things on a boat and it is an education in itself to get used to them.

As the day progressed, the boat did well and we made good mileage. Although I thought it might make things a lot rougher, I wanted to get more westerly so I adjusted our course from its slightly too-southerly route to a straight shot for Kauai. *Black Feathers* held her speed even though she endured more slaps against her hull and the now regular spray across her bow and over the dome. I, however, experienced a smoother ride than anticipated. Each time I looked aft, I couldn't help but be thankful for such a reliable and durable windvane that held its course impeccably. There is nothing like a good self-steering device.

By evening, things imitated the night before. This would be another "night of survival." Nothing to do but sit there, monitor things, try to control the wetness and hang on—too rough to read, too wet to practice my concertina and too uncertain to sleep. The life raft and ditch bag were again moved into position for quick access. Sitting there, I could feel frustration creeping over me. Things weren't going as I had hoped, and as I became more and more fatigued, my spirits began to sag. The boat was a mess. Supplies were everywhere. Little room remained for me. I was getting weary, and most of all, everything was becoming wet. This wasn't pretty. I felt I had planned better. Where did I go wrong?

Fortunately, the frustration did not turn to despair. As I sat there, a bit like a pouting child, I came to realize it made no difference if "it wasn't pretty." So what if things got wet? If all I have to complain about is things getting wet, is that really insurmountable? All things would eventually dry—and long before we arrived in Hawaii. As long as the boat remained secure and we were moving through the water with things working, I had nothing to complain about or apologize for. In fact, unless I told anyone how wet things got, no one would ever know. What a revelation! Within minutes, my attitude turned around and my sense of confidence returned. This renewed confidence allowed me to sit back and accept the situation, embracing just how pleased I felt being there, even as uncomfortable as it was.

The night continued, messy, somewhat uncomfortable, but productive in the number of miles covered. I knew then that the mileage during those last 24 hours would be our best of the race—and it proved to be, 143 nm.

I tend not to have many decorative things inside the cabin even though their presence may be comforting at times. This is because of the limited space and my desire to limit clutter. But in spite of this, I do keep a stone with a symbol engraved on it hanging from the VHF radio. It is the Japanese symbol for "patience" and it acts as my constant reminder to strive to maintain this critical quality. A sailor must have patience. When he runs short of it, he becomes vulnerable and can be overcome by frustration, anger and despair. When things got tiresome, I felt reassured when my eyes would rest upon this important symbol.

Chapter 7
The Ridge Transition

The TransPac race can be loosely divided into three sections. The first: Rough, cold, wet and mostly into the wind. The second: A transition where the wind veers and starts to come from astern. And the last: The run downwind through the northeast trade winds to Kauai. As the sun rose on the seventh day of the race, I found myself 570 miles off the coast of Los Angeles and 1728 miles from Hanalei. This transition phase of the race is most encouraging because the trades are not far away. Sailing in trade wind conditions is what most people think of and dream about when considering a sail to Hawaii—a steady, fresh breeze, warm air, clear skies with distant puffy clouds and water full of color and allure.

By early afternoon, the sun had come out to give us our first sunny day since the beginning of the race. It energized both the soul AND the batteries. The solar panel had done very well to keep up with our energy needs. Even without direct sun it had no problem charging. The battery monitor had also done well providing information on energy use and charging strength, but it had not been able to credit the proper number of amp hours being charged back into the batteries. Evidently, the battery monitor was set to record recharging at a threshold too high to credit all recharging by the solar panel. So even though the batteries were being fully charged during the day, the monitor indicated a slight loss of charge. Once aware of this anomaly, I paid no attention to the misinformation. I would, however, want to address this issue sometime after the race.

After two days with a double-reefed main, the wind slackened enough to shake out one reef and we maintained a steady 5 - 6 knots. Despite a fair amount of slapping of waves against the hull, the Monitor held a steady course.

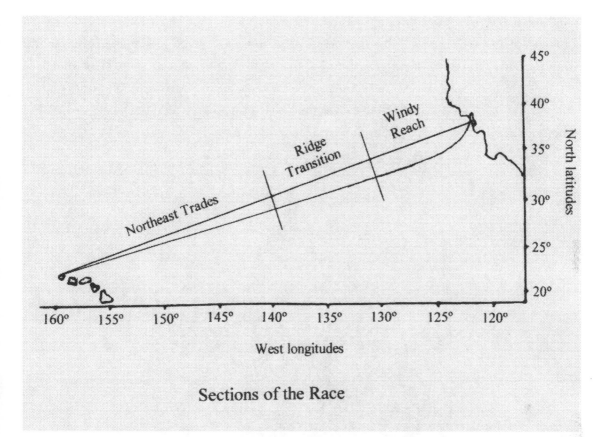

Sections of the Race

Each day, things need to be inspected to make sure all is well. The challenge: To do so thoroughly, and in the spirit of TRYING to locate problems rather than HOPING not to find any. On this day, I realized that the lines that allow the Monitor to move the tiller were rubbing against the line that adjusted the backstay. The rubbing had not harmed the Monitor lines, but had chafed the backstay adjuster line considerably. Since I don't alter my backstay tension very often, I simply attached a line to the adjuster and pulled it out of the way, resulting in a quick, easy fix for something that could have developed into a problem. Also when inspecting these lines, I found the tension on the Monitor lines to be excessive. Too much tension creates friction, and friction will greatly reduce the effectiveness of the Monitor's steering. It was a simple matter to lessen the tension. I expected the Monitor lines to stretch with time and use, and therefore, need to have their tension increased, but it proved precisely the opposite. During the race, I had to reduce the tension on these lines three or four times.

The morning of July 19th marked the eighth day of the race and was, as usual, overcast. After I shook out the one remaining reef, we were making a steady 6 knots. The consistent wind made the tiresome calm days of the beginning of the race seem long ago. We began a pattern of 125 - 130 nm per day that should last until we arrived in Hanalei Bay. Feeling confident this would be the case, when I spoke with Jeanne that morning I predicted if existing conditions continued, we should arrive in Hanalai Bay around noon on July 31st.

It felt good to have a projected arrival time based on an educated guess. It became my rabbit to chase.

Early Morning

As darkness descended on us, the wind freshened so I put in a reef. It had been a good day with much time spent reading and practicing my concertina. Also, the boat began drying out and the comfort level greatly improved. This sense of relaxation and control abruptly ended when around midnight the CARD alarm sounded. During the last couple of days we had encountered no commercial vessels so I had begun to forget about this ever-present danger.

The CARD picks up a radar emission and displays the direction it comes from. I popped my head into the dome, but the spray on the dome prevented clear vision so I opened the hatch to look around. The overcast night sky barred me from seeing any light from the stars or moon. I saw nothing but blackness. The absence of any light gives no sense of a horizon. There is no way to detect direction. My eyes strained to see anything in the direction the CARD had indicated the radar was emitting from, but there was nothing visible. From experience, I knew to have faith in the CARD and as I continued to scan what I thought might be the horizon, I saw two faint lights—a green and a red. The only way you see a green and a red together is when a vessel is coming AT you. Something needed to be done soon as we approached each other head-on. I scurried inside to check the AIS for a plotted position of the oncoming vessel. I knew the CARD would always pick up a target vessel before the AIS, and once the AIS responded, it would take several seconds before the relevant data would appear on the plot. I tried to be patient but nothing came up on the screen. I popped my head out of the cabin again to check the boat. Even without my glasses, I could see the green and red lights as we moved closer toward one another. There was no time to worry about the AIS; I had to evade the oncoming ship.

Earlier that day, I tried improving our boat speed by poling out the jib and thereby sailing wing-on-wing. The wind angle for that procedure, however, wasn't right so I eventually gave up on it and let the jib go back to its original side. Instead of totally securing the spinnaker pole (now being used as a whisker pole), I left it attached to the mast since I thought I might be using it again later in the day. Little did I realize that when doing this I allowed one of the jib sheets to fall under the pole. An understandable, but very un-seaman-like mistake—and like most such mistakes, one which would eventually come back to haunt me.

To evade the ship I simply needed to tack and sail off in a different direction. This normally would be no big deal even in the fresh breeze, but as I tacked, the jib sheet hung up under the pole causing it to swing up in the air and get wrapped around the jib. In a fresh breeze you need a smooth jib action to help you through the tack. This tack failed from the start. I not only had no help from the jib, its baggy, out-of-control shape caused it to become back-winded and I fell back onto my original course. With the spinnaker pole sticking up in an obscene gesture, I quickly realized my earlier mistake. Another attempt to tack would likely be met with failure, so with no other choice I could think of, I quickly let the main out in an effort to fall off onto a more favorable course. As the main went out and the boat now steered from our original course, I found we were not clear of the ship and the possibility still remained that our paths would cross. Therefore, I had to drastically alter our course—I needed to gybe the main. To gybe is to change your boat's course so the wind crosses your path not from the front (which is a tack) but from the stern. This will cause the mainsail to quickly slam across the cockpit to the other side as the wind crosses astern. Damage to one's body or the boat can be a resulting factor. To minimize any damage, as the wind was nearing the stern, I frantically pulled in the main sheet to lessen the degree of slam that might occur. Our timing proved good and the slam of the boom, as it swung across the cockpit, mercifully mild. We were now heading clear of any possible encounter with the ship. With my heart racing, I tried to assess WHERE we were heading. Without the ship's lights as a reference, I had no idea of our direction in the pitch-black night. In order to save battery power, the compass light is not routinely kept on so I had no point of reference until I could turn my headlight on and check the compass. I could then take time to scan what I hoped was the horizon to see the ship again. I swiveled around and felt relieved to see only red and white lights indicating the vessel no longer posed a menace.

In order to change course, I had previously disengaged the Monitor's steering. Once re-engaged, I proceeded forward to the bow and untangled the mess with the spinnaker pole and jib. It always takes longer to do things than you think it should. When it's dark you must rely on your headlight to see, and whenever you go outside the cabin, you must tether yourself to the boat to prevent falling overboard. These encumbrances, along with the heel angle of the boat, demand more caution, and inevitably slow you down, but slowly things get done and before long you can return to the relative peace, quiet and inviting calmness of the cabin. With the alarm of the CARD still alerting me of a ship in the area, I again checked the AIS—still no trace of the ship indicated. The AIS simply had not detected the ship, possibly because the ship did not have its transponder on. This would remain a mystery.

The night passed without further incident, but the mishap with the spinnaker pole weighed heavy on my mind. It seems that when problems occur on a boat they tend to escalate given any opportunity. You must be ever vigilant to observe and listen for anything that doesn't look or sound right—and once detected, these things must be investigated as soon as possible. Also when a boating maneuver is completed, such as a tack, the area must be inspected and made ready for future maneuvers. To disregard this, is to ask for unexpected surprises that may come at the most inopportune time. I vowed to be more conscientious in my seamanship.

During the next couple of days, the persistent overcast skies gave way to ever-increasing clearing, both day and night. For the first time since the beginning of the race we had a real sunset. As we sailed toward the west it surprisingly reassured me to have a celestial body confirm our direction of sail instead of having to rely solely on the impersonal data of a GPS or compass.

Due to our latitude, now equivalent to the border of Mexico, things were clearly warming, especially during the day. None of my clothing resembled what I started out wearing. Instead of the warm, breathable, but bulky sailing boots of the start, I had now switched to tabis footwear. These odd-looking lightweight felt-soled mittens for your feet provide excellent traction on slippery surfaces, as well as protection for your feet and toes. They dry quickly, and if washed every couple of days, don't develop an odor. Besides being a great warm water boat shoe, they are highly recommended as footwear in Hawaii for hikes and reef walking.

This part of the race course seems to be the most frustrating. As we approach and cross a weather ridge created by the Pacific High pressure area, the wind veers, coming more from the stern. Once we pass this transition area and enter the trade winds, the wind will primarily be from astern and we can make a straight run for the islands. At least that is the theory. Here in the transition, it was tempting to set our spinnaker or twins, but the wind didn't seem right for that and I found it difficult to hold a steady course. The sails would periodically become back-winded due to the limits of the pole angle. During this time, I needed to glance at my "patience" symbol and relax. Our time would come. We had to wait and earn the position for effective downwind sailing. In reality, our time came sooner rather than later, for during the following afternoon with the sun casting a yellow-gold glow on the clouds against the blue sky, *Black Feathers* flew her black and white spinnaker for several hours. The next day she would fly it for 24 hours straight—a record for her.

Unless it is an overcast night with no stars or moon, it is surprising how well you can see your spinnaker at night. If there are lots of stars, it will block them out and create a dark silhouette of the sail's shape. If the spinnaker has black borders, these will stand out against a dark gray sky. I had heard it is helpful to have your spinnaker lined with black but I had never seen one. *Black Feathers'* spinnaker has areas of black randomly scattered throughout and some of the areas create a border. This concept truly works. Yes, the black portions along the border did stand out against the dark gray sky.

Black Feathers' Spinnaker

A couple of days had passed since our encounter with the ship, and neither the CARD nor the AIS had sounded an alarm. The failure of the AIS to display the last ship we encountered created some doubt in my mind about the AIS's effectiveness so I was almost relieved when the CARD's alarm again went off. It was a clear, beautiful day so I knew this would be a much more controlled situation. At first, I could see nothing looking in the direction the CARD had indicated, but on closer inspection, a ship could be seen coming off the horizon and our paths would definitely cross if no evasive action were taken. As our paths continued toward one another I wondered about the AIS, but I also wondered if we showed up on their radar. Before the AIS announced their presence, I decided to try to call them on the VHF.

You sound a bit vague calling out on the VHF to a vessel whose name is unknown to you.

Do you say: "Oncoming freighter, oncoming freighter, this is the sailing vessel *Black Feathers*, come in please"?

Or, do you instead say: "Commercial vessel heading NW, —"?

Or say what you really feel: "Big scary ship heading straight for me, —"?

I tried the "Oncoming freighter" version, and to my surprise, got an immediate response.

Many times a call to an unidentified vessel goes unanswered, but the voice from this vessel called back clear and precise, carrying a distinguished accent from what sounded to me like India or Pakistan. The voice informed me that the oncoming ship was a car container, not a freighter, and carried the name of *Pegasus Leader*.

I responded, "*Pegasus Leader*, this is *Black Feathers*, a small sailing vessel heading for Hawaii. Do I appear on your radar? Over."

I was quite relieved to hear, "*Black Feathers*, yes, we have visual and radar contact. Over."

As our paths narrowed, I, unsure if I would pass ahead of or behind her, decided to declare my intentions by saying, "*Pegasus Leader*, it is my intention to hold my course. Is that okay? Over."

To this, I received a rather indignant response. "*Black Feathers*, you MUST hold your course. Over."

I had just been scolded. Aware that a sailing vessel is expected to hold her course and allow the powered vessel to alter course if necessary (and if possible), I still wanted to give the ship the option as she was MUCH bigger and faster than *Black Feathers*, and she could make a much greater impression on us than we on her.

I humbly responded, "*Pegasus Leader*, this is *Black Feathers*. I will hold my course. Thank you very much for the information and have a nice day. Over."

Our conversation ended with, "*Black Feathers*, have a nice voyage. *Pegasus Leader*—Out."

By this time, I could see they had slightly altered their course to allow me to cross their path in front of them. The alarm on the AIS had gone off just after I called the ship, and when I entered the cabin I could see *Pegasus Leader's* location, speed, course and name on the plotter of the AIS. The AIS picked her up at four miles. The CARD had done so at about 10 miles.

I felt good about this encounter. Several things went right. It confirmed the AIS was functioning properly, I learned that my radar reflector allowed me to show up on the ship's radar, I felt reassured knowing the vessel intended to avoid me and that I possibly might confuse them if I unnecessarily altered my course. These were all good things to keep in mind for my next encounter.

The beautiful day turned into an enchanting night with a sky so full of stars it became difficult to identify any particular one. Although still chilly, it felt magical to lie down in the cockpit and look up at the heavens. To save energy, unless I detected a ship, the only navigation light I kept on was the masthead strobe. If a ship were seen, I would then turn on the stern and red/green running lights. But now, in the darkness, with no one around, I lazed there watching my strobe blinking away as if trying to signal the millions and millions of stars above me. *Black Feathers* sailed wing-on-wing through the night, trailing in her wake a stream of phosphorescent glitter that seemingly tried to compete with the diamonds overhead. Our speed would always feel greater at night. Often I would stand in the hatch, 10 feet of boat in front of me and 10 feet behind, and marvel at how it all works. How can it be that I, the only one aboard, can be riding along as a passive observer watching this incredible machine carrying me across this ocean? I would look forward into the darkness and see the sails as they blocked out the shine of the stars. I would look behind and see the Monitor, ever vigilant, creating constant but subtle movements of the tiller to keep us on course. With a steady breeze in my face I would feel the stern rise, as an overtaking wave would lift us, and then let us fall as we would slide down its face, and the resultant wake would leave a glittery trail as a reminder of where we had been. It was all a bit too much to take in and fully appreciate at one time. Fortunately I would experience this time after time and come to accept it as truth.

Chapter 8

The Northeast Trade Winds

The transition phase of the race where we try to get into the northeast trade winds has always been a bit confusing to me. The winds get variable both in their speed and direction causing the wretched sailor to try one sailing configuration after another in hopes of getting the most speed out of his boat. It can be trying and tiresome to stay attentive when all the while you remain uncertain whether your efforts are effective or not. I fear I find myself taking the lazy man's path of doing nothing far too often. In spite of that tendency, we tried all sorts of sailing the last few days as we neared mid-point in the race. The repertoire of sailing configurations used in the race at that point generally involved sailing wing-on-wing with the pole on starboard or port, sailing with the spinnaker with the pole on starboard or port, and sailing with the spinnaker both with and without the main. With *Black Feathers* being so short and lightweight, the actions of the wind and waves would kick her around quite a bit and I often found our course resembled a snake's path. Holding a straight course became my constant concern.

The day of July 23rd would be marked with memorable events. The first: We passed longitude 140°W and I felt comfortable we were at last in the trades, our latitude at that time being 29°N. The second: A surprise visit. On this overcast day, a large squall-like mass of rain approached from astern in the afternoon. As I watched it nearing, a red spinnaker emerged from the gray mass, and slowly a sailboat appeared.

I could see them, but I wondered how well they might see me, so I called them on the VHF radio. They did not respond, but I wasn't surprised. With their spinnaker keeping them in the heavy air at the leading edge of the squall, I figured they were busy and would call me as they passed. It didn't take long. The boat, *Rage*, a Sunrise 70 out of Portland, Oregon participating in the PacCup, is a well-known boat in the racing community. A welcome sight for me, it confirmed I was still heading in the right direction and possibly in a good location. During the race I steered a more southerly positioned course than most of my competitors, and I had hoped this would not work against me. Seeing another boat in the area didn't necessarily confirm anything, but reassured me nonetheless.

Typical Trade Swells

As *Rage* sailed abeam she called me and we had a good conversation. Her skipper, Steve Rander, informed me, as had *Rain Drop* a few days earlier, that Portland has a large Cal 20 fleet with considerable interest being expressed in my efforts. He mentioned that several of his crewmembers were past Cal 20 sailors. I must admit this attention and encouragement honored me. Such support goes a long way and may even prove critically important if things get tough. As with the other Pacific Cup boats, I couldn't help but feel a little lonely as *Rage* pulled ahead and eventually disappeared over the horizon. Alone again. Well, maybe alone physically, but not in spirit.

The night passed without incident as *Black Feathers* sailed wing-on-wing with a reefed main.

The morning of July 24th brought with it a celebration. *Black Feathers* had crossed the halfway point of the race during the night—I called Jeanne. It was our regular morning call, but not our normal conversation. There is a tradition in the TransPac for the skipper to open a halfway gift from his or her loved one as they reach this point of the race. Also, the loved one may receive a halfway gift from the skipper. After giving Jeanne my race update, we opened our gifts together as we talked. A sensitive time, a time of loneliness, yes, but more a time of closeness. With each mile of the race, the mundane details of life become less important and the deeper feelings that take their place can be felt and expressed much more easily and openly.

As a halfway gift, Jeanne had written a small book for me—a tale of a mermaid and a knight. The storyline blended our own lives with those of her characters—a story of searching and of love, a fairy tale, yet true. Such things tighten the throat and bring tears to the eyes but lift the heart and add strength for the second half of the race yet to come. At the end of the book, Jeanne had placed a photo of a bronze mermaid—a sculpture I had admired at a store prior to my departure. She bought the mermaid, but because it was much too heavy to put onboard *Black Feathers*, she wrote the story. I would receive the bronze version when we returned home in August.

A charm from my mother's antique charm bracelet represented my halfway gift to Jeanne. Not surprisingly, the charm's likeness of a small sailboat resembled *Black Feathers*. It would rest near Jeanne's heart, just as her story would play on my mind.

After my halfway celebration with Jeanne, I settled myself in the cabin and spent the next couple of hours reading the book she had written for me.

The morning was overcast as usual. I spent the day reveling in *Black Feathers'* sailing—straight and smooth. We were doing great.

Halfway. A slow start had put us behind our projected schedule by two days, but that applied to the entire fleet. *Black Feathers'* position remained very competitive.

That afternoon with thoughts of my halfway gift fresh in my mind, I sat comfortably in the cockpit taking in the sights and sounds of the wind and sea—and *Black Feathers*. As stated before, the sounds on a boat are of paramount importance. Changes from normal don't happen without a reason, so when I first noticed a scratchy sound coming from the stern of the boat, I immediately grew concerned. My first thought: The mounting plates for the Monitor Windvane might be loosening and the Monitor torquing from side-to-side. This wonderful piece of equipment had endured so much strain for such a distance, it seemed reasonable it might be coming loose. This thought ran through my mind as I stepped across the solar panel supports to the back of the boat. When I looked down I saw one of those sights that induces nausea and leaves your mind fighting trying to comprehend what to do next, while imagining all the sickening downside consequences of what you are observing. OUR RUDDER HAD BROKEN! I knew I needed to avoid panic and to think things through before I reacted. However, I obviously also needed to address this catastrophic failure quickly, because without a rudder, the boat would lose control.

The underwater portion of *Black Feathers'* fiberglass rudder had split apart at the waterline and that loose portion had risen up to lay flat on the surface of the water. It must have JUST happened because we had not yet fallen off course.

There are an infinite number of developments that can present catastrophic problems on a sailboat. The two most common are a broken mast and a broken rudder. Realizing this, the SSS requires all racers to carry an emergency rudder. The problem is that rarely do we test our emergency rudders under stressful open ocean conditions, and if we did, many emergency rudders would fail. This was precisely the case for the smallest boat in the 2006 Transpac—a 23' vessel by the name of *Hesperus*. In that case, when the emergency rudder was installed, it too broke, leaving the skipper, Paul Woodward, with few efficient steering options. Paul, approximately 300 miles from the finish, met the challenge, however, and managed to bring his boat into Hanalei Bay after several days. A fellow skipper in that race, Chris Humann of *Carroll E*, chose to drop out of the race to be on stand-by as *Hesperus* limped toward the finish. This act of collegiality and sportsmanship demonstrated the highest qualities a racer can possess. Chris Humann returned in 2008 and was now within 30 miles of *Black Feathers* when my boat broke her rudder. Being familiar with what had happened to *Hesperus*, I knew if I experienced the same difficulties, my TransPac objective "to keep alive the dream of the common man doing the race in a rather basic craft," would be totally lost. I needed to think through my plan of action for I might only get one chance to achieve an effective remedy.

In spite of some obvious disadvantages, a simple Cal 20 has some very real advantages, and one of those concerns the rudder. Whereas all racers in larger boats have some form of emergency rudder; many, if not most of these emergency rudders, are smaller versions of their normal rudder. These small versions will not be as effective, and although the boat will get to the finish, it will not do so in a true racing mode. *Black Feathers'* emergency rudder was her original 1961, solid mahogany rudder which had graced her stern until I replaced it with the modern fiberglass rudder which had just broken. If all went well, once replaced, we should be able to carry on in full racing mode. A great fix appeared possible. All I needed to do: Plan it out and do it. It was late afternoon in normal trade wind conditions.

The first thing I needed to do was to take down the sails, as there is no way to replace a rudder with the boat moving along out of control under sail. Once the sails were down, the boat turned so the swells were meeting the boat on the beam. This orientation can create issues because if the swells are breaking, the boat can suddenly take on large amounts of water and the motion can be difficult to work in as it creates unstable footing. But since the swells were not breaking, I didn't have to deal with water coming over the side and the boat's movement actually calmed down much more than I had anticipated.

Next, I had to remove the broken rudder and stow it away in the cockpit where I could later examine it and remove its various fixtures. I disengaged the Monitor from the tiller and then worked under the solar panel to remove the tiller from the rudder. With the tiller removed, I could disengage the pintles from the gudgeons and lift the rudder off the transom and out from the confines of the surrounding windvane. This done, I secured the broken rudder to one of the cockpit seats.

Now it was time to retrieve the spare rudder from under everything in the V-berth in the bow area. I tried to create as little disarray as possible, but the already cramped cabin quickly became a jumble of storage bins, sail bags, water bottles, spare parts, etc. The boat seemed to be fairly stable as she bobbed around, or at least it seemed stable until I stood up holding the large, fairly heavy mahogany rudder. The walk back to the stern definitely tested my balancing abilities. As I stepped over the first of two solar panel supports the moving surfaces proved too much for me and I fell onto the top of the solar panel. A crunch emanated as my elbow pressed on the glass and a thousand cracks instantly ran through the entire surface of the panel. It amazed me how easily I accepted what had just happened, saying to myself, "Okay, you just broke the solar panel. We should be able to get along without it! Keep going but be more careful."

One conscious thought acted like a cloud over all my other thoughts as I worked my way past the solar panel and prepared to lower the spare rudder into position. A common mistake when mounting pintles on a rudder is having them in a position requiring both the upper and lower pintles to enter the gudgeons at precisely the same time. Having them mounted in this manner requires the rudder to be perfectly aligned before the pintles will slip into place. I knew the pintles were placed in this fashion on the spare (original) rudder. It proved fairly easy to put the spare on the boat in practice at the dock, but now I would have to do the installation on the pitching open sea—NOT an easy task.

The rudder, measuring 5 1/2' feet tall and 1 1/2' wide and weighing 25 pounds, is not so heavy as it is bulky and awkward to handle. After I managed to squeeze myself and the rudder between the Monitor and the back of the solar panel, I impatiently attempted to slip it between the Monitor supports and into the water. It needed to go almost to its fully down position before the pintles would start to enter the gudgeons. Right about now, I think I should assure you—YES, I WAS tethered to the boat. The boat movement made any pintle engagement highly improbable and I almost lost my grip on the rudder. Had it been pulled from my hands, it would have quickly drifted away and I would have been left with only ineffective emergency steering alternatives. I hauled the rudder out of the water, back onboard and laid it down in the cockpit. I took a deep breath and again, I reminded myself to slow down. I could manage this situation, but I needed more control. This would at least require a more stable area to work in. To create this, I released the aft-most supports for the solar panel, which allowed me to rotate it toward the front of the boat. I expected all the thousands of cracked pieces of glass to fall out as I swiveled it over, but none did.

Now that I had a more suitable work area, I needed to secure a line to the rudder so if I lost my grip on it, it would not drift away. I could feel my confidence mounting as I prepared to reseat the rudder. Kneeling on the back of the cockpit with my arms around the rudder, I slid it down between the Monitor supports and watched the pintles as they neared their respective gudgeons. All seemed to line up until the last half-inch when the boat's movement forced the rudder off alignment. I kept trying. Each time I tried, I clutched the rudder harder against my chest for more support. It seemed there was no way I could benefit by the failures that preceded my previous attempts. The lack of consistency in the pattern of the boat movement made it impossible for me to anticipate the exact moment of the pintle alignment, which was necessary to accomplish my objective. Each attempt began with confidence but met with failure.

This went on for a half an hour as frustration and despair began to develop. My hands bled from the bangs and scrapes endured during the various attempts. My chest hurt from the pressure of the rudder against my body. And, of course, I grew more and more exhausted.

I knew if I could simply get the rudder seated on its gudgeons I would have a superb fix to a significant problem. I also knew failure to do so would leave me over a thousand miles from Hanalei Bay trying to steer the boat with some very compromised methods. The best of these methods would be to use the Monitor to steer. With no rudder, the Monitor paddle that extends into the water can be used as a rudder. It has a limited degree of swivel ability, but it would definitely work. When used in this manner, the self-steering quality of the Monitor is lost. The result: All steering would have to be done by hand using the Monitor lines. Not something I would relish doing for almost half the race.

If that failed and I needed another option, I could consider steering with just sails. Since we were in the trades, the race was pretty much a downwind run to Hanalei Bay from this point. If I set twin jibs and no main, that sail configuration could move us dead downwind fairly effectively. With poled-out twin jibs, as the boat falls off course, more force is placed on one jib. This extra force corrects the course until the forces are equal. This would definitely get us to Hawaii somewhere, but it is unlikely it would be to Hanalei Bay.

Another option would be similar to what Paul Woodward of *Hesperus* used in the 2006 TransPac wherein he drug a bucket behind the boat on one side or the other. Boats tend to turn to the side of the greatest drag.

I had various fallback plans but hoped they would be unnecessary as I had a perfect fix so close at hand. All I needed—a split second for things to line up so I could push down in time to get the pintles to seat within the gudeons.

Suddenly it came to me—as I attempted to seat the pintles, my mind had been focused more on what to do if it failed than what to do to succeed. I had to readjust my thinking. Between this mental adjustment and a bit of luck, both pintles finally found their mark at exactly the same time and the rudder dropped that last two inches into the gudgeons. As I felt it drop to its full seat, I quickly locked it in place. A sense of absolute elation came over me. *Black Feathers* was back in business!

It took only a few minutes to reposition the solar panel, attach the tiller to the spare rudder and adjust the Monitor lines to the tiller. Then up went the sails, and *Black Feathers* was back on course. The fix had taken a little over an hour. During all this, the designated time to call Jeanne had come and gone. I felt it important to solve the problem before telling her about it. She, too, was familiar with *Hesperus*. And although impressed by the skipper's success in sailing to Hanalei Bay, she understood the endurance it took, as well as the fact that he could no longer effectively race. I did not want her to worry. With the boat an absolute mess, I relaxed in the cabin and reached for the SAT phone. Jeanne and I had a good talk, and since we were back in the race, I enjoyed relating the story. When all things go well, you tend to wonder what you would have done had they not. But now with our problem resolved, we enjoyed the sense of accomplishment. Hopefully, we would not have to deal with another crisis of such magnitude.

I spent the next hour re-organizing the boat. Then I relaxed again and reached for the SAT phone—this time to call my son and wish him a happy birthday. The wind picked up and as darkness fell I placed a 2nd reef in the main. It had been a very full day.

Later when I had time to give the pintle dilemma some more in-depth thought, it came to me that I had succumbed to the temptation to use brawn rather than brains in my approach. On the transom of the boat I had placed double gudgeons for both the upper and lower pintles. The length of each pintle being sufficient to go through both gudgeons and still have half an inch of excess. Had I been unable to seat the rudder, I could have simply sawed off a half-inch portion of the upper pintle. Having done that, I would have been able to first insert the lower pintle, and then with the lower portion stable, line up the upper and push it in place. This would have been a much less stressful fix, and certainly could have been accomplished during the crisis onboard the boat, but also could have taken place before the race as I had long been aware of the pintle concern. Some things should not be ignored.

I spent the next couple of days addressing how *Black Feathers* sailed with the newly installed rudder under varying winds. I didn't expect to detect any changes and I didn't. The winds varied from 15 knots to the low 20s. Our usual sail configuration: The jib poled out on the port side with one reef in the main. When the wind got into the 20s, I placed a 2nd reef in the main. Our speed was good at 5 1/2 - 6 knots and we made a steady 125 - 135 nm per day.

Our course concerned me. Not as straight as it should be, we were sailing more miles than needed. Also, the constant adjustments due to wind and waves on the Monitor's steering stressed it more than necessary. If we could balance the sail trim better, we could sail straighter with less effort. I decided to go with twin jibs on poles. When sailing downwind, a boat can do a fair amount of its own steering by poling out a jib on each side. If I could drop the mainsail, and not lose much boat speed, that too would add to a more stable sail plan and, therefore, a straighter course. With a bit over 600 miles to the finish, I retrieved the second spinnaker (whisker) pole and a second identical-sized jib and raised them on *Black Feathers'* single headstay.

To my pleasant surprise, this procedure went smoothly. As the twins took charge, and the mainsail came down, *Black Feathers* settled onto a straight and stable course. Much less correction seemed to be necessary by the Monitor as the waves overtook and passed under us. Without a main to reef, no change was necessary as the wind increased with an oncoming squall. We had a forgiving and comfortable sail plan for this part of the race.

When things go well, there is plenty of time to do things other than actively sail. My favorite: Practicing my concertina. Other entertainment for me included educational audio CD's and reading.

I have long enjoyed Homer's *Odyssey* and thought that a reading of it would be inspiring during the TransPac. Poor Odysseus had to endure so much during his 10-year journey back to Ithaca from Troy. In contrast, my short time on the Pacific appeared as merely a mild challenge. Any TransPacer would greatly benefit by emulating Odysseus' qualities of patience and tenacity.

Trade Wind Twins

At one point in the tale, Homer refers to Odysseus as "scudding over the sea's broad back." This, in fact, is what I did in this part of our race. *Black Feathers* and I were indeed "scudding over the sea's broad back," and if we could keep it up for just a few more days we would find ourselves scudding into Hanalei Bay. I found Homer most inspiring and Odysseus certainly had the makings of a great TransPacer.

Twenty-four hours sailing under twins convinced me it was a valuable sail plan to have in my repertoire. As the winds increased, two things happened—one: There was no main to reef and, two: We didn't have to sail wing-on-wing as that creates instability in the boat's performance. I was, however, concerned about how I might de-power the poled-out jibs should the winds increase alarmingly.

Two ideas came to mind that might allow me to de-power the twins without taking them down—one: I could allow their poles to move more forward, and two: I could decrease the sails' effectiveness by raising the poles. I never did either of these but I felt reassured, having given thought to the solutions, just in case.

The night of July 28th started out being another of those anxious, survival nights. The winds approached 25 knots and it felt as if we were flying across the ocean, even though our actual boat speed was more like 6 1/2 knots. The steering required little correction. With the winds increasing, I began to feel that things could get out of control any time, and anxiety began settling in. I had been in this position several times before and knew the best solution. Simply evaluate the conditions to see if things remained stable and all continued to work well. I did my evaluation. Finding everything fine, I just relaxed and enjoyed the ride. The mental demons that occasionally attempt to take over are worthy opponents but can be slain by rational thought and a calm demeanor.

The night passed quickly and without the persistent anxieties that had plagued me at times on some earlier nights. We did well with regard to both control and mileage. I felt confident. During the next day the ever-present haunting mantra of, "This is a race. Are you doing all you can to increase your speed?" ran through my mind. I could not honestly answer "Yes"— because I could look at my mainsail and see it neatly folded upon the boom. Finally I could take it no longer so I raised the main to increase the sail area. Possibly our speed improved, but I cannot be sure that this led to a consistent improvement. What I can be sure of is that the steering became more difficult, and our course began to suffer. After a couple of hours of this sail configuration, I'd had enough, and down came the main. It would not be raised again until our final approach to Hanalei Bay. We returned to a smooth, straight course.

That night my talk with Jeanne became quite emotional for me. She had flown to Kauai that day and settled in the condo we had rented. It seems strange, but it inspired me knowing she was in Kauai and that I was sailing TO her rather than away from her—a simple change of perspective, but quite profound. Then she hit me with the news of *Sparky*. *Sparky* had dismasted the day before. Ruben Gabriel, her skipper, had been sailing with twins. With the hope of driving the boat as effectively as possible he added his main with poled-out twins. An approaching squall led him to place a reef in the main. In spite of this maneuver, the wind gusts leading the squall caused the boat to round up driving the leeward pole into the water. The resultant force broke the mast. Ruben, uninjured, had a downed mast and was trying to deal with it. That's all Jeanne knew. We soon finished our talk and with a loving goodbye, I broke into tears.

My greatest fear in the race was to be hit by a ship, but my next greatest fears were breaking a rudder or losing a mast. Luckily I averted a disabling failure by replacing my rudder, but Ruben had lost his mast. No skipper can devise a clean and complete fix for that.

He was 670 miles from Hanalei Bay and only his patience, tenacity and creativity would get him through this. My heart ached for him as I pictured him in my mind struggling to take control of his situation. The loneliness and sense of isolation must have been overwhelming. Too soon for me to have thought it through, I reacted on pure emotion and I could not control my tears. Ruben became the race's Odysseus with a perilous task ahead of him. My thoughts and hopes were with him, and I'm sure the same became true of every skipper in the TransPac.

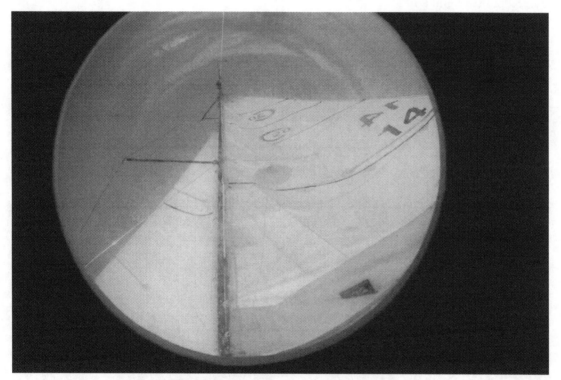

Observing the Sails Through the Dome

As I sat in *Black Feathers'* small cabin, thoughts of when I first met Ruben flashed through my mind. At the April TransPac seminar, he introduced himself saying I had inspired him to begin preparing his small boat, *Sparky*, a Pearson Electra 22, for the race. As I had rarely been told I inspired anyone to do anything, his comments touched me. Ruben is a handsome, soft-spoken guy full of enthusiasm, yet interested and patient enough to really listen to what others have to say. We talked a bit about small boats and when I left the meeting, it pleased me to know that if all worked out for him, there would be at least one other small boat in the 2008 TransPac.

Ruben showed his determination and resolve while doing his race qualifier on *Sparky*. Deadlines and other demands forced him to sail his qualifier in challenging weather conditions. Despite this, he did well and the experience added to his confidence level. The stage was set for a spirited race within the small boat division. Although the TransPac fleet would consist of 22 boats, the small boats of *Sparky, Feral, Carroll E* and *Black Feathers* would be watching each other with the greatest of interest.

Now we all had a different kind of interest in *Sparky* and Ruben—we wanted them to reach Kauai safe and sound.

Trade Wind Sunset

Chapter 9
Final Approach

At this point in the race, the sailing is as good as it gets. The days are warm and sunny with a steady trade wind breeze and beautiful azure water. *Black Feathers* was making good mileage. The final couple of days would be significant for each of the remaining smaller boats. A very close race developed among us as the small boats of this TransPac proved very competitive. Although very much in the race until her dismasting, *Sparky* now found herself out of contention.

My thoughts for these last few days would involve driving *Black Feathers* straight for Hanalei Bay with the hope of not breaking anything else. If the winds held, I would keep the poled-out jibs pulling hard. If the winds failed, I would need to react in a timely manner to alter the sail plan and do my best not to become sloppy or lazy.

I had nearly 200 miles to go to reach Hanalei Bay. As the sun began to drop below the horizon and the skies filled with the golds, yellows and reds of the developing sunset, I noticed a great deal of bird activity in the area. As always when a bird approached I energetically whistled and made friendly gestures, hoping to encourage the curious creature to visit. This oft-repeated pattern never met with any success. This day, however, proved different. One bird in particular continuously circled *Black Feathers* in ever-diminishing circles. Encouraged at first, I became alarmed as it hovered at the top of the mast, showing great interest in the wind indicator. Birds often disable these delicately swiveling sailing aids.

Another circle brought our curious feathered friend hovering near the Monitor's air vane, only a couple of feet above the cockpit. Apparently intrigued by what it saw, the bird made a final low circle, skidding to a stop on the solar panel. I couldn't believe it! This bird actually landed on *Black Feathers*. I expected it to fly off at any moment, but it stayed put, and in fact began settling in for a stay. I'd never seen a wild animal pay so little attention to a nearby human. Its only focus was in preening itself, and it did so long into the night.

Twins with No Main

The bird must have grown tired of trying to maintain its balance on the slippery and slightly inclined solar panel, so it jumped onto a nearby railing. This proved more stable, and after a few more hours of preening, it snuggled its head fully into the feathers covering its wings. It was obviously nap time. I took several flash pictures of it and checked on it regularly using my headlight. The light didn't disturb the creature one bit. I began to have the feeling this bird had done this before—perhaps on a regular basis.

The night passed peacefully and the fact the bird was still aboard amazed me. What could be better than a fresh warm breeze, a beautiful sky full of a zillion stars all competing for attention, moderate seas that allowed *Black Feathers* to gently surf the waves as they passed under us, and this creature that had chosen to hitch a ride with us. One drawback, however: Sea birds eat a lot of squid, fish and other sea inhabitants, and have a rather high rate of metabolism. Our visitor had settled in on the stern railing as we sailed downwind. That left me downwind of the bird, and it didn't take long for my olfactory nerves to acknowledge that fact. Despite the foul odor, *Black Feathers* and I were honored to have our feathered friend onboard, and welcomed it to stay as long as it wished.

My Feathered Stowaway

This bird had an appearance similar to an albatross, and that is what I hoped it was. Later I learned it was a red-footed boobie. Boobies are considered to be extreme nuisances by most sailors, but as an avid bird person, whether it would have been an albatross or a red-footed boobie, I felt honored to have such a guest aboard—and I relished the company.

As we neared the islands, I expected an increase in commercial traffic so I needed to pay more attention to my surroundings. I didn't go back to the 15-minute sleep cycle I had used coming out of San Francisco, but did implement a 30-minute cycle.

The CARD went off first, as it always did, and shortly thereafter the AIS responded. I spotted the oncoming ship. No danger, but I took my position beneath the dome choosing to keep an eye on things for a while. The night passed uneventfully.

With the dawn came a beautiful sunrise. Since much of the weather to this point had been overcast, I greatly appreciated the presence of the sun. The latitude of Kauai is almost exactly the same number of degrees as the inclination of the earth, so noon passes directly overhead. It is fascinating to watch the beautiful sunrise to the east, a noon sun directly overhead, and an explosive sunset to the west each day. You cannot help but feel in touch with nature and her daily phenomenal patterns—things that may have previously gone unnoticed.

On the morning of July 31st, I thought, "Tomorrow at this time I should be at the Kilauea Light to begin my final approach to Hanalei Bay." Realizing things were actually coming together was most exhilarating!

I sat in the cockpit visiting with my feathered friend when all of a sudden a splash of water drenched the cockpit, and plop, there on the deck landed a most surprised and concerned flying fish. It must be quite startling for such a critter to be swimming along peacefully one second, and find itself splashed aboard an oncoming boat the next. All too often, I find these flying fish a bit too late to rescue them. Sadly, they wash or fly aboard quite regularly, but mostly when I am unaware or unable to break away to help them. Fortunately for this fish, we met at a convenient time, which enabled me to return it to the sea.

The solar panel continued to do a great job recharging the batteries despite the glass protection being totally shattered and enduring several downfalls of rain. When it originally broke, I believed I could complete the race with the energy stored in the batteries at that time, but happily it had performed as if it had never been broken. I looked forward to seeing how efficiently it would continue to function.

By now, my SAT phone calls to Jeanne at 7 a.m. and 7 p.m. (PDT) provided the much needed and greatly anticipated highlight of my day. After the morning's talk I felt relieved to learn that Ruben of *Sparky* had jury rigged a mast and was again moving well. Great news! As Jeanne spoke, I couldn't help but think how exciting it would be for everyone to see Ruben sail *Sparky* across the finish line. He would have accomplished a tremendous feat. Jeanne then told me *Carroll E* had arrived that afternoon, and *Feral* and *Kali O Kalani* were due later that night or early the next morning, slightly before *Black Feathers*. The weather fax indicated "dead air" coming in directly behind me. She told me, "Put the pedal to the metal and get your fanny in gear, or you're going to spend the next two days sitting offshore with no wind." I gathered she was somewhat anxious to see me. Later I learned from Chris Humann of *Carroll E*, that as he crossed the finish line he started his stopwatch to measure our finish time separation. He had to give me about 20 hours on corrected time. We both knew it would be close.

The day provided some beautiful sailing and I spent most of the time outside. The Monitor steered its steady course, the twin jibs pulled *Black Feathers* toward the island and the bird rested, preened and took in the sights. Toward sunset, the scene very much resembled the evening before. Birds filled the skies. Instead of preening or sleeping, our feathered visitor appeared very content observing the other birds surrounding the boat. It came alive with periodic stretching of the wings. Although my wish would have been for the bird to cross the finish line with me, I had little doubt that the time was nearing when the bird would take off and rejoin its buddies.

As the sun dropped below the horizon, and the sky filled with hues of blue, red and yellow, the bird leapt from the stern railing and dropped into the water. It alarmed me as I didn't know if it could simply flap its wings and rise up out of the water, or if it needed some kind of runway to get sufficient speed for liftoff. It sat on the water a mere second before it gave a couple of forceful flaps and up it went. I had rehearsed this sad departure, and just as I was coping with the fullness of my loss, the bird closely circled the boat twice and made another skidding landing on the solar panel. Two small steps to the panel's edge and a quick hop to the railing allowed it to again settle in for the night. The critter didn't appear quite ready to take its leave. There would be less preening this night, and much more sleeping.

I don't know what woke me, but I looked about and saw the time—1 a.m. (PDT) (10 p.m. Hawaiian time). I stuck my head out the open hatch and scanned the horizon. At first I saw nothing, but I kept searching. All of a sudden the flash of an arching light crossed before me. I looked closer. It happened again. A flashing light definitely appeared before us, and upon closer inspection, I observed a slight glow on the horizon, just to the left of the flashing light. I checked my chart to see if it might be the Kilauea Light—the northern most part of Kauai. If on course, it should be the first thing I'd see. I checked the GPS and it indicated we were 44 miles from the Kilauea Light. The chart stated the light could be seen for 23 miles. Could we be seeing it from 44 miles? I saw a glow from lights to the left of the flash. The town of Kapaa? It made sense when looking at the charts, but we were seeing these things from too far away. Maybe I was all wrong and it wasn't even the right area or even the right island. No—that couldn't be. Our GPS could be off a bit, but not that much.

Staring through the darkness at the flashing light, I reached the conclusion I wasn't seeing the actual Kilauea Light—I was simply observing its light reflecting off the clouds above it. A few hours later, this phenomena became even more clear as I could actually see the Light, and also see that which I observed earlier—the light shining off the clouds above it. We were closing in on Kauai, and right on course. There were clouds on the horizon, clear skies overhead with massive amounts of stars—and pitch-blackness surrounding *Black Feathers*.

For years I came to Kauai to visit my parents in Hanalei Bay. I had sailed there twice, but both times arrived during the daylight hours. I had heard many stories about a nighttime approach so I knew it would be dark with few guiding lights, but I had no grasp of just how dark. Without a moon, it was PITCH, PITCH BLACK.

As you approach Kauai, you first come to the Kilauea Light, then you sail parallel to the northern shore of Kauai for 6 miles until you arrive at Puu Poa Point, which is the eastern entrance to Hanalei Bay. The "hole punch" shaped bay, on the north coast of Kauai, is one mile across. If you make your turn into Hanalei Bay too sharply from either the east or west, you will run into unmarked reefs. You need to carry your course to nearly the midway point of the bay and then turn into the entrance. That's extremely easy to do in daylight, but not at night, as there are no navigation lights to guide you.

As the early morning hours clicked away and our approach to Kauai was at hand, I found myself wishing the sun would rise early on this last day. Even though familiar with the area, I found this extreme blackness disquieting to me.

The end of the race doesn't just happen, at least not for me. As much as we plan for all aspects of a race, we also plan for the finish. I wanted control. I needed to think things through and act in a timely manner.

I wanted to bathe, shave and dress to be ready to greet my wife, family and fellow sailors. I had to prep the boat for anchoring in Hanalei Bay. I needed to think through the sail plan for the Bay approach. If it became necessary to make a last-minute sail change, would my twin poled-out jibs create a problem or would they be appropriate? What did I need to take ashore? What could I come back for later? These thoughts ran through my mind like a bad recurring dream. The sooner I resolved them, the sooner they would leave me alone. The miles were clicking away and we were getting closer to the finish. The Race Committee wanted each racer to contact them when they were about 15 miles from the Kilauea Light. I wanted to be ready for my arrival when I contacted them.

I spent the next few hours cleaning up both the boat and my body, getting the ground tackle ready for anchoring and putting out fresh clothing. I placed anything I would take ashore where I would remember it.

One important item I would wear ashore—a lei. This lei had a tradition, and bringing it ashore to present to my wife would be adding to its tradition and history. The lei was made of nuts that originally all clustered together in a tree commonly known as the pineapple tree. For a number of years, my parents lived in Princeville near Hanalei Bay where I visited them twice a year. When they met me at the airport, they would always greet me with a floral lei.

In September of 1992, a very powerful hurricane crossed directly over Kauai destroying all the flowers used in making lei, so when I arrived that December, my parents could find no lei. Always the resourceful one, my dad visited a neighbor's pineapple tree, gathered these curious nuts and created a lei for me by threading them together. When I returned home to California, I took the lei with me. The lei sailed with me in the 1994 TransPac Race, and as I came ashore I presented it to my mom. A picture of me with my parents, taken as I arrived at the finish of the 1994 TransPac Race, appeared in an issue of the sailing magazine, *Latitude 38*—my mom is wearing the "nut" lei. Now 14 years later, the lei had made another crossing, and I would present it to Jeanne. My parents both passed away in late 1994 so they would be present in spirit only.

The final six-mile approach to Hanalei Bay from the Kilauea Light is usually a continuation of the downwind run, but then you must turn upwind to enter the bay and anchorage area. In the mornings, however, this downwind run may become an upwind approach for the last two or three miles. If you want to cross the finish line while sailing with your spinnaker flying, this wind change can be a disappointment. I wanted to be ready for any change in sail plan that might be warranted.

During the final hours as we sailed through the darkness, I readied the boat and myself, keeping an eye on our feathery hitchhiker. It sat serenely on the stern rail sleeping soundly. We reached the 15 miles out point at about 4 a.m. Hawaiian time. The darkness was intense, but the Kilauea Light presented a forceful rotating presence every 10 seconds. Easily visible now, the actual light created an eerie arching streak across the low clouds above it.

Communication with the Race Committee using a VHF radio is rather inconsistent due to the terrain so I wasn't surprised when they failed to respond to my initial call. My back-up plan: I called Jeanne on the SAT phone and had her contact the Race Committee. This worked well, and it was wonderful to hear her voice and know she was so close. There was an understandable sense of excitement in both our voices. We spoke for a few minutes. She told me *Kali O Kalani* had arrived the night before and *Feral* had arrived just two hours before I called her. She didn't need to remind me the clock was ticking for me against my closest competitor, *Carroll E*. Jeanne and I both "hoped" out loud the wind would hold.

Aside from the lighthouse straight ahead, little indicated the presence of an island. Another less intensely flashing light could be seen off to the east and a slightly diffused glow projected on the cloud over in that same direction. The glow emanated from the lights of Kapaa and the other flashing light from a prominent point near the village of Anahola. Despite that the island was still engulfed in blackness, things seemed to make sense. I felt a little guilty hoping the sun would hurry up and rise. After all, Tom Kirschbaum of *Feral* and Nick Ratto of *Kali O Kalani* had to arrive in this blackness, and they weren't as familiar with the island. But wish I did, and I experienced great relief when I saw some light illuminating the land as we neared the Kilauea Light.

The Kilauea Lighthouse, home of the Kilauea Point National Wildlife Refuge, is known for its many seabirds. Although I hoped my feathered companion would stay with me until the finish, I knew it just would not happen. As we neared the lighthouse and began our final six miles along the north shore of Kauai, the bird activity became too appealing, and with wings spread wide, our hitchhiker lunged into the air and quickly blended in with all the other birds. How lucky for me to have had this friendly fellow ride along with me the last 200 miles of the race. In return for the companionship, it got to rest while I took it to its probable destination. And for me, my companion gave me some wonderful memories and a lot of endearing photos. Without the pictures, I might have eventually wondered if the visit had ever really happened.

A Sad Departure

It seems to take forever for the sun to start to rise, but once it does, things move quickly. As clear rays of sunlight began striking the island, the many shades of green along the shore came alive. The hills deeply saturated with hues of green, and the blues of the water mixed with the golden glow of the morning sunrise made my final six miles magical.

Approaching The Finish

The Race Committee had established VHF contact and I knew they were in position on the bluff overlooking Hanalei Bay. The wind had shifted from behind to abeam and now slightly ahead of *Black Feathers* so it would remain upwind for the finish. As I moved toward Hanalei Bay I sailed along the bluffs of Princeville. The condos and homes could easily be identified. I saw this arrival as even more beautiful than my previous TransPac of 1994, and my sense of accomplishment felt much greater with little *Black Feathers*. I fought to hold back my tears.

I strained to see the Race Committee among the trees along the bluff and just as I focused on the group, the radio came to life and Sylvia Seaberg announced, "*Black Feathers*, this is the Race Committee. We are pleased to inform you that you have just completed the 2008 Singlehanded TransPac. Congratulations!"

"Race Committee, this is *Black Feathers*. Thank you very much and thank you for all your effort and hard work."

The radio cracked to life once again and the familiar voice of my son, Winston, surprised me. He offered loving congratulations from the family, who were all congregated on the bluff. How exciting it felt to know very soon I would be able to see and hold those I love.

As I continued past Puu Poa Point and began the turn into Hanalei Bay, I was greeted by *Wildflower*, and her skipper, Skip Allan. Skip, a skilled seaman and gracious gentleman, did his best to greet each boat that came in after him. His smile and congratulations signified a special gift to me after such a long voyage. Within a short time, the red inflatable chase boat came along side and transferred members of the Race Committee onto *Black Feathers*. The welcoming committee consisted of Synthia Petroka, the Race Chair, Christine Weaver and Jonathan Gutoff of NorCal Sailing, and Mitchell "Boy," the chase boat driver. *Wildflower* led the way as I sailed into Hanalei Bay with my newly-acquired and most helpful crew. After Synthia checked the seal on the engine, we were able to motor through the early morning calm waters of the Bay and finding a good spot, we let loose the anchor.

Bluffs of Princeville at The Finish

Before we headed for shore, Jonathan filmed a short interview I had with Christine. Knowing these wonderfully emotional moments would eventually fade from memory, I appreciated knowing Jonathan and Christine had recorded the arrival of each boat. These recordings would provide a poignant and lasting documentation of a treasured time. I gathered my belongings to take ashore and climbed aboard the chase boat.

The short ride to shore was full of excitement and anxious anticipation. I could see my personal entourage assembled along the shore near the Hanalei Pier, but the exhilaration of the moment could not distract from the beauty of the morning and the majestic serenity of the setting. Hanalei Bay, with its nearby surrounding mountains rising up some 5,000 feet into the tropical sky is a spot truly blessed by nature—a feast for the eyes, as well as the soul.

Robert and *Black Feathers* after Anchoring

The committee boat mercifully took me through the mildly lapping surf all the way to the sandy beach so that my first steps on land would not be challenged by waist-deep water. There, my daughter, Kendra, enthusiastically greeted me, and happy family and friends quickly surrounded me.

Because of *Black Feathers'* size, Jeanne and I decided it best for her to wait for me on shore rather than go out with the Race Committee to greet me. Her loving embrace on the beach of Hanalei after such an adventure was worth the wait. I had worn my dad's nut lei to shore. Taking it off and placing it around Jeanne's neck led to yet another emotional moment. Jeanne presented me with a striking "cigar" lei.

Winston, Jeanne, Robert, Kendra and Sarah

Traditions abound with the TransPac, and one classic—each skipper is greeted with a lei and the drink of their choice. I had requested a Mai Tai. After I greeted my family, Synthia presented me with a cool, moist, scented washcloth and a handsome lei, PLUS my most anticipated ice-cold Mai Tai. The last 17 hours had been very busy for Synthia and her sidekick, Sylvia. They had coordinated the finishes of six racers, and although Synthia must have been exhausted, she welcomed me with her usual energy and exuberance.

Jeanne and I left the beach to head for our condo in Princeville. We would be back that afternoon to visit with all the skippers during another great TransPac tradition, Tree Time, but for now it was a time to relax and reconnect with loved ones—a time to share and a time to receive.

Chapter 10
Tree Time

Traditions are amazing institutions. They can act as guides to direct us into the future with dignity or they can be anchors that become burdensome and lead us into stagnation. Fortunately, the Singlehanded Sailing Society's tradition of Tree Time has been a guiding light to the dignity of the individual sailor and a platform for developing camaraderie within the group. Those rare competitors who only concern themselves with the race miss out on much of the TransPac experience.

Tree Time started at a most appropriate time—at the finish of the very first TransPac. Due to a few unexpected complications at the finish of that first race, no Race Committee appeared to act as finishers for the arriving skippers. The racers, as they arrived in Hanalei Bay, took their own finish times. After the first few finished, they themselves opted to become the "acting" Race Committee to help with the finishes of the remaining incoming skippers. They compiled a list of all the boats and racers as they made their entrance into Hanalei Bay, and nailed this list to a tree at Pavilion Park on the beach in Hanalei. This document still lives among the treasured sailing memorabilia of Skip Allan, one of the finishers of that 1978 race, and as you know, a skipper in the 2008 race. The tree still lives on the beach today and acts as the site for Tree Time each afternoon at 5 when those who have arrived meet to discuss the race and share their thoughts with that day's new arrivals. Tree Time has become a tradition cherished by all.

The informal gathering involves racers, family, friends, the Race Committee, and anyone else interested in the TransPac. Potluck-style appetizers and beverages provide the nourishment and lubricant for socializing, as well as serious in-depth discussions of any sailing questions that may arise. Tree Time offers a time to relax and reflect on the race; to compare notes on strategies, times of trauma and moments of exhilaration. For the friends and family of those skippers who are still out at sea, it provides information and companionship from an enthusiastic support group. Tree Time ties a face, a heart and soul, and a humanity to the name of each participant and their family members, as well as to the tireless Race Committee. We all become family.

Tree Time

Unfortunately, the small boats and their skippers miss out on much of Tree Time because they are still battling their way to Hanalei. But on the other hand, when the smaller boats arrive, everyone is there and the gathering becomes more energized. After the Awards Ceremony, held on the evening of the final race day, people begin to leave Hanalei to rejoin their former lives. Tree Time continues each day until the final few skippers take their leave of Hanalei. As each person returns home they take with them that shared experience of tradition and friendship that has become known as the TransPac Experience.

Having arrived early the morning of August 1st, I had all day to anticipate my first 2008 Tree Time. I found it exciting since almost all the racers were there and they showed enthusiasm for *Black Feathers'* finish. They looked forward to an opportunity to examine my broken rudder. I told them to "come back tomorrow—I'll have it here."

During this Tree Time, Ruben called his girlfriend, Robbie, from his SAT phone. As she strolled away from the crowd to get some privacy, it became apparent how emotional and trying *Sparky's* dismasting and the long wait for his arrival was for her.

Ruben was turning the dismasting into an adventure in itself. He had progressed from jury rig #1, intended to simply erect something to enable the boat to head downwind, to jury rig #2.

The first jury rig involved the lower 4' - 5' of the mast. It consisted of the mast base being placed back into the deck-mounted mast step and extended up to the point where the mast had folded over about 5' off the deck.

The second jury rig consisted of placing a spinnaker pole into this existing mast segment and almost doubling the height. From this, Ruben tried to get up as much sail as possible without overpowering the "mast."

From the time of the dismasting, Ruben had been considering how to use the top portion of the mast to his best advantage. By working with jury rigs #1 and #2, he continued developing his technique to move toward what would become jury rig #3.

As promised, Jeanne and I brought the broken rudder with us to Tree Time the following day. This gave us a chance to hear various opinions of why the fiberglass rudder of *Black Feathers* failed. I was most interested to learn how I might have been able to detect a developing problem prior to the rudder actually breaking. The consensus of opinion focused on the edges where the fiberglass joined together. Minor cracks could be seen along the forward edge of the upper portion of the rudder. Although it didn't fail in that area, if a de-lamination occurred as this area extended down under the water, it could have led to a separation of the two fiberglass side halves of the rudder, resulting in a break along the waterline due to stress. A guess, but certainly a strong possibility. If I saw similar cracks developing in any future fiberglass rudder, I would have cause for concern. After Tree Time, I removed the pintles and cheeks from the rudder and discarded the broken fiberglass and foam core. I knew the business firm I had purchased the rudder from would be interested in what caused it to fail, so I had plenty of pictures documenting its demise.

Ruben had booked a shared ship space with Tom Kirschbaum/*Feral*, with the intent of shipping *Sparky* back to the mainland. Now that *Sparky* had been dismasted, he and Robbie decided they would give up their space, and once he arrived in Hanalei, they would donate *Sparky* to a worthy cause. I had intended to sail *Black Feathers* home, but Robbie offered me *Sparky's* return space. Jeanne and I had already discussed this possibility, and we knew we would need to make our decision very soon for if we chose to ship *Black Feathers* home; there was much to accomplish in a very little time.

Tree Time—Robert with the Broken Rudder

Things were looking up for *Sparky*. She was regaining her energy, and with a good breeze and jury rig #3, made 100 miles during the last 24 hours. Jury rig #3 involved approximately the top 10' - 11' of *Sparky's* original mast. Ruben had secured the mast to the boat using several lines that could be adjusted to keep them taut, thus making the rig stable. Twin jibs were used to create as much sail area as possible. This rig proved to be *Sparky's* final version and would eventually bring her all the way into Hanalei Bay.

The Beach at Hanalei Bay

Chapter 11
Awards Ceremony

Unless an extension is granted, the racers have until noon of the 21st day of the race to cross the finish line. Any boat that finishes after the deadline will go down in TransPac history as an FAD (Finished After Deadline). On the evening of that 21st day, the Race Committee holds the Awards Ceremony. For this TransPac, Jeanne, working with Synthia, had arranged for it to be held at the Princeville Hotel on Hanalei Bay. Like Tree Time, this event joined together anyone involved or interested in the TransPac, but with a more Hawaiian theme. Clad in Aloha shirts and bright, festive attire, the skippers, wives, significant others, family members and enthusiasts all mingled to enjoy drinks and dinner. Jeanne and I shared the celebration with my family.

The awards for the TransPac come in many varieties and it's always a pleasure to watch the oft-unassuming skippers receive recognition for their hard-fought accomplishments. Something always revered is a record-setting performance, but the most coveted award—the Fleet Honor, goes to the fastest corrected time in the fleet. Light winds plagued the first three days of the 2008 TransPac so no records were broken. Notwithstanding, however, is the performance of the Open 60' monohull, *Dogbark*, skippered by Al Hughes, which arrived only one day off the all-time monohull record—quite a feat given he lost considerable time to light winds. When considering corrected times for all boats the best performances went to:

Wildflower/Wylie Custom 27	Skip Allan	1st in fleet
		1st in division
Polar Bear/Olson30	Eric Thomas	2nd in fleet
		1st in division
Ragtime!/J92	Bob Johnston	3rd in fleet
		2nd in division
Alchera/J120	Mark Deppe	4th in fleet
		1st in division

Black Feathers, the smallest boat ever to complete the SSS TransPac, and the oldest boat in the fleet, finished second in her division and eighth in fleet.

It was a warm, enchanting evening. As the sun dropped lower and lower toward the horizon, all eyes shifted to the west as the sky exploded into an array of brilliant colors. The dinner festivities paused while many of us went out to the shoreline to capture that highly sought-after photograph that might forever encapsulate our Kauai experience.

Black Feathers and *Carroll E* at Sunset

By night's end, several skippers were heavy-laden with trophies that had been bestowed upon them, but all the skippers left with the most meaningful award that the SSS gives, that being the belt buckle of the Singlehanded TransPac. There are no losers in the TransPac. No matter how you finish, the fact that you accomplish what you set out to do makes you a solid winner in the eyes of the Singlehanded Sailing Society, your fellow racers and the sailing community at large.

TransPac Skippers Cheer *Sparky's* Anticipated Arrival

Chapter 12
Honolulu Bound

Two common ways exist to get a boat back to San Francisco from Hanalei Bay. You or someone else can sail it back, or you can sail it to Honolulu and then ship it back.

I originally planned to sail *Black Feathers* back. I made this decision for several reasons, the most compelling being, 1) to save money, 2) to experience the return sail as I had in 1994, and 3) recently retired, I had the time. Working against this plan were the thoughts that, 1) I would have to begin my sail later in the season than thought ideal, 2) I would need to plan on at least 30 days for the return, and 3) I had no effective motoring capabilities so I would need to be prepared to sail even further north than usual to avoid the lack of wind in the High, and/or wait for the High to move away if I got stuck in it.

After the rudder broke and the solar panel was damaged, I knew I would have to order a replacement for each of these items in preparation for the return trip. These replacements would need to be delivered to Kauai, and then installed on the boat before I could leave. Certainly possible to do, but I knew some real potential existed for delays in actually getting it all accomplished. Too much of a delay would increase the chance of running into some bad weather on the return.

With *Sparky* dismasted, Ruben would not be shipping his boat home as planned, so the opportunity to ship *Black Feathers* back in *Sparky's* stead presented itself. Generally when shipping a boat, you have to provide your own trailer or cradle. *Black Feathers* had neither. Fortunately the contracted shipping company provides adjustable trailers, a rather unique service, so there would be no problem with the substitution.

Jeanne and I now had the option to rather conveniently ship *Black Feathers* home, but with a narrow window of opportunity, we had to move fast. *Black Feathers* needed to be loaded onto the shipper's trailer in Honolulu on August 6th. The trailer would be shared with Tom Kirschbaum's *Feral*.

Tempting, for sure. *Black Feathers* and I had experienced a beautiful sail to Hanalei, and the thought of spending my post race time in Kauai relaxing with Jeanne seemed much more appealing than dealing with boat repairs! It didn't take much to decide to ship *Black Feathers* home even though we knew it would mean a significant unplanned financial hit.

I had long heard that the upwind sail from Hanalei Bay to Honolulu makes for a rough, but memorable adventure. It is easiest and most pleasurable to sail downwind among the Hawaiian Islands traveling from south to north. Hanalei Bay sits at the northern most point of the most northerly island (of the major islands), so going east to Oahu entails sailing against the wind and this can get nasty, and usually does.

In 1994 I sailed my Ericson 32 back to San Francisco so I never had to do this upwind passage to Oahu. But now I would have to tackle it, and surprisingly, I looked forward to the challenge. Since I wasn't sailing *Black Feathers* back to the mainland, I reasoned that this known-to-be rough jaunt would be my "rite of passage," affording me the privilege of shipping my boat home.

I had arrived in Hanalei Bay on August 1st. The shipping schedule required me to sail out of Hanalei Bay early the morning of August 5th.

Skip Allan had completed many crossings from Hanalei Bay to Honolulu and graciously wrote out some sailing instructions for me to use as a guide on the transit. They proved to be of immense value, and I was glad I had copied them to distribute to the other skippers who planned to make the crossing.

Skip's step-by-step sailing directions provided great detail with sailing instructions, latitudes/longitudes of key points, phone numbers of relevant harbor masters, bail-out harbors in case it became too rough, and even the phone number of the Coast Guard. I was set!

As strongly suggested by Skip, I began my sail in the early morning. A significant trade wind breeze already existed at 6, so the upwind battle began right away.

The plan: Sail from Hanalei Bay to Ala Wai Harbor in Honolulu, a distance of 120 miles. This takes a small boat 30 - 36 hours. *Feral*, the International Folkboat, would leave Hanalei Bay the same day, but her skipper planned to sail the passage with his daughter and opted to leave a few hours later.

By noon, I could still identify landmarks on Kauai, and it wasn't until 6 p.m. that Kauai was no longer visible. Things were going well, but slower than anticipated. I didn't enjoy my sailing options. If I sailed hard-on-the-wind, I would pretty much stay on course. If I fell off a bit (went slightly less upwind), it would be more comfortable, but be on a course that fell away to the southwest of Oahu. I chose to hold a tight course and beat into the wind. The waves would periodically slap against *Black Feathers* so hard that I would look around the cabin half expecting to see water entering a newly-formed crack in the hull, but fortunately no such cracks appeared.

The sun fell below the horizon as *Black Feathers* and I fought our way toward Honolulu. Several times the CARD alarm sounded, but never the AIS. This caused me to reason that the approaching vessels had radar but were not large commercial ships. Twice during the night I could see ship lights indicating we were on intersecting courses. We had the strobe light on at the masthead, as well as the navigation lights on the stern and bow, but with such low-positioned bow lights on the bow pulpit, I doubted anyone could see them. As the approaching vessels became alarmingly close, I made a general VHF radio call on channel 16 to anyone listening, informing them of my presence and intentions. I received no response, but with a bit of time, our courses diverged. The waves sprayed over the bow and dome every couple of minutes, and as some spray entered the cabin, things began getting wet. Because we only had to make it through the one night, the wetness didn't concern me. This would be one of those nights when you don't even try to sleep.

At 9 p.m. I called Jeanne on the SAT phone as planned. It comforted me to hear her voice—something stable in an otherwise very unstable world. I mused it would be such a shame to have the waves crack *Black Feathers'* hull on this short beat to Honolulu after sailing so far to Hawaii. I was half joking, half serious. Even today, Jeanne cringes when she speaks of that phone call. During our conversation she could hear the waves slapping against the hull and alarmingly loud "bangs" as the oncoming waves picked up the bow, held it momentarily, and then SLAMMED *Black Feathers* down into each wave's trough. It was good I had already reached the conclusion and acceptance that some nights will simply be wet, rough and uncertain. Given a bit of time, they will turn into a new day and bring a fresh outlook on life.

At some point during the darkness of the early morning, probably about 2, I began seeing two flashing lights rather widely separated. These lights emanated from Kaena Point and Barbers Point on Oahu. I didn't have the appropriate navigation chart for this journey because mine lacked the degree of detail I would have liked. Instead, my chart included all of the islands from the Big Island to Niihau (NOAA Chart #19004). Despite the anxiety I experienced due to the roughness of the ride, I felt confident we were headed in the right direction. A few more hours passed and my mind slipped into the misty fogginess of a troubled sleep.

Stillness woke me. No sound. No roughness. Things were way too peaceful. As I gained my senses, it became evident that my surroundings had been greatly altered. The early dawn brought with it a lack of wind, and therefore a stillness to the water. I sat up and stuck my head inside the dome to look around. The rough seas and wind of a few hours before had vanished and now *Black Feathers* found her sails listless as we drifted. The land I had imagined a few hours before now lay in front of me. It astounded me at how the insecurities of the night before could melt into an early dawn of such peaceful beauty.

Too impatient to wait for the wind to fill in, I got out our little outboard engine and started it up. We motored a couple of hours before the wind joined us. At that point, I returned the engine to its storage bin, and we were off under sail, but this time in a mild breeze that lightened the heart and raised my spirits. The sail along Oahu's western shore proved delightful.

Barbers Point marks the southwest corner of Oahu where you turn to head for Honolulu. I arrived there a bit after noon. Since I was beginning my final 3 - 4 hour approach to Honolulu, I felt I needed to contact the boat shipper, Larry Cummins, of Load-a-Boat. A cell phone probably would have worked for this call, but since Jeanne had mine, I used the SAT phone. To my surprise, Larry informed me it would be best if I could put in at Koolina Harbor instead of Honolulu. Koolina Harbor was within an easy sail, much easier than the continual beat to Honolulu. When checking the chart and reviewing Skip Allan's instructions, I noticed Koolina Harbor listed as one of the harbors where I could seek refuge if needed. Skip had provided all pertinent information. At 4:00 p.m. I found myself sailing into Koolina Harbor.

Usually intended for 60' - 80' fishing boats, *Black Feathers* barely weighed enough to take up the slack in the lifting slings at the Koolina boatlift. The lift operator raised her from the water with me on the boat readying her for the return. By the time the operator had her fully positioned on the trailer, her rig was ready to come down. Several of the yard hands implied, in rather "manly" terms, that they were impressed and amazed that I would have sailed a Cal 20 solo across the Pacific.

I hate taking the rig down. Since I seldom do it, it seems like each time I have to relearn the procedure. A Cal 20 is designed to be easily trailered, therefore, dropping the rig should not be a big chore. The mast meets the deck in a tabernacle that, once released, allows the mast to tilt to the stern. Once down, the mast is released from the tabernacle and the mast base is brought forward so the mast lies across the length of the boat. Not really a problem for most Cal 20s, but when you put a Monitor Windvane, solar panel and dome in the way, and when you have electrical wires and masthead antennas, lights and wind gauges to deal with, the mast gets heavy and the cockpit space maneuverability becomes restricted. Also the internal wires of the mast need to be disconnected from the electrical panel. In reality, with the help of a pulley system to lessen the weight, and a clear idea as to what you are intending to do, the rig comes down fairly easy with two people. Larry, the Load-a-Boat shipper, and I lowered the mast and secured it safely to the trailer.

Jeanne had received a call from Larry, and therefore, knew when to schedule my return flight to Kauai. Things moved along very smoothly and quickly, but I unfortunately had no time to tidy up the cabin and dry things off. Instead, what little order existed in the cabin before I arrived in Koolina, was quickly destroyed by the addition of the rudder, boom, jib and mainsail.

My last act of love: To remove the fragile wind indicator from the masthead so it would not be damaged during the trip home, place it in the cramped, cluttered and a bit moist cabin, cover the dome so it would not get scratched and lock the hatch. My tasks in Koolina were finished and *Black Feathers* sat atop the trailer that would bring her and *Feral*, who had not yet arrived at the harbor, back to the mainland.

The time from when I arrived in Koolina until my flight left Honolulu to return me to Kauai seemed but a hectic blur. My fatigue contributed to the fuzziness. I left Hanalei Bay at 6 a.m. the day before and now is was nearing 6:30 p.m. of this "new" day. Larry and I made a final inspection of *Black Feathers* as she coyly sat on the trailer. *Feral* would arrive shortly to join her, and then they would be homeward bound. I would not see her for a month at which time she would arrive at the boatyard of the San Francisco Boat Works, the company that knew her from doing her hull inspections and bottom paintings.

The time had come for me to be off as well—back to Kauai. Jeanne managed to get me a convenient, and timely flight. Larry had been great to work with, and after all his help in readying and loading *Black Feathers*; he even drove me to the airport. As we pulled out of the boatyard at Koolina, I glanced back to see little Miss *Black Feathers* one last time. Boats always seem so big when out of the water. She sat there appearing serene and regal among the other boats in the yard. She had earned such dignity for she had taken us far, and I felt greatly in her debt.

The flight back to Kauai had a different feel to it from the several previous times I had made this short inter-island hop. When we took off, it was still daylight. I sat facing the window watching the shoreline as we flew across the very landmarks I had passed just hours before. Miles I had fought so hard for, sailing against the wind, gave themselves up easily to the jet engines. Somehow it just didn't seem fair!

Chapter 13
Sparky Arrives

As Jeanne and I drove across the island from the airport to Hanalei Bay, she gave me the latest news from Tree Time. *Sparky* would be arriving tomorrow morning! I had so hoped to be at her arrival, but feared the trip to Honolulu would make that impossible. Great news! Since Synthia and Sylvia, who had been timing all the finishes, had returned to the mainland the day after the Awards Ceremony, our task would be to act as the Race Committee for *Sparky*'s arrival. From the bluffs above Hanalei Bay's entrance, we would announce *Sparky*'s finish once she crossed the line. If I had not returned from Honolulu in time for *Sparky's* arrival, Jeanne would have taken the finish time herself, but now it would be our pleasure and honor to do so as a team.

You never really know how accurate an estimated arrival time will prove to be, so Jeanne and I got up extra early the next morning to be ready when the call came from Robbie that Ruben was close. It was August 7th, a little over 10 days since *Sparky's* rig had come crashing to the deck and fell into the water. Ruben's odyssey began at that moment some 670 miles out in the open sea. He had dealt with fear, loneliness, isolation, pain and fatigue, but countered these feelings with hope, desire, persistence, ingenuity, creativity, and the knowledge that a world of love and support was being offered by known and unknown friends, family, fellow sailors, and of course, ROBBIE!

We jumped when Robbie's greatly anticipated call came in. Jeanne grabbed the VHF radio, and within minutes we positioned ourselves on the bluff a few blocks from our condo. It was an overcast morning, the early sun attempting to break through. As you look out over the vast ocean from the 200' high cliff, you try to imagine how large or small the boat will appear when you finally see it. No sign of *Sparky,* so we did our best to relax as we waited. We were anxious.

After several minutes, we attempted a call to Ruben on the VHF radio.

"*Sparky, Sparky, Sparky,* this is *Black Feathers*, come in please."

To our surprise and delight, the radio cracked back, "*Black Feathers*, this is *Sparky*."

"Ruben, great to hear you! Jeanne and I will be acting as the Race Committee to announce your finish. We don't see you yet, but I'm sure we will soon. Over."

In an exhilarated voice, Ruben gave his location, stating how happy he felt to be finishing. Within minutes, he would appear.

The tiny white speck of a boat could easily be overlooked if you weren't watching for it. *Sparky's* light blue hull with her white deck and twin jibs all showed white as they reflected the early-morning sunrays. The overcast skies began clearing. A marvelous morning lay ahead.

Unlike Odysseus' return to Ithaca, which was fraught with danger because he had to deal with his enemies, Ruben's arrival in Hanalei Bay was a greatly anticipated festive affair. He had done what we all hoped we could do if ever the need arose, but we had not yet been tested, and hoped we never would be. During the 10-day, 670-mile ordeal, a lesser person would have thrown in the towel and called for help, especially after making the decision to give up their boat. Later at Tree Time we learned Ruben never even considered abandoning his race. Instead he devoted all his energies to applying what resources he had at-hand that would allow him to create an effective rig while at the same time doing no further damage to the boat or himself.

Ruben did one other task aside from the necessary mechanical achievements, and he accomplished this with utmost success. During this stressful ordeal, he reached out to his loved one, Robbie, keeping their minds and hearts connected. A skillful sailor in her own right, she added to his strength and determination.

A few of the other skippers provided ideas for Ruben to consider in developing his various jury rigs. At Tree Time when Ruben would call Robbie on the SAT phone, she would slowly walk away and talk, but always return to pull a skipper aside to speak with Ruben. It is a wise man that will seek the advice of others.

As we stood on the bluff awaiting *Sparky's* finish, we heard various other skippers calling Ruben on the VHF welcoming him home—Ken Roper, "The General" who had been in contact with him since the day he broke his mast and had offered his "learned from experience" expertise; Skip Allan, Dwight Odom, and even Jeanne Socrates, who had planned to do the race but had lost her boat to a reef just days before the start of the race (she came to Kauai to support the other racers), and many more, all eagerly awaiting his arrival on shore.

The tiny white speck that was *Sparky* grew in size, but not by much, as she made her way along the bluffs. Jeanne and I sighted along the established finish line. Even though the race had been over five days ago, we knew this exact finish time would be as important to Ruben, as the finish time for Al Hughes of the 60' *Dogbark*, the first to finish the race some fourteen days earlier. As *Sparky's* bow broke the line of sight, Jeanne excitedly called out, "Now!" and I pushed the button on the VHF radio, announcing, "*Sparky*, this is the Race Committee. It is my great pleasure to inform you that you have successfully completed the 2008 Singlehanded TransPac at 06:37:12 Hawaii Time on August 7th, 2008. Congratulations on a job well done!"

Sparky Finishes The TransPac

Skip Allan motored *Wildflower* out of the Bay to greet *Sparky* and assist Ruben to the anchorage. From the bluffs, Jeanne and I held each other as we watched the red inflatable chase boat as it went out to photograph *Sparky's* arrival and bring Ruben ashore once he anchored. Mitchell, who would later become *Sparky's* new owner, operated the chase boat. Christine and Jonathan of NorCal Sailing went onboard to document the event, along with Chris Humann, Ruben's close friend, and of course, Robbie. Now we had to get ourselves down to the beach where we could join everyone else to greet Ruben when he came ashore. We felt the excitement in the air.

We made the short jaunt from the bluffs of Princeville down to the beach of Hanalei, traveling the winding highway lush with the green vegetation of Kauai that grows abundantly everywhere. Once across the one-lane bridge spanning the Hanalei River, we entered the small village of Hanalei.

We joined the other skippers, family and friends who had gathered on the beach. Robbie had flown in Ruben's parents and brother as a surprise for him. You could see the relief in their eyes now that they knew Ruben had arrived safely and would be coming ashore soon.

We had anticipated Ruben's arrival for so long, that the wait as they anchored *Sparky* and made their way to shore, seemed to pass in a flash. Robbie and Ruben stepped out of the red inflatable and made their way the last few steps through the gentle breaking surf to the outstretched arms of Ruben's family. He was home at last, and the hugging group grew as fellow skippers and friends gathered round him.

I felt a bit like an outsider infringing on an intensely emotional event intended for but an intimate few, but I also wanted to show the respect and support I felt in my heart, so Jeanne and I joined the welcoming crowd. Ruben's eyes appeared somewhat glazed—you could see the ordeal had taken its toll, at least temporarily. Everyone wanted their moment with Ruben, but they also wanted him to rejoin his life with Robbie and his family, so with assurances that we would see him later that afternoon at Tree Time, we all took our leave. Finally alone with the ones he loved—Ruben's ordeal was over, our Odysseus had come home.

Each day at Tree Time we would hear the various skippers planning their return trip to the mainland. Although a few had already left, most had delayed their departure to herald *Sparky*'s arrival. The general consensus seemed to be that his arrival day would be our last big Tree Time.

Ruben came to Tree Time with Robbie and his family looking as if he had just arrived on the island for a vacation. He had not slept. He had even gone on a hike! And now he actually sported a very refreshed appearance. His eyes sparkled as much as his smile. The atmosphere had relaxed now that the concerns for Ruben were behind us. Everyone gathered around Ruben to hear of his dismasting and how he worked his way through the various jury rigs. As he spoke, I wondered how many of the skippers were trying to visualize how they would deal with a similar failure on their boats. I felt somewhat relieved in knowing that at least on a small boat the weight involved in trying to manage an effective repair would be greatly reduced.

The highlight for this special Tree Time came when Skip Allan awarded the Singlehanded TransPac belt buckle to Ruben. Of the nearly 300 buckles given out since the TransPac began, only a handful has been so deservedly earned. We all shared in his joy, and Jeanne and I were glad we could share in his experience.

Ruben Aboard *Sparky* in Hanalei Bay

Chapter 14
The Fleet Returns

Following the Awards Ceremony, those skippers planning to sail their boats home began to take their leave. If one is not a sailor, you might automatically assume the skippers would simply retrace their "steps" to return to San Francisco, however, that is not the case. TransPac returnees need to begin their voyage by sailing north for several hundred miles. Then they can head east for 1,000 miles or so before heading for their final destination on the mainland. No sailing the rhumb line back. You want to get to a latitude that will take you north of the Pacific High pressure area so the wind will begin to come from behind you, eliminating the necessity to sail into the wind the entire way. If you make your turn east at too low a latitude, you will run into the calm of the center of the High and have to motor for a few days.

Once beyond the High, boats returning to Southern California would head more southerly. Boats heading for the Seattle area would not have turned so sharply once above the High and would sail more northerly back to the mainland.

In 2008, the returnees encountered rougher than expected weather and several boats had to deal with quite a few days of gale conditions (34 - 47 knots of sustained wind). Skip Allan, sailing *Wildflower*, endured the roughest weather. Toward the end of his return, after several days of continual strong gale conditions and facing the likelihood the gales would continue for several more, Skip made the difficult decision to transfer from his boat to a passing commercial vessel. He chose not to abandon *Wildflower* to the open sea because by doing so she would have become a navigational hazard for others. Just before making his transfer to the ship, he opened a thru-hull so she sank quickly. This occurred approximately 350 miles off the California Coast. Some other returning skippers were also battered but managed to continue. The rest of the fleet made it safely to their respective ports.

The loss of *Wildflower* was a sad and emotional time for all the TransPac participants and friends, but nothing when compared with Skip's grief. *Wildflower* had been his sailing companion for 30 years. They did the first TransPac in 1978 and now had won the 2008 race. In between was a lifetime of races and adventures. What a legacy! (See Chapter 31 for more information on sailing the return.)

Chapter 15
Looking Forward

The finish of the TransPac can also be considered the beginning of a new era of problem solving. The race answers many questions of performance and ability concerning both the boat and her skipper, but various circumstances that occur during the race leave you with many concerns to ponder. There is much I want to explore with *Black Feathers*, as well as with myself. For myself it becomes concerns about performance. How hard did I push myself? Did I manage the boat well? How much better could I have done with a keener understanding of *Black Feathers'* outer limits—her full potential in all points of sailing? The concept of "don't break the boat and don't hurt myself" was always uppermost in my mind, but then I really didn't know how far I could push both of us and still remain true to that mantra. These questions will become the impetus for future projects I will face over the next few years. This strong yearning to fine tune one's boat and oneself may be the reason so many TransPac skippers return, often several times, to do the race.

Few things could have been anticipated more than *Black Feathers'* arrival home in San Francisco. Jeanne and I stayed in Kauai for three weeks after the race, so the boat shipper delayed the land travel of *Black Feathers* from San Diego to San Francisco an extra week. When I received a definite arrival date and time, I scheduled her transfer from the truck to the boatyard. She would have her bottom painted and then be returned to the water.

I had last seen *Black Feathers* sitting atop a truck trailer at Koolina Harbor on Oahu. Now, a month later, she arrived at the boatyard ready to be offloaded. After *Feral* had been delivered in Los Angeles, the shippers transferred *Black Feathers* to a larger trailer, a MUCH larger trailer. This was so they could pick up a 58' powerboat in Northern California after delivering *Black Feathers* to the San Francisco Boat Works. She was indeed a sight to see, this tiny Cal 20 atop a sophisticated heavy-duty trailer designed to haul boats up to 60'. Sitting squarely in the middle of the massive trailer bed, four giant hydraulic pads supported her pint-sized hull. The truck operator found it quite difficult to get the mechanical pads adjusted correctly because of so little weight resting on them. She appeared totally unaware of anything out of the ordinary. Quite serene, she accepted any and all attention coming her way.

Within minutes of her arrival, the yard's travel lift engulfed the trailer, and *Black Feathers* found herself being gently lifted from the trailer and moved to her spot in the yard where she would rest on blocks. A short time later I could once again climb aboard. She was home!

When I unlocked her cabin and slid the hatch open I feared I would pay dearly for the haste in which I left her, but everything appeared fine. During the month most things had dried out, but not all. That which did not dry, surprisingly did not mold either! Everything came out of the boat so she could get a good cleaning and receive a planned improvement. Now the fun of preparing for the future could begin—and I had spent much time thinking about how to proceed.

I left the mast down while *Black Feathers* resided in the yard so I could make some additions once she returned to her slip at South Beach Harbor, only a 12-minute motoring from the yard.

The projects I had planned were: 1) Install a red/green navigation light on the mast, 2) Improve the deck organization of the lines as they come off the mast and go aft, 3) Address the challenge of the large cockpit, 4) Waterproof the dome hatch cover to curtail spray that might enter the cabin. (For a discussion of these improvements, please see the appropriate sections in Part III: "Thoughts on Small Boat Preparation—")

Chapter 16
Results in Perspective

So how did this race turn out? Because we had gone to the Awards Ceremony, we all knew the major winners of the various divisions, and who took Line Honors (First to Finish) and Fleet Honors (First on Corrected Time). In spite of this, it took several months for me to really look at the times and divisions of the various boats, and analyze how exciting the race truly was when viewing the overall fleet.

Imagine a fleet of 22 boats racing a course of 2,200 miles. Eight of the boats actually finished within two hours of their closest competitor. Six boats finished within one 17-hour period, and two boats finished just eight minutes apart!

Black Feathers finished with the group of six boats that all finished within one 17-hour period. Interestingly, as close as we were during the race, I never saw another competitor! Despite that you feel alone out there on the ocean, your competitors can be just over the horizon. Within that group of six boats finishing in a 17-hour period, four of them were in the Small Boat division. So even though the small boats arrived after most of the fleet, our division provided a most exciting finish. And as hoped, the larger boats could not rest easy until we all completed the race.

Within the six boats of the Small Boat division, we won the most coveted Singlehanded TransPac trophy of First on Corrected Time (Skip Allan's *Wildflower*), and three of these six boats finished in the top half of the fleet on corrected time:

Wildflower	-	1st in fleet
Black Feathers	-	8th in fleet
Carroll E	-	11th in fleet

Followed by:

Feral	-	12th in fleet
Kali O Kalani	-	17th in fleet
Sparky	-	21st in fleet

Sparky, due to circumstances, finished after the deadline, but her skipper's performance in bringing her the last 670 miles to the finish with a jury rig after being dismasted stands as one of the most admirable achievements of all TransPac races. I believe it is safe to say that in the 2008 Singlehanded TransPac the small boats made a strong showing. (For a discussion of how boats are handicapped to determine their corrected time, see Chapter 30, Elapsed Time, Corrected Time and Boat Handicap Ratings.)

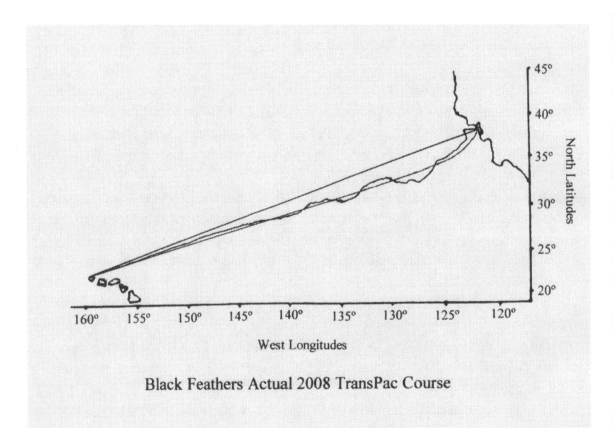

Black Feathers Actual 2008 TransPac Course

Final Finish Report

Boat Name	Boat Type	PHRF	Skipper	Elapse Time	Corrected Time	Order of Finish	Fleet Rank
Multihulls							
Hecla	Hammerhead 54	-30	Jeff Lebesch	12d12h48m	13d06h28m	2nd	9th
Sport Boats							
Polar Bear	Olson 30	99	Eric Thomas	14d01h53m	11d15h35m	4th	2nd
Ragtime!	J/92	105	Bob Johnston	15d00h34m	12d01h19m	6th	3rd
Warriors Wish	Jutson 30	54	Don Gray	16d02h35m	14d04h39m	8th	14th
Ankle Biter	Santa Cruz 27	141	Alan Hebert	17d20h48m	14d05h39m	13th	15th
Large Monohulls							
Alchera	J/120	51	Mark Deppe	13d19h06m	12d03h03m	3rd	4th
Chesapeake	Outbound 46	96	Jim Fair	14d19h43m	12d12h57m	5th	6th
Dogbark	X-Open 60	-60	Al Hughes	11d20h59m	13d07h08m	1st	10th
NaNa	Saga 43	81	Dwight Odom	17d11h56m	15d08h42m	12th	19th
Wenlemir	Swan 47	75	Wen Lin				DNF
Medium Monohulls							
Haulback	Spencer 35	201	Jim Kellam	16d23h44m	12d05h30m	9th	5th
Harrier	Finn Flyer 31	162	Ken Roper	17d06h51m	12d18h29m	11th	7th
Dream Chaser	Valiant 40	135	John Hayward	17d01h45m	13d19h25m	10th	13th
Sunquest	Westsail 32	216	Joshua Siegel	19d06h46m	14d09h35m	16th	16th
Feolena	Valiant 32	174	Rob Tryon	19d06h38m	14d19h27m	15th	18th
Islander	Bristol 34	198	Barbara Euser	21d03h33m	FAD	20th	20th
Small Monohulls							
Wildflower	Wylie Custom 27	183	Skip Allan	16d00h06m	10d21h37m	7th	1st
Black Feathers	Cal 20	267	Robert Crawford	19d21h49m	13d03h17m	19th	8th
Carroll E	Dana 24	243	Christian Humann	19d05h17m	13d07h22m	14th	11th
Feral	International Folk Boat 26	234	Thomas Kirschbaum	19d16h44m	13d15h52m	18th	12th
Kali O Kalani	Hawkfarm 28	171	Nicholas Ratto	19d11h55m	14d19h15m	17th	17th
Sparky	Pearson Electra 22	270	Ruben Gabriel	25d21h22m	FAD	21st	21st

DNF = Did Not Finish
FAD = Finished After Deadline

Epilogue

The TransPac experience does not end, at least not for me, and it colors much of what I do. I don't look at other boats the same as I did before, and I don't look at *Black Feathers* the same either. I have tried to seek out any weakness, and strengthen it; and if I cannot, I have tried to adapt to the fact it will continue. It costs a fair amount of time and money to do a TransPac. I have done it twice, each time for a very different reason, and under quite different circumstances. I cherish both experiences. Both adventures were time and money well spent.

Jeanne and I wanted to show our appreciation to an aging lady for whom we both owe a serious debt of gratitude—that lady is *Black Feathers*. Since my 1994 TransPac belt buckle has served me well in its intended purpose, we decided to inlay the 2008 TransPac buckle in a teak plaque and mount it on the cabin bulkhead of *Black Feathers*. Simple and elegant it is, just as she is.

The 1961 solid mahogany rudder is back in our living room, but with a plaque that reads:

Original Rudder
which graced the stern
of the 1961 Cal 20
Black Feathers
until replaced in 2002.
During the 2008 Singlehanded TransPac
the new fiberglass rudder failed.
This vintage mahogany rudder brought
Black Feathers
the last 1037 miles in full racing mode
placing 2nd in Division and 8th overall.

— ◆ —

Shortly after Ruben arrived in Hanalei, he and Robbie visited the Kilauea Lighthouse, just six miles from the finish. This beacon guided Ruben to Kauai through the pitch darkness of the early morning of his arrival. Here on the bluff of the Kilauea light overlooking the vast expanse of the Pacific Ocean, Ruben proposed marriage to Robbie and she accepted. Jeanne and I attended their warm and festive wedding two months later.

<u>Part</u> **II**
Jeanne's Perspective

Chapter 17

Embracing the Dream

Anyone who has ever worked with me on a project knows I am the queen of timelines. Any project I take on, big or small, I compose and work by a timeline. So it only seems natural that I would begin this scenario with, what else, but a timeline.

February 2004	Robert and Jeanne meet
July 2006	2006 TransPac begins
March 2007	St. Patrick's Day to be exact—Robert and Jeanne are married
June 2007	2007 LongPac (TransPac qualifier for Robert on *Black Feathers*)
September 2007	Caltopia in Alameda, California
July 2008	2008 TransPac begins

This doesn't appear to be much of a timeline, but as you read through the following pages, I believe knowing the order of these few events will help you understand a bit better the way things came together.

When Robert asked me to do a section outlining the TransPac experience from my perspective, I thought perhaps it would be a carbon copy of sections of his writings, but as I entered his text into the computer, I realized just how different our stories are. Perhaps it's a woman's point of view versus a man's, perhaps it's because he is the sailor and I am not, perhaps it's because I became involved in the event planning while he was immersed in his adventure, but whatever the reason our stories align, but provide independent accounts.

So let us begin.

We hurried across the street, hand-in-hand, through the parking lot of the Corinthian Yacht Club as if we were late for a very important date. Actually, we were early—three hours early to be exact. A couple of months prior to this beautiful July morning in Tiburon,

Robert told me he wanted to be at the Corinthian on this day for the start of the 2006 TransPac to take photos of the entrants as they crossed the line to begin their race. Sounded like a fun day. Little did I know the impact this day would have on our lives—and from where I sit now, I would say the rest of our lives.

All of the boats and skippers were already at the Corinthian, each tucked into their slips, ready to depart. Within a few minutes of our arrival, it started—The Magic! Robert walked the docks, giving and receiving greetings from skippers he had done the 1994 TransPac with, new friends, and introducing himself and congratulating skippers he had never met, but wanted to wish well. He was definitely "in his element."

He went onboard the *Carroll E*, a lovely Dana 24 belonging to Chris Humann. This would be Chris' first TransPac.

Tied up at the end of a dock, ironically in the very slip Robert and *Black Feathers* would be assigned for the 2008 TransPac, sat a 23' Kirby, a boat that seemed terribly small to me. Knowing she measured three feet longer than *Black Feathers* made me glad Robert was only there to take pictures. Given another hour, I would understand and accept what was actually taking place.

As the time drew near for the start, all the boats were towed out to ready themselves for the start—that is all but one. "The General" sailed out.

I stood on the deck of the Corinthian next to Robert as he took photos of each skipper as they crossed the start. I could see his excitement building, but in addition I could also see the longing in his eyes. He so wanted to be one of those skippers sailing out the Gate, headed for Kauai.

"2008 will be your TransPac."

"What?"

"You heard me. I just wanted you to know I KNOW. You don't have to tell me."

"We'll see."

"We already see. You are SO out there with them. You ARE sailing away to Kauai, right this very minute."

We walked back to the car. Even the parking ticket we found on our windshield couldn't dampen our day. We live three and a half hours from the Corinthian—Robert talked about the TransPac all the way home.

—◆—

When I first met Robert, there was little talk of sailing. He did show me a photo of *Black Feathers* the first day I met him, but if I am the queen of timelines, Robert is the king of understatement when it comes to himself. He is not one to "puff" things up, and if he thinks something could be perceived as bragging, he will gloss over it or just not mention it at all. So I knew he had a small sailboat, eventually I knew he used to have a larger boat and had sailed it in the 1994 TransPac, and I knew he hadn't spent much time recently on *Black Feathers* and felt he should sometime soon put some time into cleaning her up.

Our first two years we spent every moment we could together, mostly hiking and kayaking, with Robert taking lots and lots of black and white photos—mostly of me. Robert practiced his concertina, and even tried to teach me to play, but with little success—okay, no success. I worked in Folsom, California and lived in nearby Placerville. Robert worked three days a week in Palo Alto and then drove to Mi Wuk, above Sonora. So we would trade off being one place or the other in order to keep both abodes up to snuff. We focused on each other and, if he missed his sailing, I didn't know it.

BUT now things were different. Now I knew with total certainty that to fulfill his dreams, he HAD to sail the TransPac. There was nothing to do but get onboard and hang on.

Chapter 18

Robert Sails The LongPac

The first big hurdle for Robert and *Black Feathers* was their qualifier—the 2007 LongPac, which took place in June, meaning much preparation lie ahead for *Black Feathers*, Robert—and me. The LongPac is supposedly, and historically, the roughest portion of the TransPac so one needs to approach the preparation for this race much the same way one would prepare for the TransPac. The only real difference—the distance and the amount of food and water onboard.

Robert set to work. We had spent some time with "domestic" chores aboard the little vessel—cleaning, painting, refurbishing and of course, I made such things as a V-berth cover and curtains, but now it was time to get down to the serious stuff.

But first we had a personal distraction. In November of 2006, we went for a walk one afternoon. A pickup stopped and the driver asked if we had seen his missing black lab, Onyx. We had not. As soon as the pick-up disappeared over the hill Onyx walked right past us. We hadn't thought to ask how to contact the owner. Robert ran home and got a makeshift leash, actually a sailboat line, while I waited with our newfound friend. He called the number we found on the dog's tag, but got a voicemail—the number was out of the area. The area where we live is in the mountains and many who own homes here are weekend residents. When Robert returned with the leash, we decided I should walk up to the "four-way stop" (the ONLY four-way stop sign in our village) and he would "cruise" the area in the car looking for the pickup. It didn't take long. The pickup appeared at the four-way stop, with Robert hot on his tail, and Onyx's tail wagging in delight that he had been reunited with his owner. Now you wonder—so what!!!

Well, later that evening, Robert proposed to me in a very romantic setting in front of the fireplace—and later informed me that he had been quite anxious as to how he would have pulled it off if we hadn't found the owner of the dog. The proposal was perfect, AND it was just the two of us. Only one glitch—one I didn't know about until later. He had major trouble removing the band from the cigar!

We were married on Saint Patrick's Day 2007 in a private ceremony in front of our fireplace. The cigar band sat in our kitchen window, where it remains to this day, and on my finger Robert placed a brilliant ring. We wanted to get married in Ireland, but the red tape proved too confining, so we opted to make it as Celtic as we could at home. We wrote our vows, I wore a green Renaissance frock and Robert donned his Crawford tartan kilt and Prince Charlie jacket. He played *Clare De Lune* as I descended the stairs. Our friend, Judy Molloy, who loves doing things "once" got a one-day license and performed our ceremony. As part of the ceremony, Robert presented me with a Crawford tartan sash and family crest broach.

THEN in April we went to Ireland for our honeymoon. I searched the Internet until I found the perfect location, which was a 300-year-old house on a 25-mile lake, complete with sailboat rentals. A word of advice—never take a honeymoon when your groom's mind is busy preparing a boat for a long race. Robert wanted to be in Ireland with me, but his mind and heart were aboard *Black Feathers*—planning, researching, ordering, building, installing. It created an emotional and frustrating tug-o-war for him.

When we returned home, he again found himself in his element. He could now fully focus on his project.

The self-steering caused a major concern. Nicholas Odlum, Robert's friend from South Beach Harbor, had a 1974 Riebandt Windvane he donated to our TransPac cause. Robert brought it home, obtained the entire patent from the U. S. Patent Office and spent a couple of weeks working it over to see if he could adapt it to fit, and work, on *Black Feathers*. A good starting point and he learned a lot, but eventually he had to abandon his efforts and move on to something else. He and his friend, John Hill, spent hours and several weeks constructing various versions of a device Robert hoped would suffice and save money, but as the deadline for ordering a Monitor Windvane neared, we sat down and had a serious discussion. Thankfully, we concluded that the money spent on the Monitor would be well worth the peace of mind it would give both of us as he sailed the 2007 LongPac, and then the TransPac the following year. He ordered the Monitor. The Collision Avoidance Radar Detector (CARD), and later the Automatic Identification System (AIS), fell into the same category—safety first!

One afternoon he described an item he wanted but was at a loss as to where to find it.

"It's a clear observation dome. I can mount it in the hatch and then I can sit inside out of the weather but still have a clear view of what's going on outside as I sail along."

What had become my usual response popped right out of my mouth. "How 'bout the Internet?"

"If you can find it, I'll love you forever."

A challenge I could not ignore, although even if I couldn't find it, I planned to hold him to his promise of undying love and devotion. I headed for the computer and went immediately to www.ask.com. Five minutes later, I had his dome up on the screen having done a search on "marine domes." It was exactly what he wanted.

The LongPac prep was coming together. It took more time and money than anticipated, but isn't that true of most projects?

Robert went over paperwork with me so I would have a handle on things should anything happen to him while he was out at sea. We had a pre-nuptial agreement in place that would make things easier for his children should the need arise. He told me, then told me again, then reiterated over and over again that I should not worry if I didn't hear from him. I knew that his being the smallest boat, he would quickly be left behind and the VHF radio would probably be useless after the first night or so, because it could not reach the bigger, faster boats. He did not have a single sideband or a satellite phone. Either of those would have enabled him to call me directly, but with the VHF, once out beyond the Farallones, the best we could hope for was he would be close enough to another racer to call them, and they would relay his location to the Race Committee who would call or e-mail me. He gave me explicit instructions as to how long to wait before I would call the Race Committee and/or the Coast Guard.

"Plan NOT to hear from me. Don't worry."

Easy for him to say.

Food, clothing and layout planning were our final steps to get him ready to go. Fortunately, Robert is an "easy" feed. He likes simple and convenient. He just wants something that will keep him alive. I, of course, wanted something that would keep him well. In today's world lots of airtight/watertight-packaged foods exist that travel well, open easily and take no preparation, AND there are selections that are somewhat in the realm of healthy. We shopped together so both our requirements would be met. Kern drinks were a must. And of course there was a bottle of Captain Morgan's Rum with a tiny plastic Hawaiian-motif jigger for his greatly appreciated nightcaps. Daily vitamin packets (see Chapter 27 for specific vitamins and dosage), mainly to help him avoid leg cramps in such a tiny space, were my contribution. We packed the food in plastic bins. We packed what he thought he would use for sure in a readily accessible bin, with back-up items in another bin tucked further back. We would add fresh items such as bananas, apples and hard-boiled eggs the morning of his departure.

Clothing, he had covered. He did the Farallones Race on a regular basis, which can be quite cold and windy, so he felt confident his "foul weather gear" was suitable for the LongPac. He had back-up clothing and towels. We packed it all in double plastic bags, writing on the outside of each bag its contents with a permanent black marker.

He did sweat the proverbial bullets over the layout. Since the boat is only 20' long, every inch was critical. He would draw out the "perfect" schematic and then two days later improve it, only to fine-tune it again the next day. We drew up a final draft, labeled the sections, had it laminated (waterproofed), and then attached it to the bulkhead in the tiny cabin.

Black Feathers WAS ready. Robert WAS ready. Many months had gone into the preparation and a good deal of money, heart and soul. Now the time had come to just "do it." He WAS excited. I WAS excited for him, but also anxious. My friends and family WERE concerned about his safety and my sanity.

We drove to San Francisco the night before the race. We made a final check of the boat and turned in at a favorite nearby motel. Nothing more to do now but sail the race.

Early the next morning, I watched him as he dressed. I kept swallowing, then swallowing again. I knew his competence as a sailor. I knew he really wanted to do this adventure, but I still felt nervous. I usually have no trouble making conversation, especially with Robert, but this morning I fell unusually quiet. I had to accept the fact that some things are beyond our control—sometimes Mother Nature takes matters into her own hands. I kept trying to find words, but my mind was too pre-occupied to make small talk possible.

We said our goodbyes at the boat. I slowly walked to the end of the dock as he steered *Black Feathers* out of the slip at South Beach Harbor and headed around the Bay to the Golden Gate Yacht Club for the start of the race. Once he disappeared from sight, I hurried to my car and drove to the Yacht Club so I could see his start.

In time I would come to know many of the Singlehanded Sailing Society people and view them as family, but that was still some months away. At this point, I knew no one, only a few names, and although I wanted to be a part of the "group," especially at this moment, especially with the hope they could help me put things in proper perspective, it WASN'T happening.

When I arrived at the Yacht Club, the building was locked and one member of the committee was trying to gain entrance. She hadn't been able to contact anyone from the club to assist her. I offered to walk across the parking lot to the Saint Francis Yacht Club to see if perhaps someone there could help. I headed out, not knowing how spunky the SSS committee member was. She knew she had a race to run so she figured out a way to get into the building—setting off the security alarm. The police called and spoke with her. She explained the circumstances. She laughingly assured them the bar liquor was safe. They said they would come by later, but never did. Other committee members arrived shortly after and everybody got right to work. Soon the Yacht Club personnel arrived. Everything was in order.

I offered to help, assisted with unloading a few items, saw things were well under control and headed back to the parking lot, but not before having a short conversation with Justine who was also sending off her fella—Chris Humann on *Carroll E.* A lovely blonde with an endearing manner and smile, Justine gave me a hug and told me I could call her if I needed someone to talk to during the next few days. She had experienced her own anxious moments toward the end of the 2006 TransPac when Chris opted to assist a fellow racer who lost his rudder. She assured me, "It does get easier with each race." I hoped she was right.

Shortly after I returned to the parking lot, Robert and *Black Feathers* came into view. As pre-arranged, I had a large piece of bright yellow fabric that I "flew" off one of the dock pillars. Robert spotted it and headed my way. I hadn't expected he would be able to come so close to shore so it was a definite treat for me to see his smile. He and *Black Feathers* spent the next hour traversing the area in front of the Golden Gate Yacht Club, testing the wind with the other racers. *Black Feathers* never looked so tiny.

As Robert's start time drew near, he headed back over toward my yellow "banner." Even after his starting gun fired, he still headed my way instead of out toward the Golden Gate Bridge. He needed to get going, but wanted to let me know my importance to him. I KNEW. I rolled up the banner, shaped the roll into a heart and held it over the side of a pillar. Then I quickly waved the banner over my head and blew him a kiss motioning to him to begin his race. He waved back and turned *Black Feathers* toward the bridge. Their journey had begun. I watched them until they were out of sight and then watched a bit longer thinking perhaps one of those distant white specks was actually them. Then I headed for home.

The house felt eerie and unusually quiet. The plan: Twice a day, IF he could, Robert would report into the Race Committee and then the Race Committee would relay his location to me. I knew it was too early to check, but I went on e-mail anyway. Nothing yet from the Race Committee.

"You silly thing. It's two hours before they will hear from him and you are already chomping at the bit. Calm down. He's fine. He's having fun. Be happy for him." The pep talk helped. I made some soup and called my daughter to let her know Robert and *Black Feathers* were underway.

A few hours later, an e-mail arrived from the Race Committee as anticipated. All was fine.

Things didn't stay fine. The weather turned rough and heavy fog engulfed the fleet. Reportedly one boat narrowly missed being hit by a ship. Mark Deppe, the skipper of *Alchera*, had an AIS detection device onboard and did his best to alert ships in the area of the presence of the TransPac fleet. Four TransPac boats, of course all larger than Robert's, turned back, one due to extreme seasickness. One boat was hit by a whale, or two, but escaped unharmed. AND now the Race Committee told me they had not heard from Robert. It was Friday, the second day of the race.

"Plan on NOT hearing from me. Don't worry." Robert's words played over and over in my head like a recording.

On Saturday, my neighbors came to keep me company. They all had encouraging words. I heard their words, and the recording of Robert's assurance, but my mind and heart would not listen.

My neighbors left. I immediately checked the e-mail again—nothing concerning Robert from the Race Committee. Three days into the race and no word from Robert since the first night, that first night when the larger boats turned back and the whale(s) hit one of the boats.

I sat at the dining room table. I saw something shiny on the floor by the leg of my chair. A dime—a head's up dime. I picked up the coin and immediately "knew" Robert was all right. I guess if people can grasp at straws, I could certainly grasp onto a dime. Silly, yes, but I didn't care. I was calm.

Sunday afternoon, a Race Committee member called informing me there had been a mistake. Another boat had relayed Robert's position to the Committee, but somehow his communiqué had gone astray. The Committee member apologized for the oversight and reassured me, saying that after a few of these races, I would know not to worry.

Monday morning the phone rang at 5:45 a.m. I jumped out of bed and shot down the hall. Robert was within cell phone range, just inside the Farallones, and would be arriving at South Beach Harbor in about four hours. My clothes were laid out, my gas tank full and I was eager. In 20 minutes I was out the door and on my way.

When I got to South Beach Harbor, I still had another hour to wait. I walked to the end of the pier, back up the pier and over to the other side, then back down the pier. Finally

I saw the tip of *Black Feathers'* mast bobbing as she came through the opening to the harbor. I walked up the dock along the little waterway to the slip as Robert motored her into place.

His first words to me, even before he stepped off the boat, "We have to improve our communications!"

Shortly thereafter he bought a SAT phone. The best $2,000 dollars we ever spent.

—◆—

Now, Robert grew anxious and excited, as did I. The decision had been made—he would be sailing the 2008 TransPac. He had qualified by completing the LongPac in *Black Feathers*. True to form, no grass would grow under his feet. Preparation reached "full speed ahead" mode and, as soon as registration opened, he submitted his forms. Each TransPac entrant is assigned a boat number. They can take a random number or request a number. One reason Robert registered early: He wanted to align his TransPac race number with *Black Feathers'* hull number. He requested and was assigned number 14 by the 2008 TransPac Race Committee. He immediately ordered, received and applied the number 14 to *Black Feathers'* hull in the font that matched the oversized name emblazoned on the side of his tiny vessel.

—◆—

In late August of 2007, Robert heard about the upcoming Caltopia event, taking place in September at the Encinal Yacht Club in Alameda, California. This weekend boat show features only Cal boats. These 20' - 48' foot boats, built in the 1960s and 1970s, are quite respected and treasured vessels, especially up and down the Pacific Coast.

"I think Caltopia would be a great event for us to attend, but I'm not sure they would want *Black Feathers*."

My response, "Why on earth would they not want *Black Feathers*?"

Robert went on to explain that Cal boat owners usually prided themselves on having pristine boats. *Black Feathers* was far from a virgin Cal 20 at this point. Among other things, she now sported, the 18" observation dome, two 73-amp hour West Marine SeaGel batteries, a Sunsei 4000 Solar Panel, a Monitor Windvane, the CARD, a mid-boom Harken Windward Sheeting Traveler Car and a beautiful new, and quite obvious, electrical panel.

"The only way to find out is to ask. Send Jim Williams an e-mail and tell him we are the black sheep and see what he says."

Jim's response was immediate and enthusiastic. They would be delighted to have *Black Feathers* at Caltopia.

So we put on her best "Sunday-go-to-meeting" appearance, made up some fliers and posters outlining what had been added, plus some defining color photos. Of course, Robert mentioned he had just completed the 2007 LongPac and had every intention of sailing the 2008 TransPac.

And again, we made our plans. We would arrive at Caltopia early, set up, and then he and I would kick back on the boat and entertain what few visitors we would encounter, attend the luncheon, listen to the speakers, attend the evening's barbeque and entertainment, then head back to our nearby motel early.

It didn't happen. I never got near the boat. Little Miss *Black Feathers* took Best of Show in her class (20' - 29') and it appeared she also stole the hearts of many in attendance. Robert had visitors onboard the tiny vessel the entire day—both days!

Chapter 19

Here Comes The TransPac

The LongPac was, in itself, a great adventure for Robert, but also helped us better prepare for the upcoming TransPac.

He purchased and installed the AIS, integrating it with its own dedicated GPS.

It became obvious that we needed to purchase some better boots, sox and insulation layers to keep Robert more comfortable under wet and/or cold conditions. He had given me an awesome set of foul weather gear for Christmas. Yes, me the non-sailor, but his togs needed upgrading. We found great sox online through Cabela's. His boots, a West Marine find, proved to be a perfect birthday present. Trips to various outdoor recreation stores, and he had all three layers necessary to keep him warm—only keeping his original outer layer.

We decided to pack the food differently. Our favorite local thrift store turned up four zippered travel bags, weatherproof of course. Each one would hold a week's worth of food, including the "mandatory" Kern drinks and vitamin packets. Four bags, and he had the required month's worth of food storage covered.

He addressed the water requirement—biggest issue being where to store it to distribute the weight properly.

Synthia Petroka, the 2008 TransPac chairman, is also a 2006 TransPac veteran. Having served as an event coordinator as my profession and as a volunteer for a number of years, I asked if I could be of assistance. And with that, I began one of the most rewarding event adventures I've ever known. Working with Synthia proved to be a true treat. She is forthright in a pleasant and supportive manner, the trivial never throws her and she has a way of making major obstacles become benign.

When I first volunteered, neither Robert nor I realized quite what I/we were in for. I could have taken on less, but never thought to do so. And afterward, treasured every moment.

Basically, I facilitated the Aloha Banquet at the Corinthian in Tiburon, the Awards Ceremony at the Princeville Resort in Kauai, arranged for the "swag" items (I perceived a swag to be a decorative piece above a door, but I learned in the sailing community it means "optional items" the racers can order), ordered the belt buckles (which is what the race is all about), arranged for engraving, bought picture frames to attach the engravings to, worked on the skippers' manuals and collected money wherever applicable.

In mid-December 2007, I spoke with Leila Hayman of the Corinthian and reserved July 10, 2008 for our Aloha Banquet. One down—one to go.

In late December, Robert and I flew to Kauai for the holidays. While there, he investigated and photographed for Synthia what would become the 2008 TransPac finish line. We met with the Princeville catering contacts, meeting Mary Hall, who would become a personal treasure to us, as well as an asset to the TransPac.

Luck was with us in many ways. Our budget for the Awards Ceremony was $50 per person, not exactly Princeville Resort kind of money, BUT the Princeville, due to undergo a major renovation, felt they could relax their prices during the construction period. Then I said I wanted the $50 to include tax and tip. I believe I heard a "GULP" from Ria Turnbull, the Catering Manager, but she remained ever-gracious and accepted our limited funds with the stipulation we would take a block of rooms. These rooms normally garner $565 per night, but she offered them to us, double occupancy, for $150 with the understanding we were out nothing if we didn't use them as long as we gave adequate notice. They would provide a parking space for our finish line on the bluff off the tip of the Princeville Resort property, and they would display a matted 2008 TransPac poster on an easel in their lobby. Done! The contract was on the way to Synthia for signature and deposit. Mary Hall presented me with fliers and we agreed I would make up an addendum outlining the $150 room particulars and run it past her for approval in January so we could begin handing out the fliers at our February seminar.

Robert and I dropped off TransPac posters to local vendors, as well as the *Garden Island News*, making contact for later publicity for the race. We made arrangements with Lynn and Mitchell Alapa for the escort boat service. We also made arrangements for the lei that are presented as the skippers finish their race.

While in Kauai, Robert told me everything would be finished and ready for the TransPac by February and then we would have time "just for us" until the race started in July. Sound familiar? Robert was sincere in his "plan." It's just that by now we should have both known that when he does a project, he is meticulous, methodical and beyond focused. It's kind of like finishing one's holiday shopping in July. Come December 24th you find yourself still fine-tuning the gift list.

I formatted the Aloha Banquet and Awards Ceremony forms and sent them via e-mail out to the entrant list. Synthia, as time went on, would furnish me with other names to invite, e.g. seminar speakers, previous TransPac racers, etc. I learned a lesson on this one—I wanted to make the forms colorful so I added WAY TOO MANY nautical and tropical graphics, making them ravenous printer ink consumers. If I had it to do again, black and white text, and just the necessary information would suffice. They were not keepsakes. The forms and checks began to arrive and I set about tracking the meals. Soon I would do the same with the swag orders.

Enter Lin and Brad Menary of Business First in Twain Harte, California. Synthia was open to which swag items she wanted to offer the TransPac racers, but she also knew she wanted something different from previous races and she really wanted to use a purple and gray color scheme for all the items. Synthia LOVES purple! So I set to work and quite by accident stumbled upon Lin right in my own backyard. She was heaven to work with. She searched high and low for the quality, price and colors we wanted. She ordered samples and showed me how to cut cost. In addition to the optional clothing items, we also needed a mug to present to each skipper as he/she finished in Kauai. We found a tankard we liked, BUT it WASN'T PURPLE—it only came in blue. Synthia loved it. We decided on a lightweight tech jacket in gray, a matching baseball cap and a grape colored polo, all to be embroidered in shades of purple. Synthia planned to present inexpensive ukuleles to each skipper at the Aloha Banquet so Lin would provide the embroidered SSS logo on the ukulele bags. We decided we would purchase all embroidered items from Lin; and Ken from Pirates Lair would do the screened items for us—dry shorts that Synthia would purchase, dry shirts and laundry bags which Ken could provide. I made up the order forms, adding the 1986 SHTP *Across Alone* DVD that I would order separately from Amazon.com. The order forms complete, I had my samples in hand and would begin taking orders at the March seminar.

Robert, semi-retired, still worked two days a week. Then off he would go to the boat for two days. The days he was home, he would research items on the Internet or get things ready to take to the boat the following week. It became our norm.

In our county we have a literacy program through our main library and their primary fundraiser is a trivia bee. I understood the bee took place every two years so in 2007 I volunteered to chair it "next time." Next thing I knew I was the 2008 Trivia Bee chair, a yearlong commitment. Things became a TAD busy with the bee AND the TransPac.

Robert took *Black Feathers* to the San Francisco Boat Works to have her hauled out, inspected and her bottom painted. Captain Alan Hugenot completed the required survey and sent Robert a hard copy of the results. *Black Feathers* received a clean bill of health.

There are as many reasons as entrants as to why sailors attempt the TransPac, BUT one truly universal reason exists for all of them—the TransPac belt buckle. Each person who completes the TransPac race receives one. The buckle only cost $9.95, but to the TransPac racer it is priceless. In March, I called the Baker Art Foundry in Placerville, California to give them a "heads-up." I needed to make sure they were still in business and familiar with our buckle. Still very much in business, they were anticipating our order. They assured me they would be poised and waiting for our final count May 4th, the day after the registration deadline. I called May 4th and had the buckles three days later—that's service!

I, of course, had my timelines (now fleshed out with dates, tasks and vendor information), approximately 20 pages for the TransPac and 15 for the Trivia Bee at this point, and doing my best to stick to them. I have a tendency to do whatever I can ahead of time just in case a "truck hits me." Well, a truck didn't hit me, but I hit a concrete floor. In April of 2008, I fell while cleaning up after an event at our local library. I fell on my face, which was black and blue for a month, but most significant, I injured my arm, breaking the ball off the left humerus and splitting the ball. It appeared I would have permanent pins because the break refused to heal. I could not drive. I could not type. My TransPac prep came to a screeching halt, save what I could do one-handed. AND what can I say—Synthia just turned lemons into lemonade. Her take on the predicament, "I'd be worried except you are so far ahead of the game, I know we will be fine."

Robert and I attended monthly TransPac prep seminars that Synthia arranged, and at one of the gatherings we met a very special young man, Ruben Gabriel. He approached Robert and told Robert he had inspired him to do the TransPac in his boat, *Sparky*. *Sparky* was a bit longer than *Black Feathers*, two feet longer to be exact. The "small boat fleet" was beginning to shape up. The thought of having a true competitive race with "peers" instead of just tagging along after the larger, faster boats elated Robert.

Ruben won both our hearts with his wonderful smile and warmth. THEN he came to a meeting with an enhancement—Robbie. Robbie was new in Ruben's life. Both a sailor and a boat owner, she was most supportive of his upcoming TransPac adventure. As charming as she was beautiful, everyone involved in the race would come to love her before the end of the TransPac.

With the aid of a bone growth stimulator apparatus and a couple of months' time, things began to improve with my arm and soon I could type and get back to work on the race. I still couldn't drive, but my dear friend, Margie Bowen, and Robert made sure I got wherever I needed to be. Things were coming together on the event end—And Robert was making great progress on the race end.

Margaret Gustafson, our friend and the office manager in the dental office where Robert worked, called quite excited. She had organized a group of friends to take Robert and me to see a sailing movie being featured at a local theatre.

We all marched into the theatre and took our seats. The movie, *The Deep*, began. In a nutshell, this is the true account of Donald Crowhurst, a man who definitely did not fully prepare for an around-the-world solo sailboat race in 1968, but heads out anyway. When he gets in trouble, he bails out of the race, but writes up false logs indicating he still continued as a competitor. He plans to re-enter the race when the other racers head for the finish. He figures he'll come in third or fourth and be forgotten, but the lead racers drop out for various reasons and he will now to be the winner. As such his logs will undergo critical evaluation, embarrassing his family, his country and himself. So he pulls out of the race again and apparently commits suicide.

When the movie ended, all of our friends, gathered in the row in front of me facing me, and one-by-one profusely apologized for subjecting me to the movie. Interesting, because I actually appreciated the film, and didn't really equate it with Robert because I know Robert's very well prepared for his races. An excellent sailor, he is not motivated by what others think of him.

We all filed into the lobby where we met a couple some of our friends knew. Robert's upcoming adventure plans were related to the couple.

"YOU'RE going to LET him go?" they asked, a question I had heard countless times by now.

I smiled and replied, "No, I'm not going to let him go. He doesn't need my permission, but he does have my support."

Few people seemed to understand that I knew Robert would sail the TransPac prior to accepting his proposal of marriage. It would not have made any difference had his dream been revealed after our wedding, but knowing ahead of time, I would have been doubly remiss to argue the point.

May was very busy. Lots to do with the Trivia Bee and I was chomping at the bit for the May 3rd TransPac registration deadline. And then it arrived. In addition to calling in the final order on the belt buckles, I now knew how many binders to order for the skippers' manuals, how many picture frames to order for the skippers' "start" photos, how many tankards to order (Lin arranged for them to be shipped directly to Synthia in Kauai to save us shipping fees) and I could place the order for the personalized plaques for each picture frame. Ray Tai of EngravIT in Castro Valley, California did an excellent job with the engraving. Synthia ordered the race burgees (individual flags specific to the 2008 TransPac).

About this time, I had two diverse experiences—one thing went smooth as glass and the other was a story according to Murphy's Law. I wanted purple binders for the skippers' manuals. I went to Staples. They had exactly what I wanted, but not nearly enough in stock. Two clerks, who were certain they could make it happen for me, spent quite some time on the computer contacting other stores, then made a couple of phone calls, but to no avail. We finally determined the purple binders were a "back to school" item from "last year." They suggested I give Walmart a try. Walmart had purple binders but they didn't have enough in stock, but they could order them in packs of two, HOWEVER, the packs came with one black and one purple. The person in charge of the department was sure she could order 24 sets and give me only the purple. I went for it. Eventually, they came in, but then they really didn't. I went to the store three times, and then decided I'd better make other arrangements. I went online—couldn't find anything in purple within our budget, so back to Staples I went, purchased navy blue binders and used a Hawaiian insert sheet. I don't think anyone but Robert and I knew to be disappointed—actually he preferred the navy. AND then there were the picture frames. Margie took me to Modesto, over an hour away because I couldn't find anything with a wide enough frame border to accept the mounted plaques top and bottom in Twain Harte or Sonora. She dropped me off at Aaron Brothers and went to Costco to buy a couple of items. She returned less than twenty minutes later to find me sitting on a planter wall outside the store.

"They didn't have what you wanted?"

"Actually, they not only had what I wanted, they were on sale AND they will be here next week."

One week later, I got a phone call. Robert and I picked them up, took them to Synthia at the seminar that night and she took them from there.

In late May, Robert retired. Margaret and close friends surprised Robert with a lovely weekend party gathering in Bear Valley near where we live. She planned for us to kayak and picnic, then spend the night in a cabin owned by one of her long-time friends (a great supporter of Robert's race), but the weather surprised us. We had a foot of snow. But Robert appreciated the celebration even more because instead of everyone being strewn around the lake, we all enjoyed a delightful intimate dinner accompanied by lots of great conversation at the cabin. We took pleasure in the original entertainment, great food and wonderful friends who helped celebrate the end of his dental career—for the "second time." He closed his own practice in 1999 and retired to Hawaii, but later returned to California where he began working part-time.

With just over a month until the start at the Corinthian Yacht Club, he could now devote full time to the TransPac. Bill Merrick, a member of the TransPac Committee, did the honors of the TransPac inspection of *Black Feathers*. She now qualified as a totally official 2008 TransPac race entrant.

Presenting "your" TransPac skipper with a gift when he/she arrives at the halfway point of the race has become a race tradition, which presented a bit of a challenge for me. Finding gifts for Robert is never a problem, but in this case I had to find something that would touch his heart, lift his spirits and be of absolute minimal weight. At an out-of-town garden landscaping firm we saw the perfect halfway gift—a bronze mermaid. She didn't weigh the proverbial "ton," but she might as well have. Sending her along on the TransPac on *Black Feathers* was completely out of the question. BUT SHE WAS PERFECT! So I had to devise an alternate plan. I bought the mermaid (Lin and Brad graciously transported her for me), draped her with bright turquoise lingerie and took her picture. Then I hid the mermaid. THEN I went into overdrive. I wrote a 12-chapter book entitled *Cherish*—a tale of a knight and a mermaid that takes place in the 14th century. The story blended fantasy with various aspects of our relationship. Anytime Robert was away or preoccupied I took to the keyboard, then I would get up in the middle of the night and type some more. We were coming down to the wire, but I finished it with a few days to spare. I printed it out on some nice watermark paper, put the picture at the end with a note telling Robert the mermaid awaited his return home—sitting on his desk. The book was wrapped and ready to go aboard. Little did I know he had plans of his own. I, too, would be receiving a halfway present.

Synthia and Robert had a bit of a tug-o-war. Synthia won for several reasons. Robert respected that she was the race chair, AND he understood that the rules should apply to everyone. Since *Black Feathers* is small and Robert never turns on a stove anyway whether on land or sea, he preferred to do the TransPac without a stove, BUT Synthia saw it different. Several e-mails went back and forth with Robert telling her he would not use the stove, and her telling him every racer should have the ability to have hot food, regardless of the boat size. After a few discussions, Robert relinquished, purchased a gimbaled stove, and did a masterful job of mounting it on the cabin bulkhead. Since he now had a stove, we decided he should be prepared to use it. He spent over a week tracking down the perfect coffee pot. We opted for coffee pods to eliminate messy coffee grounds. As a backup, I bought him some coffee candy and our friend, Pam Silveira, gave him some chocolate covered coffee beans. As it turned out, he put the stove up for his boat inspection, but then tucked it away and never used the stove or the coffee pot or the pods, but he was in compliance with the race regulations. Thank goodness, he had the coffee candy and coffee beans onboard.

I would spend a few days working on the TransPac and then scoot over to the Trivia Bee for a couple of days, and then back to the TransPac. Thankfully, the time allotments always seemed to align with the demands of each commitment. The TransPac was coming together. The Trivia Bee was in good shape. Publicity was lined up, sponsors and teams were coming forward, the hall was rented, decorations were underway, food and liquor was set, but we had no master of ceremonies. The one from the year before had done an outstanding job, but he had moved from the area. Enter Maryann Curmi. Maryann is a most energetic lady. A prolific actress, director and radio personality, she was not only excited about being our m.c., she helped pose our publicity shots to give them life, she donated a whiteboard we needed and came up with ideas of how to energize the event. We added our own "Vanna White" at the whiteboard in the form of our ever-lovely friend, Pam Silveira— and then it was time to go back to TransPac prep.

June 2nd marked the deadline for placing the swag orders. June 30th I had the items in hand. Robert and I sorted and bagged the orders, and would deliver them at the July 7th seminar.

The skippers' manuals were a looming task. We had the binders, the Hawaiian paper for the covers and the watermark paper to create the certification from Synthia. We were ready to roll. Synthia provided a picture of her in a lei holding her 2006 belt buckle that was perfect to place at the top of the individual certification letters. She came up with a mantra coined by Blues Image: "Ride captain ride upon your mystery ship. Be amazed at the friends you have here on your trip." We would sprinkle this theme throughout the manual, including at the bottom of each personalized cover page. We did color coordinated spines for each manual, and a table of contents with insert tabs. Then it was just a matter of compiling the Hanalei finish line photo and information, various forms and instructions, plus the fleet list and the emergency phone number list. AND of course, the copying—lots of copying. Sylvia Seaberg would graciously take on the task of gathering the emergency phone numbers and preparing the contact list. We hoped to have the manuals ready a week before the TransPac, but those plans went awry because some items just could not be readied until the very last minute. Synthia stepped in and did the final copying, etc.

Sylvia also took on a last-minute chore—getting the various trophies engraved. She and Synthia rounded them up from their assorted previous winners, had some trophies refurbished, and then Sylvia made Kauai arrangements to have them engraved once we knew who would receive each trophy.

Next came dealing with the menus for the Aloha Banquet and Awards Ceremony. Both facilities provided me with menus. Ironically, both menus were nearly identical and far from what I had in mind. I do believe both catering contacts would have liked to strangle me before we settled the issue of what to serve, BUT both affairs were so beautifully and tastefully presented, I think all concerned overlooked our struggles. For the Aloha Banquet, because the racers would be out at sea for a varying number of days with less and less fresh fruit, etc., I was adamant that I wanted a refreshing, colorful meal—and of course, I wanted the same elements, but a different selection for the Awards Ceremony in Kauai on August 2.

And then, BAM, I ran into a snag. Okay, the good news first. We had an overwhelming response from our racers and their families. They booked our entire block of rooms at the Princeville, AND NOW the Princeville had decided to push out their remodel until September, which meant our people would not have to deal with construction noise and disruption—AND the Princeville, would still honor its price of $150 per room. NOW for the bad news. While working on the menus for the Princeville, a challenge in itself, I requested a drink price list and it didn't come. I asked again and it didn't come, so finally I called the Princeville and asked for the bar. I needed prices so I could budget for drink tickets for the racers. I almost fainted when I heard the drink prices—$12 to $15 per drink and up!! I called Synthia and we fainted together. I knew I should have asked for the prices when I was there in December, it just never occurred to me they would be so expensive (even though it should have—It WAS the Princeville). I am not one to assume anything when it comes to such things and over the years I have facilitated many functions of all shapes and sizes. I always ask questions, even the questions with "evident" answers. Why had I chosen this time to go brain dead? BUT now for some more good news—and to make a long and embarrassing "moment" short—one of the TransPac skippers happened to call Synthia and ask if he could contribute to the race, monetarily speaking. She said, "Call Jeanne." It was a call from an angel. He said he wanted to do something to make things extra special for the racers. We discussed the particulars and I told him not to feel obligated to send a lot. I suggested $400. He said he would send what fell in his comfort zone. Two days later I received his check for $1,000! His only request—that he remain anonymous. So I printed up Mai Tai tickets for the skippers for the Aloha Banquet (Corinthian Mai Tais were $6 each/Princeville $15) and the Awards Ceremony, and what remained went to Synthia to provide food and beverages at The Tree. Never have I been so grateful for a guardian angel.

Robert taught me how to determine longitude and latitude, and made up various "daily" forms for me so I could accurately record his progress when he called. With the SAT phone calls costing $1 a minute, we wanted to make sure our transfer of race information was as succinct as possible so we would have time for some personal exchange. His son, Winston, and Robert's friend and previous employer, Charlie McKelvey, both informed us they were composing individual blogs to follow Robert's race as he progressed across the Pacific. Dr. McKelvey, Dr. Grossman and their Twain Harte Family Dental staff had been most supportive and excited about Robert's upcoming adventure.

The time to depart grew near. Except for food and fresh water, we took everything to the boat and loaded it AFTER weighing each and every item, including the food and water. All his clothing, extra towels, etc. were packaged and ready to go. He had lots of extra batteries, three GPS devices, an extra headlamp, etc., etc., ETC. Captain Morgan, Robert's much anticipated rum nightcap, had to be left on dry land—it had become the last straw. NOW, I knew Robert was serious about weight! Robert drew up a final layout drawing, again had it laminated and attached it to the bulkhead.

As we arrived at the boat one afternoon, Robert's long-time cherished friend, Virginia, came up the ramp. She dropped by a Bon Voyage gift. Robert introduced us, as we had not yet met. We visited for a few minutes and then I went on to the boat, leaving them to say their goodbyes.

I took a few hours out to write notes on napkins for Robert's voyage. To date, every lunch I ever packed for him came with a note written on his napkin. I could not break with tradition now. I had a stash of short notes I had been compiling for several weeks so I had plenty to cover each anticipated meal of his race. Hiding out in my workroom gave me the privacy I needed to write out the napkin inscriptions, stack them in order and tuck them in a plastic bag. Robert smiled from ear-to-ear when I handed the napkins to him along with his halfway gift.

Our Kauai condo was in order—I would be staying a month, Robert approximately three weeks. My arm injury still left me unable to lift much, including a packed suitcase. Robert and I had boxed up everything we would need in Kauai, including a spare anchor for his mooring in Hanalei, and shipped it via the U. S. Postal Service. Another $200 we hadn't planned on.

My Trivia Bee committee members were working smoothly, things were well ahead of schedule and I had a most competent stand-in in Phil Nichols. I knew I could rest easy knowing everything would be well taken care of in my absence. I would return in mid-August and the bee would take place October 11—plenty of time to complete last minute tasks.

Now the only obstacle we had to overcome—my driving. Fortunately, my arm cooperated. I would have to have arthroscopic surgery to restore my ability to lift my arm above my head but it could wait until after the TransPac. The doctor released me to drive on July 1st, 2008—the start of the race was July 12—just 11 days to go.

Jeanne at a TransPac Seminar

On July 7th we attended the seminar at the Encinal Yacht Club, but earlier in the day we met some of the TransPac skippers that we had been in contact with but had not met. The Race Committee had secured a few slips near the yacht club for those boats that arrived before time to claim their slip at the Corinthian. We decided to take a walk along the docks to visit with the early arrivals. As luck would have it, we ran into Bob Johnston of *Ragtime!* We visited for a few minutes and he showed us his boat. Then he offered to show us where the other TransPac racers were "residing." He introduced us to Don Gray and his friends on Don's Jutson 30, *Warriors Wish*. Then Bob escorted us down a dock to Skip Allan's Wylie Custom 27, *Wildflower*. Both Robert and I had communicated with Skip, but had not yet met him in person. As we walked up to the boat, Bob announced our names.

Skip came bounding across the boat, went down on his knees, reached over the edge and gave me a bear hug. I thought he was going to lift me right off the dock. In a booming voice he said, "Jeanne and Robert Crawford from Mi Wuk!" You would have thought we were celebrities or long-lost loved ones. What a great welcome!

Jim Kellam and Jeanne Socrates joined us. Jim would race his Spencer 35, *Haulback.* Jeanne planned to be in the race, but during a global circumnavigation, her boat, *Nereida,* a Najad 361, tangled with a reef and she lost her boat and most of her possessions. She came to see the start of the race, and then she would fly to Kauai to help celebrate the arrival of the other entrants.

That night we attended the final seminar and handed out the swag items.

We rented a condo in Tiburon—a gorgeous apartment with a more-than-reasonable price. Again, we planned to have everything in order when we arrived so those last two days prior to the race start would be ours. Again, Robert meant it and I counted on it. It didn't happen.

Robert printed out charts of the area of the race, water-colored them, giving them to family members so they could chart his course as he progressed. One chart he left for me. He typed up a statement for Dr. McKelvey to post on his blog. He went over final personal paperwork with me, and since I would be taking care of bills, etc. for the household, plus a couple of rentals he's involved in, we sat down and gave the "process" a final run-thru.

I sent press releases regarding the upcoming race to 11 publications, including various newspapers in the Bay area and Kauai, as well as several sailing magazines.

The night before we left for Tiburon, unbeknownst to me, Robert placed a letter and his halfway gift to me under my copy of the race chart, knowing I would find it as soon as I returned home from Tiburon.

Wednesday morning, July 9th, we headed for San Francisco. We arrived at South Beach Harbor mid-day. He said a few final goodbyes—a number of people at South Beach were excited for him and *Black Feathers,* and wanted to wish them well.

He told me he would meet me at the Corinthian at 3 p.m. and motored out. I watched him go, then got in my car and headed out. It brought back memories of his LongPac departure.

I drove to Tiburon and got us settled into our condo. I rented it through Vacation Rentals By Owner (www.vrbo.com), where I found the Ireland house for our honeymoon—and just like the Irish home, this condo exceeded what I anticipated even after viewing the beautiful online photos. I set the table and prepared dinner so we could have more time for ourselves, once Robert arrived. All I had to do was pick him up and the next few days would be ours.

I headed for the Corinthian. He hadn't docked yet, so I walked around the marina to see if any of the TransPac boats had arrived. Most would be coming in on Thursday and Thursday night would be the Aloha Banquet.

I saw an elderly gent sitting up near the clubhouse. Lauren had quite a story to tell. His boat was built in 1918. He purchased it in 1939, mooring it outside the breakwater while the Corinthian was being readied for its 1941 opening. He became one of the club's charter members and had been a member ever since. He said he came to the club every day and either sailed his boat or worked on it. At the time we spoke, he was having his vessel painted. Lauren made his home in Alameda and was going strong at 95 years of age! He and his story proved a pleasant respite while I waited for Robert.

About 5 p.m. Robert called the harbormaster to alert him of his approach. Raccoon Straights had been a bit choppier than anticipated, hence his delay, but all was well.

Once docked, he told me things onboard had gone a bit topsy-turvy and he thought he would be wise to revise his layout. He would take a couple of hours Wednesday night, come back Thursday morning to finish up and be totally mine by Thursday at 12:30 p.m. I headed back to the condo, to return a couple of hours later to retrieve him.

Thursday didn't go quite as planned. I had a final appointment with the Corinthian catering manager to discuss any last-minute adjustments. My meeting over, I left to do a few errands and relax at the condo. There was nothing I could do to help Robert and lurking wouldn't make his chore any easier. I returned at 12:30, but now things had really changed, as we both should have expected. As the other skippers arrived, excitement set in all along the dock. Lots of interaction began taking place, including visits from some of Robert's out-of-town supporters. I left and drove around the area, checking out the beautiful homes and hillside gardens. I would have much preferred to be spending time with Robert, but I was quickly realizing the race had already begun—he was elsewhere—he was where he needed to be. I returned at 4 p.m. and we hurried back to the condo to dress for the Aloha Banquet.

Robert opted to wear his Crawford kilt (burgundy and forest green plaid) and Prince Charlie jacket. He looked quite handsome—he ALWAYS looks quite handsome. I wore a long forest green dress with a Celtic bodice and the Crawford tartan sash he had presented to me on our wedding day.

Just after we arrived at the club, Wen Lin from *Wenlemir,* came up to me and asked if I would come and meet his wife, Lepa. We stood and visited for a few minutes on the balcony of the Corinthian. Wen asked if I would look out for her during his race. What a dear lady, and we would grow to lean on each other the next few days, sending e-mails to one another as we experienced the first days of the race.

I finally had the opportunity to meet Shama, a woman Robert had long admired. Many times he had commented on her dignity and rich, intriguing voice. I, too, found her a compelling and most gracious lady.

The Corinthian outdid themselves. They served an assortment of vegetables, not only the most delicious I've ever tasted, but absolutely a work of art in their presentation. The rest of the meal and the service were outstanding.

Synthia had arranged for some lively entertainment and displayed the trophies on stage for all to view. A sailmaker by trade, Synthia, as a surprise, had fashioned customized, lined canvas bags for each trophy. She presented the colorful ukuleles to each skipper. We met the families of the various racers and enjoyed our own guests, John and Mickey Hill, and Wayne and Sue Crutcher, who had been so supportive of Robert's adventure.

Friday morning Synthia held the skippers' meeting. We arrived early to put the finishing touches on the skippers' manuals and attend the meeting. LaDonna Bubak from the *Latitude 38* Magazine presented all the skippers with *Latitude 38* t-shirts (I got one too—the ladies' version) and took the 2008 TransPac fleet photo.

The rest of Friday progressed much like Thursday. Robert fine-tuned the boat and visited with the various skippers. I took him some lunch and stayed for a bit but obviously my presence created more of a distraction than an enhancement. I stopped by a local store and purchased fresh fruit and eggs to put on the boat. Then I went back to the condo, boiled the eggs, prepared dinner, set the table and packed what I could to help with the next morning's departure, then went back in the late afternoon to bring him back to the condo. Things were as ready as they were going to be.

Bill Merrick and Synthia conducted the final inspections and sealed all the engines. The engines would remain sealed until the boats crossed the finish line in Kauai and face Race Committee inspection to certify the seals remained intact. If any seal were broken, the skipper would face disqualification unless he could come up with an acceptable explanation. All was ready. Tomorrow morning could not come soon enough for these racers.

We spent our final evening with Robert going over last-minute weather reports and entering into his SAT phone the phone numbers he had received that day at the skippers' meeting.

Our time together would have to come in Kauai.

Chapter 20
Finally!

Neither of us slept well that night, both of us experiencing those first-day-of-school type jitters. We rose early, had a light breakfast, put the towels in the washer (as requested in our rental agreement), finished loading the car and headed off to the Corinthian. Among the first to arrive, we could already feel the excitement mounting dockside.

Robert and I (as did most of the other skippers) went out along each dock wishing each racer well. These people had become family. We were fortunate in that we not only knew them through the race prep process, but also had the added privilege of being involved with them in the event portion. Many of the people who had just been names a few months ago now had become personalities we knew and cared about. AND of course, there were a few who Robert had known on the '94 TransPac who he liked and highly respected. A happy man, you could see Robert's eagerness to actually begin the race he had been sailing in his mind for quite some time.

At 9 a.m. family and friends began to arrive. We were overwhelmed with how many came, some driving more than three hours, some even arriving the night before. Dr. McKelvey and his wife, Gloria, came, as did Dr. Ed Russell and his wife, Linda. Several of the women from the dental office made a weekend of it, staying in Half Moon Bay with Jane, the lady who provided the Bear Valley cabin for Robert's retirement party in May. Winston and his wife, Sarah; Sarah's parents who were visiting from Germany and Robert's daughter, Kendra, were on the dock as well. The excitement was contagious.

The time came for Robert to don his foul weather gear, so he took his leave of the group and disappeared up the ramp to the Clubhouse. In a few minutes, he returned, walking and talking with Jonathan Gutoff. Selected skippers would be carrying small video cameras provided by NorCal Sailing to record snippets of their TransPac adventure. *Black Feathers* had been selected and Jonathan gave Robert his last-minute instructions on how to operate the tiny stowaway equipment. When Robert arrived back at the dock, he looked the part of a true TransPac racer, his departure evidently imminent.

Robert and Jonathan

Cameras clicked capturing lots of photos of smiling faces. I felt an overwhelming kaleidoscope of emotion. Definitely excited about Robert's impending adventure, but I couldn't help but realize Mother Nature was the one truly in control of his destiny. I focused on my breathing, wanting to appear relaxed and calm.

I knew Gloria McKelvey liked Robert, enjoyed working with him and appreciated his black and white photography, but I had never had much contact with her. I stood at the edge of the dock listening to all the laughter trying very hard to deal with my conflicting emotions. I didn't realize she was standing next to me until she touched my shoulder.

"Are you alright?"

I nodded, but I guess not convincingly.

"This must be difficult for you even though you know he is quite capable. Please know we are all here for you."

It was as if she had touched my heart.

I nodded and smiled and almost inaudibly said, "Thank you." I hoped she understood how much those few moments meant to me. My backbone felt just a tad stronger. It reiterated my true belief—that I could reach out to any of these treasured people if I needed to.

The escort boats began to tow the racers out into the bay where they would spend an hour or so maneuvering about waiting for the starting guns—various classes would begin at different times.

I watched as the various boats took their leave. The largest boat was *Dogbark* an X-Open 60 skippered by Al Hughes. I watched as this huge boat, in comparison to *Black Feathers*, was backed out of her slip, turned and towed out the entrance to the Corinthian Harbor. I waved at Al along with all the other people standing on the docks and suddenly I realized I also had concerns about his welfare. Robert's boat is tiny, but being alone on such a large boat would present its own challenges should there be trouble. I waved harder, choking back tears. All of these skippers had become precious to me. I wanted all of them to finish the race safely and relish in their sense of accomplishment. Who won the race didn't matter—their accomplished adventure was the priority.

One by one they went around the corner into the bay—Dwight Odom on *NaNa*, a man Robert had sailed with in the 1994 TransPac with and respected and liked immensely; Bob Johnston on *Ragtime!*, one of the most gracious people I've ever encountered; Alan Hebert aboard *Ankle Biter*, a fellow kilt wearer with a great sense of humor; Jeff Lebesch on *Hecla*, a Hammerhead 54, a trimaran and a VERY FAST boat; Barbara Euser, the only remaining woman entrant, on *Islander*, a Bristol 34; Jim Fair sailing *Chesapeake*, an Outbound 46—Jim being the man who sailed the 1986 TransPac in a Merit 25 and firmly believes "you don't sail a small boat, you wear it"—and now he prided himself on being the only skipper with an onboard freezer which would allow him to enjoy ice cream all the way to Hanalei; Chis Humann on *Carroll E*, the only sailboat I've ever seen that I would truly feel blessed to own and call "home;" and of course, Ruben Gabriel on *Sparky*—and the parade would go on and on until all 22 entrants were ready to go.

Winston and Kendra helped their father prepare for his departure. He opted to join "The General." Yes, Ken Roper doing his tenth TransPac—all on the same boat—*Harrier* (a 31-foot Finn Flyer), and Robert would be the only two boats to sail out to the start rather than be towed.

A few minutes before Robert stepped on the boat, he received a phone call from his children's mother, Sue. They spoke for a few moments and she wished him well. Kendra told us she had taken her mother and stepfather to South Beach Harbor a few days before to see *Black Feathers'* transformation. It was a nice gesture that Sue took the time to call. Hopefully seeing all the safety equipment he had onboard would reassure her that her children would still have a father in three weeks. I took one last look at the boat and gained some reassurance of my own.

Ready to Sail

It was time for Robert to take his leave. I wanted to go—me who gets seasick standing in a puddle.

I stood next to Robert and he asked, "Is there anyone I've missed?"

"A lot of people have moved to the dock across the way."

"Oh, thanks, I'm having trouble concentrating on anything but the race. I don't want to slight anyone. I can't believe they all came to see me off."

"They love you."

He waved to the people across the way.

He said his goodbyes to his children and stepped onto the boat, motioning for Winston and Kendra to push him off. The boat started to move. My heart sank. Winston said, "Dad, aren't you forgetting something? You didn't say goodbye to Jeanne."

AND THEN Robert did the one thing that made forgetting to say goodbye to me special. He stepped off the boat and taking me in his arms said, "I thought you were going with me."

Goodbye Embrace

We stood on the dock for what seemed an eternity—and at the same time, a split second—he enveloping me in his arms with my head snuggled into his shoulder. It was as if everyone else had disappeared.

Then he stepped onboard and his son and daughter did the honors of pushing him off.

We all watched him as he sailed out to join his fellow race entrants. I could see the excitement in his eyes, but I also could see him reaching for me. I really was going with him.

The next few minutes were a blur. The McKelveys had to head home for a previous engagement. Kendra, Winston and Sarah, and Sarah's parents headed out for breakfast. Winston would return to take pictures of the start from the race deck, and then head for the headlands to take pictures as his father and *Black Feathers* headed out toward the Farallones. As planned, I wound up on the upper race deck surrounded by our friends. I believe it was Margaret who offered to get me a glass of orange juice, but it might have been Ed Russell. Either way, I found myself plopped up on a bar stool at the rail, with a cool drink and a clear view of what was going on before me. I hadn't told Robert that I brought the piece of bright yellow cloth—Margaret and I hung it over the side of the railing and kept it moving so he could spot us. Using binoculars, we were able to keep him pinpointed. Even without them, we could spot *Black Feathers,* the diminutive one scooting around out there like a tiny mosquito.

All were present to give Robert a great send-off, but also in total support of me. Margaret informed me, "We gals are all going to lunch as soon as you are ready to leave. AND if you want to come back to Half Moon Bay with us and spend the night, you are welcome. If you need me to drive back with you, I can do that too."

I gratefully accepted the luncheon invitation, but knew I would want to head home as soon as possible to begin my vigil of Robert's journey. I didn't need Margaret to disrupt her weekend, but certainly appreciated her offer. She promised she would check in on me later that evening.

We all settled in at the rail to watch the final moments before the start of the race. Holly, Pam, Kristi, Jane, Margaret, the Russells and me—it was a family of friends all anxious to see Robert succeed in his adventure.

The various warning and start guns fired, then finally Robert's gun sounded and he gave a final enthusiastic wave and headed off toward the gate. A nice steady wind made for a good start for the fleet. Hopefully it would hold. He had hoped to clear the Farallones and beyond the first night, and then make at least 100 miles per day. My eyes filled with tears. I was going to miss him so much, but I was so proud of him, and I realized that only I knew just how much he had sacrificed to be in this race. I knew how diligently he had worked to take his $1,000 boat and make it into a safe transport to take him to Kauai—and I extremely appreciated that the extensive safety equipment he had installed was primarily to ASSURE ME he would be safe and comfortable.

As with the LongPac, we watched the boats until we could see only tiny specks and had no idea which boat was which, or even it we were actually looking at boats. Then I joined the ladies for lunch at a colorful Mexican restaurant in Tiburon. The food was delicious, the service excellent and the company delightful, but my mind stayed anchored to Robert and *Black Feathers*. As soon as we finished lunch, I said my goodbyes, thanking each of them for their friendship and support, and started my three-hour trek home.

Much remained to be done before I left for Kauai. This was July 12th and I would depart on July 27th. In addition to my now 27-page TransPac Timeline, I had a 14-page personal Kauai trip timeline. Yes, still lots to do.

When I arrived home, the house seemed inviting, not as lonely as when Robert had done the LongPac, perhaps because I did have so much to keep me busy—and because we had added the SAT phone to the equation. If he could, he would call each morning and evening at 7, then I would forward his location to the Race Committee. It was mandatory that we report in to the Race Committee at least once in every 24-hour period. Failing to do so would result in a time penalty.

I went upstairs to his office and picked up the chart. There under the chart lay a letter and a gift; the envelope telling me it was my halfway gift. I smiled and put them on his desk for safekeeping. It would be 10 days or so before we would be opening our halfway presents.

I took the chart downstairs and checked the online weather reports. Things looked mighty calm out there.

At 6:50 p.m. Robert called and confirmed—CALM it was. They had a great "getaway," but now sat waiting. Little did we know at that point, but this would be the beginning of a very long, CALM three days.

He sounded lonely and for a moment I thought he was going to come home, which I knew would not be a good thing. I was wrong. He missed me, but he had no intention of turning back. He told me he was making good use of his time—practicing his concertina. We said good night.

I sent his first report via e-mail to the Race Committee. Over the past few weeks, a number of people had requested that I let them know his progress so I had compiled quite a list. I sent an e-mail telling them the particulars of that first night and that he was fine. I also gave them the blog addresses of Charlie McKelvey and Winston. And then to my surprise, and later to Robert's, the "on land" adventure began. Each morning and afternoon, I would check weather reports and chart Robert's location, then he would call and I would send out his current information. I began to get questions, so I decided to include something "extra" about the race in each e-mail. The e-mails normally were a several paragraph, twice-daily update and informational tabloid. AND my list grew. I would receive an e-mail from someone I didn't know asking about Robert's TransPac (thank goodness for subject lines because I normally won't open e-mails from unknown sources) and after checking back through the string of forwarded e-mails find someone in our area had forwarded my e-mail to a family member or friend, one as far away as Australia. The two reports, the research and the e-mailing took up four to six hours a day, and became my true focus for the 19 days Robert was at sea. Some people told me they anxiously waited my e-mails every morning to start their day with their morning coffee, while others tuned in religiously to Charlie and/or Winston's blogs. Both faithfully added my daily updates.

Wayne Crutcher was a godsend. He would send me weather information sources to add to my repertoire. A few days into the race, when Hurricane Elida loomed, he took a look, and told me the chances of it having any oomph by the time it hit Kauai were slim to none, plus it would travel through to Kauai long before *Black Feathers* arrived.

Robert sat, along with most everyone else, quite still for three days. Then things picked up and he experienced a few days of wet and cold, however, he would not tell me about this situation until after he had come to terms with it. There were only two good things about the lull: He would not reach Kauai before I arrived (I really wanted to be there to greet him) AND he did not get seasick. Due to rough seas, seasickness usually becomes a factor the first two days of such a sail. Margaret had gifted him with an ample supply of candied ginger to help ease any bouts, and we had shared his stash with Ruben. Thankfully neither of them needed the remedy, although you can bet good money both would certainly have preferred to have the wind and partake of the ginger confection.

It disappointed Robert to learn Dwight Odom had to drop out of the race due to battery issues. Also we were saddened to learn Wen Lin had dropped out of the race. We both really liked Wen and his wife, Lepa, plus Wen had dedicated his sailing of the TransPac to the memory of parents. Hopefully, his intentions would serve just as well.

On July 14th, a quite extensive article appeared in *The Union Democrat* (our local Sonora, California newspaper), authored by Lenore Rutherford and featuring Robert and *Black Feathers'* saga.

That morning a deer sauntered across our backyard—the first I'd seen in our yard. Robert and I both took it as a good omen. I worked on the yard and the Trivia Bee, keeping busy, but missing Robert.

On July 16th, the winds picked up and Robert had advanced to making about 100 miles per day. His food and clothing were working well, AND the SAT phone made it possible for him to call each day right on time! The next few days he would average 120 - 140 miles per day, exceeding his goal of 110 - 120.

Good news! Dwight got back in the race. He dropped out a second time and restarted again. Third time was a charm. He could still do quite well as his boat was out of commission while everyone else was sitting almost "still."

On the home front things were taking shape also. Margie's husband, Denny, took our last two boxes to the Post Office for me. Driving was fine; lifting still presented an issue for me. Margie made sure I had good company and very fine meals almost every night, and when she didn't bring me dinner, she made sure I had leftovers to carry me through. She refused to let Campbell's Chicken Noodle become my meal of choice. All the bills were paid and recorded. I had an appointment to meet with Mary Hall at the Princeville on July 30th to go over the final arrangements for the Awards Ceremony. The Kauai condo was confirmed. I held my final Trivia Bee meeting and turned the reins over to my trusty sidekick, Phil. That timeline was up to 17 pages, and all but the last two completed. Those items would either be accomplished in my absence or needed to wait until closer to the date of the event.

By July 19th, Robert had made it out beyond the ship traffic for the most part and could relax and get more sleep. He spent most of his spare time reading because things were too wet to chance practicing his concertina. Due to his daily averages, he was gaining on *Sparky* and *Carroll E.* The smaller boats had their own race going. He was quite pleased with his progress. In 1994, when he did his first TransPac in *Now or Never,* he averaged 120 - 130 miles per day on good-wind days, so little Ms. *Black Feathers* was doing herself proud. At this point, he projected a July 31st arrival in Kauai. He had 1543 miles of the 2120-mile trip left. The winds were 15 knots, perfect for *Black Feathers*. And for the first time since he began the race, he saw a patch of blue sky and hoped for more the following day.

When I e-mailed the report to the Race Committee, I received my usual confirmation, but this time, in addition to the normal concise wording, Shama sent me a hello and a very nice supportive message.

The evening of July 21st Robert actually called a few minutes late. He overslept. Great news, because at this point, he could sleep about an hour at a time. A marked improvement over the 15-minute stints he began with. He encountered light winds but he kept his spinnaker up for 12 hours and still gained 40 and 20 miles on *Carroll E* and *Sparky*, respectively. All three boats were doing beautifully. With *Sparky's* handicap, Robert needed to arrive in Kauai nine hours before her, but having *Sparky* win would be a great treat. She was a small boat sailing an excellent race. *Black Feathers* gained speed by heading further south, averaging 4 knots of speed while the other two boats were getting 2 and 2 1/2 knots. He was looking forward to gaining a bit more on them over the next few days. His spirits were high.

Synthia Petroka and Sylvia Seaberg arrived in Kauai and set up in the Race Committee condo in Hanalei. Tankards arrived right on time. All the other materials were either transported by the two ladies or by the various skippers. All I had to bring—my timeline with all my contact information, some Mai Tai drink tickets, and me.

I received an e-mail from my friend, Jeanne Hannon. While on vacation in Paris, she and her husband passed a man crossing the street wearing a TransPac t-shirt. What a kick!

On July 22nd, Robert reported things on the boat were drying out well and he was happy to report nothing had broken. He was surrounded by six other TransPac boats—all less than 50 miles away and he was ahead of some of them. Our neighbor, a fellow sailor, said given Robert's size and handicap he was progressing quite well and should do even better once he reached the trade winds out in front of him. He was closing in on the halfway mark.

Robert informed me, "We will never be apart like this again. Where I go, you go. I've had a great adventure, but we need to be together." Music to my ears, but I would come to understand what is said during a race can quickly become foggy and forgotten once the sailor arrives back on dry land and starts yearning for his next adventure.

Brad Menary (Business First) was out in his front yard in the small neighboring town of Twain Harte, and overheard two of his neighbors talking about "that dude who's out there in the middle of the Pacific in a 20' boat."

At the July 24th 7 a.m. call-in, we opened our halfway gifts together. Robert appreciated his book, *Cherish*. I read my letter, and cried, then opened my gift—a small silver sailboat charm with a swiveling mainsail and rudder—it belonged to his mother, the original Jeanne Crawford. We planned to read *Cherish* together in Kauai on the beach. The bronze mermaid waited for him on his desk at home.

Well, we counted our blessings a bit too soon. Robert called about 30 minutes late the evening of July 24th. I knew something was wrong—he'd never been more than 10 minutes late. I felt tremendous relief when the phone rang. He hadn't wanted to call until he had everything under control.

While sailing along quite nicely, he heard a suspicious scratching sound at the back of the boat. Going to investigate, he discovered his fiberglass rudder broken in half. He spent two hours removing the broken rudder and installing the refinished original 1961 mahogany rudder that usually graces a corner of our living room. The Monitor (steering mechanism) was now attached to the replacement rudder and all was well, except he was exhausted and had some serious housekeeping to do before dark.

In the process of installing his back-up rudder, he fell against his solar panel and watched it crackle craze into a "million" pieces, BUT like him, it was still going strong.

Of course, he didn't tell me until he arrived in Kauai that the installation of the rudder also left him with quite sore ribs for a couple of days.

With all this, he still managed to get 60 miles closer to Kauai in 12 hours. He chose to sail a bit more cautiously the next couple of days because should his replacement rudder fail, the Monitor could serve as a back-up, but he didn't relish losing yet another rudder.

He needn't have worried. They just don't make rudders like they used to. The mahogany rudder sailed perfectly the rest of the race, and has been returned to our living room only now she sports a plaque touting her accomplishment in the 2008 TransPac. He has a new fiberglass rudder on the boat. Apparently the failed fiberglass rudder was defective. Too bad it had to make that fact known during the TransPac, but all's well that ends well.

Right about now he broached the subject of NOT sailing *Black Feathers* back.

"If you tell me you don't want me to sail back, I won't."

"I can't tell you not to sail back. This is your journey. I can't make that decision for you."

The next night when he called, he said, "I've had a really good race, and I'm thinking it would not be wise to jeopardize the TransPac experience, because any delays in leaving due to repairs, might cause problems with the return. Is it okay with you if I ship her back? It will be expensive."

"Makes my day! I'm happy to spend the money and have you sitting next to me on the plane home. Are you sure?"

"I'm pretty sure. We'll talk about it when I get to Kauai."

"Whatever you decide, that's what we'll do."

I really didn't think he would ship her back, but I didn't think it would hurt to hope.

Dogbark was the first to finish the race early the morning of the 24th, followed later that evening by *Hecla.* Now they just had to sit back and wait for the other boats to come in and see how they corrected out according to their various handicaps. One of the smaller boats could still take the winner's trophy. Robert said all along he believed the boat to beat would be *Wildflower* because she was a wonderful boat, had a favorable handicap, plus sported a professional and competitive skipper in Skip Allan. Skip and *Wildflower* did the first TransPac in 1978, finishing 3rd. It would indeed be a pleasure to see them win this one.

On July 25th, I ordered a new rudder from Steve Seal of Seal's Spars and Rigging in Alameda, California, expecting to have it delivered to Kauai. Plans would change.

On July 26th, Robert and *Black Feathers'* photo appeared in `Lectronic Latitude 38. The solar panel was doing fine, but even if it failed, Robert felt confident he had enough stored battery power to complete his trip with power to spare. There is a lot to be said for these little boats when it comes to power consumption—tight quarters for sure, but you can't have everything. The winds were keeping him on his toes—up to 20 knots, five knots above what he desired, but presenting no problem.

On the 27th, Robert took down his mainsail and put up twin jibs on poles. The boat moved along smoothly and he hoped to finish the race with this configuration. The next morning he reported he'd had a blustery night, but the boat remained stable and the Monitor held its arrow-straight course so he opted to maintain his sail configuration.

Skip Allan woke up in the dark of the morning to find his boat in the midst of a squall. At the time he was flying two headsails (jibs) on two poles. The storm overpowered his windvane and had him tipped over to the side in the wrong direction. One of his poles broke. He righted things and climbed 12 feet up to release his "wind chiming" pole. In good shape, he finished the race the following day.

Disaster struck. *Sparky* dismasted. Ruben had twin jibs up and decided to put up a reefed main to obtain more speed. A gust of wind caught him and that was all it took to break his mast. He spent several hours getting his rigging, etc. fished out of the sea. He devised a makeshift mast but failed to make good time. He hoped to finish by August 12th. I hated to give Robert the news, but I knew he would want to know. He took it hard. He cried and I cried. The Race Committee was slated to depart on August 3rd. Robert and I were staying in Kauai until the end of August so we would definitely be there to greet Ruben and celebrate his finish, but that served as no consolation. Given time, this grave mishap would turn into a true catalyst for all the racers, but for now everyone worried about the outcome.

Time for me to head for Kauai. I drove to Sacramento and spent the night with my daughter, Lisa, and her family. Lisa drove me to the airport, gave me a hug and waved me on my way. I could hardly wait to arrive in Hawaii. Winston's wife, Sarah, would take the report call from Robert and send in the update to the Race Committee in my absence. Robert was within 500 miles of the finish line.

I arrived in Kauai Monday evening, July 28th, just a few hours after Kendra. She had already settled in at the condo and added a couple of most welcoming surprises. As I entered the condo, in the middle of the glass dining table, sat the most incredible assortment of tropical flowers along with a very lovely card. And later that night she came to my rescue. When it came time for me to e-mail that night's report to the Race Committee, I could not get the DSL connection to work. Kendra had gone to bed so I kept trying, but finally I had to admit defeat and ask her help. She sat cross-legged on my bed and worked with the computer and cords until she got it up and running. We laughed and hugged. Then she went back to bed, and this time she actually got to go to sleep. She would stay with me for a couple of days then move to the Princeville Resort when Winston and Sarah arrived. They would stay a couple of days then join her at the Princeville. Those $150 prices proved too good to pass up, plus they wanted to give Robert and me a few days alone.

Even though he called me in Hawaii, the Race rules still required Robert to call me on Pacific Daylight Time. So instead of hearing from him at 7 a.m. and 7 p.m., I now heard from him at 4 a.m. and 4 p.m. Hawaii time. It actually worked out better because Tree Time was at 5 p.m. so I had time to take his call, report his information and drive from Princeville to Hanalei. An added bonus, I had his update to share at Tree Time. When he reported in to me on the 29th, he told me he had made his decision. He would not be sailing *Black Feathers* home to San Francisco. We would ship her back—particulars to be worked out when he arrived in Kauai. He asked me to contact Steve Seal and let him know we still wanted the new fiberglass rudder, but would pick it up after we returned from Kauai. I didn't share that update at Tree. I figured Robert could give out such information when he arrived.

My first Tree Time proved super. All of the "in" skippers attended with their family and friends. The camaraderie and the "munchies" were terrific. We only had two concerns. One, of course, being Ruben and *Sparky*. Concern for their safety occupied everyone's mind. Ruben had been in touch with Ken Roper, "The General." Ken, having had experience with dismasting, became a great source of knowledge for Ruben. Ruben, out there alone, would hopefully make more effective decisions by having such expertise to rely on. Our other concern—Barbara User on *Islander*. There had been no word from her for a week. The last contact the Race Committee had with her came via a relayed communiqué from a ship she had radioed stating she was fine, but had no long-distance communication capabilities. Her latitude and longitude at that time indicated she sat far north of the other racers in a high. She had not set off her EPIRB to notify the Coast Guard of any emergency, so we had to assume all was well. We hoped to see her coming in by the end of the race.

Gayle, Tom Kirschbaum's wife (*Feral*), came up to me and said she enjoyed following Robert on the "dedicated" website. I couldn't figure out how she found the McKelvey's Travel website. She said she went online and entered "*Black Feathers*" and somehow found the web address. Little Miss *Black Feathers* was becoming quite a celebrity!

Linda Powers, whose fella, Jim Fair, skippered *Chesapeake* told me about ALL the wonderful farmers markets on the island. We vowed to get together to check some of them out, a promise we did our best to honor, but never quite made come to fruition. And speaking of Jim, I learned that his freezer indeed proved quite functional all the way to Kauai. When Synthia greeted him on *Chesapeake*, after his finish—he presented her with ice cream! Definitely not something that would happen when she would go to greet *Black Feathers* in a few days.

I met Tom and Susan Hayward, the brother and sister-in-law of John Hayward, the skipper of *Dream Chaser*. Tom and Susan live in Peru aboard their own boat. I immediately felt I had known Susan forever. She and Tom would quickly become people I would seek out each time I went to The Tree.

After Tree, Sylvia (Race Committee/Finish Line) invited me to keep her company on the bluff while Dwight Odom/*NaNa* came in. Quite an exciting happening. Dwight called in saying he would be arriving in about 45 minutes. Definitely dark, but in about 30 minutes, we saw his lights as he headed into the bay. Sylvia monitored his finish and then the escort boat headed out to meet him. Synthia and Dwight's wife went onboard and presented him with his arrival lei and beverage of choice. Then he turned on his engine and motored in the rest of the way. You may recall *NaNa* is the boat that restarted the race twice due to battery issues. The third time WAS definitely a charm for him—and his family waiting for him in Kauai.

Ankle Biter also came in during the night and then we would start seeing our small boats making their appearance. Six of them arrived in a cluster, with *Sparky* unfortunately quite a ways out by himself. Several skippers spoke with him, but he had to conserve his power so "limited contact" remained best at that point.

July 30th, I kept busy, a blessing because I was getting very anxious to be with Robert. He started my day off in a most romantic way stating it had become much easier for him knowing my being in Kauai now meant he sailed toward me rather than away from me.

As pre-arranged, I met with Mary Hall at the Princeville Resort to go over any last-minute issues with the Awards Ceremony. Everything appeared under control at this point. She had stepped in, and working with the chef, came up with a beautiful, refreshing and delicious buffet. She would add subtle Hawaiian print overskirts to the dinner tables giving the entire outdoor event a most festive flavor. Her true, and ulterior purpose for the meeting: To treat me to a lovely lunch overlooking the bay where Robert would be appearing in just a matter of hours, and to present me with two incredibly beautiful lei, compliments of The Princeville. For me, a Christina (stacked white orchid petals with fuchsia edges) and for Robert, a handsome cigar lei. Mary collects lei and she outlined the history of the Christina for me. Designed as a memorial by a mother who lost her young daughter, Christina, it is a most fitting tribute—very lovely.

One of my tasks for the 2008 TransPac: To arrange for the welcome lei (yes, lei is both singular and plural). Well, I thought I had done a good thing. We made arrangements to have the lei made by a local hula group in support of their school at only $5 each. On paper it looked perfect. Hanalei, the location of the TransPac finish line, was in close proximity to the place where we made the arrangements. I understood the place we would pick them up was just a "few blocks further away." It turned out we needed to pick up the lei in Lihue, the FAR side of Lihue on the other end of the island. In addition, the racers prefer flowered lei, which is what we ordered, but the islander who made the lei thought it would be best to make masculine lei since most of our skippers were men. Of course, a number of the lei had been picked up before I arrived, and even after I arrived, I didn't hear of any disappointment right away. A lesson learned. The market just a couple of blocks from the bay has very nice lei—they are a bit more expensive but the time and gas were a bigger factor than the dollars spent, or saved, on the lei. Hopefully the hula group reaped some benefit.

At his evening report, Robert's excitement showed—he was ready to come ashore. Within 200 miles of the finish, he had his clothes laid out on the ready. Some of the racers come ashore as they "are," but Robert is not one to be untidy in anyone's presence. I knew he would be bathed, shaved and dressed in what he saw as appropriate arrival attire. A bird had taken up residence on *Black Feathers* and Robert hoped it would stay put and come across the finish line with him, although he doubted that would be the case. I had good news for him. Ruben's jury rig had grown from three feet to 10 feet in three stages enabling him to make 80 miles per day. Robert spoke with elation and pride of Ruben's tenacity and ingenuity, and expressed his pleasure in learning that a number of the skippers planned to be in Kauai through August 9th. This meant numerous skippers would be on-hand too greet *Sparky*. An added bonus for both Ruben and Robert—there would be Tree Times for both of them to attend, not always the case for the later arrivals.

Just before I left California, Pam Silveira called and told me some very dear friends of hers, Deb and Greg DeBree, had moved to Princeville and suggested we look them up while we were in Kauai.

"Is Jeanne Crawford here?" I turned to see who was asking for me. I didn't recognize the couple standing directly behind me. It turned out to be Deb and Greg. They had come to The Tree. They stayed for a couple of hours, visiting with me and the other "Tree" folk as if we had all been friends forever. This couple had only been in Kauai for ten days, moving there from Turlock, California, just a couple of hours from where we live in Mi Wuk Village.

Robert had lost track of days and thought his son and daughter-in-law were not arriving until Sunday, August 2nd, and voiced disappointment as they would miss his finish, but actually they were coming in Friday evening. I didn't correct his thinking. A surprise seemed in order.

Down to the final hours. Now July 31st, Robert was within 100 miles of Kauai—by evening report, 76 miles to be exact. Traditionally, one's spouse will go out on the escort boat to meet the incoming skippers, but since *Black Feathers* is so small, we mutually agreed I would greet Robert onshore. Anxious to see him and because I had looked forward to being a part of his welcoming ceremony, I felt disappointed. Christine and Jonathan went on the boats to film each skipper's arrival so I knew I would at least have the opportunity to watch him arrive on film.

One would think this would be a great Tree Time day, but in fact it turned out to be the most difficult for me. *Carroll E* finished on the 31st, an hour earlier than anticipated. Then Joshua Siegel of *Sunquest* and Rob Tryon of *Feolena* finished within eight minutes of each other just before Tree Time. Nick Ratto of *Kale O Kalani* would be in late that evening. All of a sudden, it seemed like Robert sailed out there in a great big sea all by himself. And to make matters worse, a few of the skippers made comments about how he had no business being out there in the first place. All along everyone had been so supportive of Robert and *Black Feathers*, always assuring me of his sailing strengths and telling me how *Black Feathers,* although small, certainly was seaworthy—and now this. I had the feeling they wanted the information to go through me to Robert, as they had no plans to address their issues with him directly. And I worried about Ruben and Barbara. Barbara's husband had come in from China and anyone could see his stress over the situation. Robbie, Ruben's girlfriend, was absent from Tree that night. A trooper for sure, but she had every reason to worry. I left and went home for an hour, and then went out to the bluff to join Sylvia to await Nick's arrival.

Nick's wife and four-year-old daughter joined Sylvia and me up on the dark bluff. Most excited about her daddy's arrival, the little girl told me "all about" his adventure.

"Who are you waiting for?" she asked.

"Well, tonight I'm waiting for your daddy with you. Tomorrow morning I'll be waiting for my husband."

"Which boat is he in?"

"A boat called *Black Feathers*."

"I know *Black Feathers*," she exclaimed. "*Black Feathers* is little. It's my FAVORITE boat—" then quickly added "other than my daddy's boat." Somehow this little girl's excitement over *Black Feathers* raised my spirits.

I went back to the condo, laid out my clothes for the morning, picking a white eyelet sundress, because Robert loves white cotton clothing, and tried to sleep.

Chapter 21

Finis

Synthia asked that Robert call me when he got within two hours of the finish and then I would call her. The phone rang at 4:30 a.m.

He was making good time, but according to the weather reports I had just checked, "no wind" conditions were chasing him.

"I know we've said we would be cautious, but now you had better put the pedal to the metal and get your fanny in gear, or you are going to spend the next two days sitting offshore with no wind."

He laughed. "Sounds like you are eager to see me."

I called Synthia. She and Sylvia had had a rough night. After Nick, Thomas Kirschbaum on *Feral* had crossed the finish, and now the two ladies would have to facilitate Robert's finish in *Black Feathers*.

At this point, Winston and Sarah were staying at the condo and said they would join me on the bluff shortly. We put in a call to Kendra at the Princeville. I dressed quickly, retrieved the Princeville lei from the refrigerator and headed for the bluff in the dark. Sylvia arrived shortly after I did. We waited.

Suddenly through the blackness came a crackle and Robert hailed Sylvia on the VHF radio, telling her his location—in the vicinity of the Kilauea Light. Later we would learn the bird took its leave about this time, joining its friends onshore, but Robert still had a ways to go in the darkness.

Daybreak came and with it a most welcome and glorious sunrise shining through the clouds. People in condos along the shore saw him first, but of course we didn't know that until later in the day.

Kendra, Winston, Sarah, and me—all pacing the bluff reaching with our eyes for a glimpse of him. AND THEN, there appeared a tiny twinkle on the horizon.

Sylvia carefully watched the alignment of the finish line to the boat and then announced over the VHF that *Black Feathers* had successfully completed the 2008 TransPac and congratulated Robert.

As directed by us, Sylvia handed the radio receiver/transmitter to Winston and he welcomed his father home, much to Robert's surprise. Kendra opted to wait to greet her father on the beach.

Jeanne on The Bluffs

I departed the bluff and headed for Hanalei Bay so I could watch him be escorted in. It seemed like he would never come ashore, but actually all ran quite efficiently and timely.

Later on film, Christine would comment on Robert's MacArthur-style landing. All dressed in white cotton (casual pants and a Renaissance shirt he had stowed away), he wore webbed tabis with the "nut" lei around his neck, topped off by his SSS 2008 TransPac baseball cap. He rode in on the red inflatable with Synthia and her entourage, waved, stepped out into the surf and waded ashore. He looked incredibly handsome—and certainly refreshed for having made such a long voyage in his tiny craft.

Coming Ashore

Just as Robert stepped out of the water onto the shore, Kendra and Sarah came bounding down the beach to welcome him with exuberant hugs. I stood on a little sandy knoll about 30 feet away. I'm afraid Robert somewhat snubbed his son because after hugging the girls, he ran up the hill toward me, leaving Winston standing at the shoreline. Hopefully delivering his "surprise" on the bluff served as his special moment with his father.

Robert ran up to me and hugged me—a delightfully long hug. He presented me the "nut" lei that his parents had given him years before (I had no idea he had it onboard), and I draped the cigar lei around his neck—the one the Princeville had so graciously provided.

We held each other and said words I can't remember. I felt overwhelmed seeing him—nothing else mattered.

A Warm Embrace

Apparently, both Robert and Synthia thought outside the box because Synthia had checked the engine seal and Christine had filmed a short discussion on the boat, but they finished up the filming of his welcome ceremony onshore. Synthia presented Robert with a lei, a cool herbed washcloth and a Mai Tai, the drink of his choice, in the blue 2008 TransPac tankard. And I got to see it all, along with his children.

When you are away from your spouse for a long time, assuming you love that spouse, and assuming you are me, you envision your reunion as something very romantic. I saw us in the famous "rolling in the surf in each other's arms" movie scene, spending hours in romantic interludes complete with candlelight and soft music. I didn't picture what actually took place. Winston and Sarah made plans for the day giving us plenty of time alone. I figured I would take Robert to breakfast in Hanalei and then have the rest of the time to get reacquainted. Robert wanted to go directly to the condo. Hmmmm—sounded promising. He marched straight to the bedroom—we're on the right track. AND then for the next two and a half hours we sat on the edge of the bed while he talked and talked and talked about the TransPac. At 11a.m. we finally went for breakfast in Hanalei, only of course now, no place was serving breakfast, so we wound up getting a Bubba Burger and sat while he talked more about the TransPac. And so it went for the next several days. This man had spent days alone at sea and he had lots of pent-up adventures to get out of his system. So I listened. Not sure I retained as much of it as I should have, but it didn't prove to be an issue because I was hearing for the first time, accounts I would memorize from the re-telling in the months that followed. Another lesson learned. Sailors home from the sea just need to unwind. Romance will come later.

Lenore Rutherford from *The Union Democrat* called Robert for an interview. This extensive article and photos of his arrival in Kauai appeared in the paper the next day. Friends had lots of copies waiting for us when we returned.

We had a couple of pressing matters to address, but the day after he arrived, we spent mainly dealing with the Awards Ceremony. We drove into Kapaa and Robert patiently went through a number of shops with me looking for a tropical sundress for me to wear to the event. After a good deal of searching, we settled on a very bright long cotton fuchsia-colored strapless dress sprinkled with large white flowers. We found a shell bracelet that I could put in my hair. AND we went to lunch at a great sidewalk cafe that LaDonna and Christine had shared with me a couple of days before. Back to the condo to shower and then off we went to the Awards Ceremony.

An ideal setting—next to the pool down by the beach with a bright and sunny atmosphere made warm and inviting by the skippers, friends and family. Barbara Euser of *Islander,* a most welcome sight, had arrived just 30 minutes AFTER the deadline for finishing the race, but safe and sound. As with any finisher, she would still receive her belt buckle, but show in the record books as an FAD (Finished After Deadline). Power issues deterred her from contacting the Race Committee and then light winds kept her from finishing the race on time. Her husband appeared quite relaxed and happy. The food, beautifully displayed, the tables perfectly tropical. The wait staff seemed overjoyed to be a part of the event adding an extra special, and unexpected, touch.

I watched Robbie from across the room as she so graciously went from group to group saying hello and giving out the update on *Sparky's* situation in response to the eager requests from the various skippers. Ruben's absence created such a hole in the evening's festivities. When I envisioned this evening, I always viewed it with Ruben and Robbie together.

I also missed Wen and Lepa. Wen had returned safely to San Francisco, but it would have meant so much to have them at the Awards Ceremony celebrating with the rest of us.

Susan and Tom Hayward approached me. Susan showed me a lovely Peruvian mola (a colorful layered piece of fine stitchery she purchased from one of the ladies in Peru who came to her boat to sell their wares). She told me they brought this one knowing they would meet someone special on the trip to give it to. She and Tom had agreed to gift it to me. I had only known these people for a few days but knew I would always treasure them— and their fine gift.

The evening ended with a lovely Hawaiian sunset, various skippers receiving trophies (Skip Allan and *Wildflower* taking top honors); and of course, ALL the skippers receiving their much- coveted 2008 TransPac belt buckles. Robert had his buckle from his 1994 TransPac so he planned to make a plaque featuring his 2008 buckle and mount it inside *Black Feathers* when we returned home. He felt she had earned the honor.

It was indeed a grand finale for the 2008 TransPac adventure.

Now we had to buckle down. The original plan had been for *Sparky* and *Feral* to share a trailer on the ship that would return them to the mainland. Robbie informed Robert that Ruben had decided to donate *Sparky,* therefore, making trailer space available for *Black Feathers*. Robert spoke with Tom Kirschbaum, and then called Larry Cummins at Load-A-Boat to make the arrangements. All Larry required: Confirmation of the space's availability from Robbie, and then we went into overdrive knowing little time remained to get our tiny vessel ready to head home. Robert would have to have *Black Feathers* in Honolulu by August 6th. A lot to do to make that happen. We knew we could get done what we needed to do. Our only real concern: Ruben and *Sparky* were due in the morning of August 6th, and Robert really wanted to be in Princeville to announce their finish. If he didn't make it back in time, I would fill in for him.

Robert spent the better part of August 3rd, rowing his inflatable raft out to *Black Feathers* anchored in Hanalei Bay, cleaning her up and then loading the raft with things we needed to bring ashore. Then he would jump in the water and swim back to shore, pushing the fully loaded raft ahead of him. Thank heavens we had a washer and dryer at the condo because we dealt with a LOT of laundry. Then back he went with his raft full of the items that would be stowed onboard. Originally we thought we had to ship the boat back empty, which meant deciding what we were willing to part with or pay to ship separately, so hearing we could "fill her up" was music to our ears—and pocketbook.

Black Feathers Rests Quietly

Skip Allan helped tremendously by providing sailing instructions to Honolulu along with some key landmarks and pitfalls to watch for.

As dawn broke on August 5th, Robert headed out of Hanalei Bay for Honolulu. We had been warned by Skip Allan and various other skippers that this short 120-mile crossing would be a tough one, and it certainly proved to be.

That evening as pre-arranged, Robert called me from the boat. I could barely hear him because the boat was pounding so hard on the water. We knew it would be rough, neither of us had any idea it would be as rough as it was. Thomas Kirschbaum's daughter sailed to Honolulu with him. I hoped she felt much more comfortable on a sailboat than I, otherwise she would be terrified.

Robert called the next morning and much to our relief, the weather and the seas had turned calm and beautiful. Later that morning a steady breeze developed. The rest of the day would be smooth sailing. Now his only concern: Finding the port and getting there on time.

That afternoon I received a call from Larry Cummins. He informed me that *Feral* had been unable to make it to Honolulu due to the lack of an engine and the early morning calm. Larry, therefore, planned to come down to Koolina and meet both *Feral* and *Black Feathers*. He had already made contact with Robert, and Robert had turned back a few miles and would soon arrive at his updated destination. Larry told me he would make sure Robert got some food and could use his shower if he wished. Then he would drop him at the airport. NOW, that's service. I went online and booked Robert's flight back to Kauai.

Robert called me for his flight information. I told him it was thought Ruben would arrive early the next morning. He got quiet for a moment and then said, "Looks like I'll be there in time to see *Sparky* come in." I nodded my head as if he could see me through the phone line. Each of us knew how much we wanted BOTH of us to be on the bluff to announce the finish as *Sparky* crossed the line. By the time Robert arrived in Kauai, I had confirmation from Robbie—Ruben was indeed scheduled to arrive the next morning, news I took great pleasure in delivering to Robert.

August 7th—a VERY BIG day! Ruben sailed *Sparky* in under her own power.

In the early-morning darkness, Robbie called and told us, "It's time." She sounded like a little child who had just seen her first Christmas tree.

Out the door in five, we headed for the bluff. The skies, overcast when we arrived, soon cleared, providing a glorious morning—beautiful skies and blue sea that stretched to the horizon.

The VHF crackled and then it became truly real—we heard Ruben's voice. THEN we saw the tiny glistening speck. Ruben had arrived!

Many of the skippers who had remained in Hanalei to welcome Ruben began sending their welcoming messages to him out over the air. You could hear the exhilaration in each message—in every word.

I aligned myself with the finish line and Robert readied himself on the VHF. I raised my arm and as *Sparky* sailed across the finish line, I brought my arm down and jumped for joy, calling out "Now." Robert announced Ruben's finish. We both jumped around up there on the bluff, giggling as if we were little kids stomping around in a really cool mud puddle.

At the finish line, Skip Allan on *Wildflower* waited to tow the valiant little ship and her tired, but gallant skipper, into Hanalei Bay. We watched for a few minutes as they made their way toward "home," and then drove down to the bay to join the rest of the welcoming party.

Mitchell Boy, our regular escort boat skipper, came ashore in his bright red inflatable chase boat to retrieve Robbie, Chris Humann, Christine and Jonathan who would go out to meet Ruben, leaving his parents and brother onshore as a surprise. After the official greeting and anchoring of *Sparky*, Ruben and his entourage headed back to shore where a crowd had gathered, all eager to welcome Ruben.

I was quite startled when I saw Ruben. On the bluff over the VHF, he sounded animated, happy and robust, but now as he came ashore, he appeared quite haggard and disoriented. This young man, always so full of life, looked as if he had not one ounce of energy left. It appeared to me as if Robbie supplied the force holding him upright. I so wanted to rush him and hug him, but stayed at the perimeter of the circle surrounding him, knowing it was not my place. His parents and brother were there and they were his family. His mother, a delicate, elegant lady did rush him and one could tell that all her worries flew away as she embraced her son. Indeed a joyful moment to watch his family encircle him with their love.

Ruben turned and reached out to me. I stepped quickly across the sand into his outreached arms and clung to him.

I heard a soft, "I love you."

"I love you too. I'm so glad you are safe."

Ruben Embraces Jeanne

Everyone took turns embracing Ruben and sharing their thoughts with him. And this young, exhausted man received each and every person as he always does, with total graciousness and love. Robbie stood by his side, radiant, and yet obviously feeling he should get some rest, and soon.

After a short time, Ruben, Robbie and his family headed for their condo. We wouldn't see them again until that evening at Tree.

AND what a surprise he had for us! The exhausted man of less than 10 hours before appeared the picture of health and energy. He had not slept. Instead he took a hike. Now here he stood freshly showered and shaved in a crisp Hawaiian shirt and summer slacks, laughing and sharing, what else, but his TransPac adventure. I have two photos taken that day of Ruben and me—the first that morning when he arrived, and the second that night at The Tree. Difficult to believe someone could recoup that fast. Awwwww, youth!!!

A very well attended Tree, and definitely the most emotional one of the 2008 TransPac. We all stood in silence as Ruben related his dismasting experience. Immediately following the dismasting he felt disbelief, then despair and frustration, but not for long—he got to work and started jury rigging his mast, up and up, going from three feet to 10 feet, from disabled to making 100 miles per day. His "audience" went from silent to chattering as we all joined him in the jubilation of his adventure. Skip did the honors of presenting Ruben with his 2008 TransPac belt buckle. Then the crowd cheered. Ruben was home. Our TransPac family was complete.

Within the next few days, lots of things changed. Robert's children had returned to California. The skipper "population" began to dwindle—some sailing back to the mainland, some shipping their boats home, one starting to sail home and then changing his mind and turning back to ship his boat home, and some selling their boats and flying home. Ruben and Robbie would donate *Sparky* to Mitchell Boy. We understood his uncle would help him obtain and install a new mast.

We spent one evening with Ruben and Robbie. We had hamburgers and played pool in a local "joint" in Lihue. It was great fun.

Once everyone left, we spent the next couple of weeks exploring various parts of the island, going to thrift stores and local farmers markets, and one night had a lovely dinner at the DeBree's, who it turned out lived within walking distance of our condo. They had their dining room table delivered earlier that day, so we were their first true dinner guests in their new abode.

Ruben Receives His Belt Buckle from Skip

A few days later, we were stunned to receive the news *Wildflower* had been lost. Skip and *Wildflower* had become family. Skip obviously had a deep affection for his boat and took great pride in her. We knew making the decision to scuttle her must have been agony for him.

On August 20th, Robert and I took Mary Hall from The Princeville Resort to lunch in Hanalei and presented her with a lei. We had a delightful visit. She said The Princeville would love to have the 2010 TransPac return to their resort. I told her the huge discounts due to the impending remodel were what made it possible for us to have the Awards Ceremony there in 2008. She smiled and told me they liked having us there, and certain adjustments just "might" be offered again, suggesting when the time came, to give her a call. I promised her I would put the "suggestion" into my final TransPac report.

A group of homeless people "resided" in and around The Tree. A number of them had shown great interest and support in the TransPac, and prided themselves on knowing the skippers and the boats by name. Obviously "our Tree" was normally "their Tree," but they graciously gave it up for our daily gathering. The day before we were to leave the island, I collected our extra food supplies and headed down to the Pavilion. I walked up to the small group of people sitting at the picnic tables by The Tree. One fella said, "I know you! You're from the TransPac." I smiled and nodded and told them why I had come. They were quite happy to have the bags of food. I stood and talked to them for a few minutes. They asked which boat Robert had sailed in the race. When I replied, *"Black Feathers,"* I immediately got a quite lengthy monologue outlining Robert and *Black Feathers'* race in detail. The orator knew *Black Feathers* to be the smallest boat to ever complete the TransPac, he knew Robert had broken his rudder and replaced it with the original one, he knew he had sailed to Honolulu and *Black Feathers* was on her way home aboard a ship, and he knew Robert had previously sailed the TransPac in a larger boat. I stood in amazement. As I took my leave, they thanked me for the food, wished us a safe journey home and said they hoped to see us again next TransPac. When I got back to the condo, I told Robert about my encounter. He had no idea how the man in the park had come to know so much about *Black Feathers*, but it delighted him to know the fella's information was accurate.

Robert said he wanted us to fly home on the same plane even though it would have been considerably less expensive coming back on separate flights, since I had booked my flight using frequent flier miles many months before. We'd been apart enough, so we spent $900 for a one-way ticket for him to come on the same plane with me, but then our seat assignments were not together. Luckily a very friendly and efficient United ticket agent checked us in at the Lihue Airport. One of our bags weighed four pounds over the limit, so right there at her ticket counter she let us open two bags and re-adjust things to equalize the weight and eliminate the $125 overweight baggage fee. Then she found us two seats together and we headed for home.

Home felt so good, and the best part, our homecoming day. Our treasured friend and neighbor, Margie, had outdone herself. She had custody of the key to our house and used it to provide quite the surprise for us. She decorated the dining room table in an elaborate tropical motif, complete with Hawaiian shirts (two for me and two for Robert) on the backs of the chairs. A six-pack of beer with sailboats on the labels waited in the refrigerator, flowers and a basket full of tropical fruits rested on the counter, and of course there were luscious fresh strawberries (which I love and she hates) for me. Balloons and stuffed animals (fish) contributed to the mood. A most welcome surprise indeed—and she just happened to be there when we arrived which made it even better.

We had a long and anxious wait for *Black Feathers* to arrive back in San Francisco. Prior to their departure for Honolulu, Robert spent a full day cleaning and drying out the boat, but the trek to Honolulu had rendered many items within the boat damp, if not downright wet, and the entire boat in disarray. He did what he could with his limited allotment of time to put things in order, but we had visions of alarming proportions as to what we would face since she had been closed up for over a month.

While we waited for *Black Feathers* to arrive, I had plenty to do. I had a trivia bee to pull together. I conducted the premises layout walk-thru and the event walk-thru, made signage, and completed the other last-minute tasks. Some of the TransPac skippers decided they wanted more swag items, so we offered them one more go-round and came up with a fair-sized order for Business First. Also, I needed to go through my TransPac event timeline and tidy it up to hand off to Synthia with the hope it would help those working on the 2010 TransPac. Robert and I added a page of suggestions; one being they do away with the hard copy of the skippers' manual and simply publish it online, letting the skippers print out whatever portions they deemed useful.

—◆—

In mid September, Carla and Mark Deppe of *Alchera* held a lovely post TransPac party at their hillside home in Lafayette, California. The white-clothed round tables, set up in the lush backyard were adorned with shells and other sea accoutrements. Skip Allan's brother came as a surprise for Skip. When he lost *Wildflower*, Skip managed to save his trophy for posterity, but he couldn't save such things as his collection of miniature stuffed animals, his 2008 TransPac tankard and his 2008 Transpac belt buckle—THE buckle that is so precious to all the skippers. His brother brought with him a start of a new collection of stuffed animals. Sylvia and I presented him with my tankard complete with his drink of choice—it seemed inappropriate for me to have a tankard when his was gone. AND Synthia presented him with a replacement belt buckle. Skip had pictures to share of the last minutes before *Wildflower* was laid to rest, and of him struggling to climb a Jacob's ladder on a pitching sea as he boarded a freighter.

Shama came into the party dressed in a simple understated neutral-colored outfit with a brown scarf draped around her neck. I was captured by how the simplicity of her clothing seemed somehow to enhance her electricity. She always appears relaxed, poised and open. Her laughter music, her voice and words the lyrics of the beautiful melody—the composition entitled *Shama*.

At the Awards Ceremony in Kauai, Robert received the Perseverance Trophy. This trophy normally goes to the last to finish, or the skipper who does something that shows great fortitude. The TransPac rules state that all TransPac trophies are to be awarded to skippers who finish within the official race time. Robert felt embarrassed to have this trophy for 2008 for a couple of reasons. He did quite well in the race, finishing eighth in fleet. Dwight Odom on *NaNa* certainly showed perseverance in starting the race three times, but who could argue that Ruben on *Sparky* had truly won the award, even though he finished after the deadline. We called Synthia, proposing that we present the trophy to Ruben. She said no. It had to go to a skipper who finished before the deadline and Ruben had not done so. But Synthia and Robert talked it out, and decided if the presentation came from Robert and not the Race Committee, it would be acceptable. Robert and I had the plaque engraved with Ruben and *Sparky's* names. The night of the post party, Robert presented Ruben with the trophy that so rightly belonged to him. All in attendance appeared highly supportive of the hand-off.

Robert received a call. *Black Feathers* was due to arrive at San Francisco Boat Works in a couple of days. Excited and anxious, he wondered what he would find inside his boat—mold, mildew, structural damage from the shipping. He would go from chatterbox to extremely quiet, and back to chatterbox. He really needed to see her and assess the situation before he would be normal again. On the morning he went to accept delivery of her, he woke up before daylight and scooted out the door.

Within a couple of hours of his arrival at the boatyard, the truck rolled in carrying *Black Feathers*. Tom Kirschbaum had sent Robert a photo he had taken of her sitting on the truck when she arrived in Los Angeles and now Robert would see in person just how diminutive she looked sitting atop the carrier. The truck driver told Robert he had some trouble getting his automatic pads to fit her tiny form and spent an hour making adjustments to ensure her a secure ride. The good news—she seemed in great shape inside and out. The dampness had dissipated and nothing remained to be alarmed about. Having been out of the water long enough to make her bottom paint ineffective, Robert removed what items needed to be taken home and left her at the boatyard to have her bottom paint redone.

When the boatyard completed the painting, Robert and I both made the trek back to welcome her home. Only one minor issue: A few scuffmarks on her hull from the supports she had been resting on during transport. We had a half-hour wait while they put another boat in the water, so why not remove scuffmarks while her underside was so readily accessible. Thirty minutes later, in tiptop shape, two boatyard employees eased her into the water. Robert and *Black Feathers* headed for South Beach Harbor and I hopped in the car to be there when they arrived. We still had one unforeseen obstacle to overcome.

As Robert headed into South Beach Harbor where it all began, *Black Feathers'* motor died and refused to restart. I could hear Robert's thoughts, "I took her clear across the ocean and now I'm stuck needing help to get her into her slip." Fortunately, a rescuer was close at hand. An avid group of disabled sailors regularly sail the waters of South Beach, and one thankfully was close at hand. He saw Robert in need of assistance and aptly came to his aid. Of course, then the engine started right up. It appeared *Black Feathers* just wasn't quite ready to end her adventure and be stuck in her slip.

—◆—

The mail arrived. Robbie and Ruben had originally planned an intimate wedding for their immediate family, but a friend of theirs had offered her lovely hilltop mansion for their ceremony, and now we were receiving an invitation. Robert was elated, I felt devastated. Their wedding date—October 11th in the Bay Area, three or four hours away, the same day as the Trivia Bee. I told Robert he would have to go without me, but I really, really didn't want to miss out on the celebration. My Trivia Bee Committee to the rescue. I called my sidekick, Phil, and his take, "You have everything organized—we know what to do, how can we fail, you go and have a great time." No more to be said.

Early the morning of October 11th, Robert and I went to the Opera Hall, the site of the Trivia Bee. We helped get things organized, and then headed for the wedding. And what a wedding!!!

We checked into our motel, changed our clothes and headed to the site. At the base of the hill we were met by a limo that took us up to the top of the hill to an incredibly striking home. The reflection pool appeared to fall right over the edge into a canyon with a valley view in the distance. The owner of the home, a most gracious lady and the friend of Ruben and Robbie, attended the wedding. The ceremony took place in the front yard with the mountains and valley in the background. Robbie lovely as always, Ruben as handsome as could be, and both obviously very happy. A lovely sit-down dinner, a catered affair in the terraced backyard, featured elegant and delicious food. Tiny silver sailboats supported the place cards—how appropriate can you be. Awesome music and an incredible dessert display, prepared as a wedding gift from another friend of Robbie and Ruben, topped off the evening. The Trivia Bee took in a record amount of money for the literacy program, and I have to admit I wish I could have been cloned for that one day so I could have been in two places at one time, but the wedding became the priority. Ruben and Robbie are family!

— ◆ —

The 2008 TransPac was finished. Robert, Jeanne and *Black Feathers* were all home safe and sound. Life swung back to normal, but normal had changed. People recognized Robert in parking lots, we would begin to focus on the writing of this book, and Robert would have a newfound pride in his little boat, Miss *Black Feathers*. An uncommon adventure in a quite common little boat had been rewarding and successful for both skipper and vessel. Changes were warranted to make the boat better for such future voyages, but all in all she had proved herself worthy of the honor of TransPacer. She had gained a well-deserved reputation— a little boat with a mighty spirit.

Hanalei Bay from The Princeville Bluffs

PART III
Thoughts on Small Boat Preparation For The Singlehanded TransPac

Chapter 22
Advantages and Disadvantages of Small Boats

Contrary to many people's thoughts, there are many advantages to small boats. To maintain a proper perspective, a short discussion will be offered to review both the advantages and disadvantages of small sailboats when considering offshore racing.

ADVANTAGES OF SMALL BOATS

1) Costs: Costs in general are usually less. This includes the cost of such things as services (hull cleaning, boatyard fees, etc.), slip fees, gear and sails. If the small boat happens to be a popular model, the costs often become even less and the availability of specific gear greater. Because of the potential wetness problem with small boats, you will often avoid investing in high tech electronics, thereby cutting costs even further.

2) Maintenance: Maintenance can be less expensive as well as being easier to accomplish because of size and less things to maintain.

3) Boat and Gear Handling:
   - Due to its smaller size and weight (sail carrying and folding, sail trimming, spinnaker pole handling, spinnaker packing) gear handling becomes easier.
   - Smaller spinnakers can make dealing with spinnaker performance mishaps less traumatic.
   - Boat handling under normal conditions may be easier and more forgiving because the boat is smaller and lighter.
   - Small boats are more maneuverable in limited space.
   - Small boats can easily be pushed, rowed, sculled or towed.

4) Performance: In a race, the singlehanded skipper of a small boat has a better chance of sailing his boat to its potential, thereby benefiting by a higher handicap PHRF rating. Although he will have a longer elapsed time, he has a better chance of benefiting on his corrected time.

5) Mental Outlook:
- Smaller boats are often less intimidating and easier to understand.
- Because smaller boats respond more quickly to change, a skipper can often more readily learn sailing techniques.
- Because smaller boats are less expensive, less intimidating and easier to understand, skippers may be more willing to make experimental changes since they will not be risking the value of an expensive boat.
- In a small boat you have a feeling of being more "at one" with the sea.

6) Breakage: Equipment breakage may be less because the powers generated in small boats are less.

7) Troubleshooting: Smaller boats have fewer inaccessible areas so problems may be diagnosed more readily.

8) Limited Size: The limited size of a small boat prevents the accumulation of too much "stuff" because there simply is no place to put it.

9) Emergency Repairs:
- Repairs may be easier to accomplish due to equipment and parts being of a more manageable size.
- Some repairs may have full-sized replacements available (e.g. rudder) instead of having to depend on a makeshift, partial-sized replacement.
- If dismasted, some form of repair may be easier to accomplish simply due to the lesser size and weight of the remaining mast segments.
- On small boats the mast could possibly be lowered at sea to make a repair and then re-stepped.

—◆—

DISADVANTAGES OF SMALL BOATS
1) Weather:
- Small boats are more subject to the whims of nature giving the skipper a rougher ride.
- Heavy weather affects small boats more quickly and profoundly, therefore, they need to reef earlier and discontinue sailing sooner.

2) Construction of the boat:
   - Some small boats may not be built as strongly as desired for offshore sailing because that was never their intended use.
   - Small boats generally have inadequate headroom and interior space creating more physical discomfort for the skipper.
   - You may not be able to climb the mast of many small boats due to a lack of stability with weight aloft.

3) General disadvantages:
   - Small boats generally cannot sail as fast as larger boats.
   - Small boats are more likely to provide a wet ride, which not only causes discomfort, but also limits what high tech electronics are feasible.
   - Due to the limited space of small boats, it is impossible to carry all desirable gear or people.

4) Racing:
   - In the TransPac, a lack of wind creates two particular disadvantages for small boats: 1) There probably will be little time after arrival to spend with the other skippers, and 2) The small boat may not finish the race on time if there is a lack of wind and the race committee grants no time extension.
   - In races involving tidal changes (e.g. the Farallones race) small boats are less likely to benefit from all the favorable tides, unlike the faster, larger boats.

Chapter 23

The Basic Cal 20

Cal 20s, designed by the respected C. William Lapworth, were built from 1961 to 1975. During those years Jensen Marine produced approximately 2,500 of them. Here are some of the Cal 20's statistics:

LOA (length overall)	20'
LWL (length at waterline)	18'
Beam	7'
Draft	3 1/3'
Displacement	1,950 lbs.
Sail area	
Main	115 sq. ft.
Class Jib (#3 approx. 115%)	81 sq. ft.
Spinnaker	290 sq. ft.
Ballast in keel	900 lbs.
Spars	Aluminum
Hull construction	Fiberglass
Cockpit length	8'
Sailboat type	7/8 Fractional sloop
D/WL ratio	147
2008 PHRF handicap rating	273 seconds/mile

I purchased *Black Feathers* in late 2000. She is hull #14, produced in 1961, the Cal 20's first year of production. From the boat's appearance, I felt the previous owners had held a bit of passion for her. Lifelines had been placed around her working deck and a self-tacking jib boom adorned her bow. Although thoughtful additions, these were not done in a manner appropriate for my plans for her as an offshore racer so I removed them. At that point, she would have represented about as basic a stock Cal 20 as you can get. The original aluminum mast, a Zephyr #3, was produced on the East Coast and installed on the first 50 Cal 20s. After the first 50, Jensen Marine began using masts produced on the West Coast. Most of her deck hardware, as well as her one-piece solid mahogany rudder also came with the original boat. The head had been removed as it has on most Cal 20s. The low hand railings along each side of the cockpit had also been removed. The electrical system to run the navigation lights and radio was positioned poorly for my use so I removed all electrical wiring and the small electrical panel associated with it.

Although the previous owners made four important upgrades, basically what remained was a 1961 stock Cal 20 with a bow pulpit. The original fittings attaching the spreaders to the mast had been replaced with stronger fittings. A stainless steel strap (tang) was placed to attach the headstay directly to the hull rather than to the existing forestay fitting on the deck. Her original aluminum-framed windows had been replaced by 1/4" Lexan windows that were sealed and bolted through the hull. Lastly, the deck area under the mast had been reinforced with 4" X 4" supports to prevent the deck from being affected by the compressive forces of the mast. Everything else was original— hardware, fittings, spars, tiller, rudder, etc.

As my intent was to sail this boat singlehanded in the various SSS races, I began making improvements that would make such races possible and provide additional safety at sea. Over the next several months, I put the following initial improvements in place:

1) New standing rigging. I had no idea how old the existing rigging was so I replaced it with class regulation-sized rigging. (See the Rigging section in Chapter 26 for actual sizes.)

2) Originally two gudgeons were on the rudder with two pintles on the transom. During a race to the Farallones, the lower pintle, always under more stress than the upper, broke off the transom. The repair consisted of getting a new fiberglass rudder and placing two long pintles on the rudder—and doubled gudgeons, top and bottom, on the transom.

3) New sails: main with two reef points, working class jib and a spinnaker

4) New tiller with an autopilot attachment

5) Autopilot (Raytheon ST2000)

6) Bulkhead mounted lighted compass

7) Two new Harken winches to replace the original winches

8) Mounted at the masthead were:
- VHF antenna
- Combination strobe/anchor light
- Windex wind indicator

9) A traveler was placed across the cockpit 19" aft of the companionway hatch and the mainsheet controls were moved to the mid-boom area.

These initial upgrades enabled me to compete in the various SSS races in and around San Francisco Bay. Slight improvements or changes become regular occurrences on any boat. My primary concerns were to improve sailing performance, and enhance safety and comfort at sea. The deck layout is extremely important for the singlehanded sailor. Blocks around the mast directing lines to deck organizers, and then to the cockpit, are a critical component to efficient performance. Also an essential component—the convenient location of reefing lines from the boom to the mast and cockpit. I spent a great deal of time researching what I hoped might be an ideal layout.

The further evolution of this stock Cal 20 into a TransPac-ready pocket racer extended over several years. I spent a fair amount of time, effort and money installing modern gear on the boat, but did nothing to strengthen the basic hull or mast.

The following three chapters address the various elements of a small boat and how it might be prepared for the Singlehanded TransPac race or other offshore voyaging.

Chapter 24

Electrical System

If you think you might eventually set your boat up as a TransPac racer, it is helpful to prepare for that eventuality as you plan your electrical system. The electrical system for *Black Feathers* consisted of the following general categories:

1) Electrical Panel
   - Circuit breaker panels
   - Monitor
   - Wiring
   - Solar panel regulator
   - Charging outlet for handheld devices
2) Electronics
   - VHF, SAT phone, SSB (Single Side Band) or other types of communication
   - CARD (Collision Avoidance Radar Detector)
   - AIS (Automatic Identification System) with its dedicated GPS
   - Knot/Depth meter
   - Spare GPS devices
   - Autopilot
   - Various antennas
3) Navigation Lights
   - Mast head lights (strobe and anchor)
   - Stern light
   - Red/Green bi-color lights

—◆—

Electrical Panel

For a small boat with limited battery capacity, the electrical panel should meet the following criteria:

1) Location: The panel should be positioned where it is least likely to get wet but still be easily accessible.

2) Size: The panel should be large enough to house every necessary component (monitor, charging regulator, etc.) and provide enough circuits so each individual electrical device can be exclusively selected.

3) Accessibility: The wiring within the panel should be easily accessible.

The electrical panel in *Black Feathers* was positioned within the cabin on the port side bulkhead between the V-berth and the mid-cabin. It consisted of a box measuring 14" X 20" X 4 1/2" and was constructed of 3/8" thick teak veneered plywood. A continuous/piano hinge ran along the left vertical side. I designed the panel to be large enough to house the following components:

1) Two water resistant circuit panels of six circuits each (Blue Sea System #8053)

2) Electrical monitor (Xantrex Link 20)

3) Solar panel regulator (Sunsei CC20,000 D)

4) 12-volt receptacle to charge handheld devices

5) The large mass of wiring required to make it all work

The wires placed within the panel enabled the door to swing open for easy access to the components within.

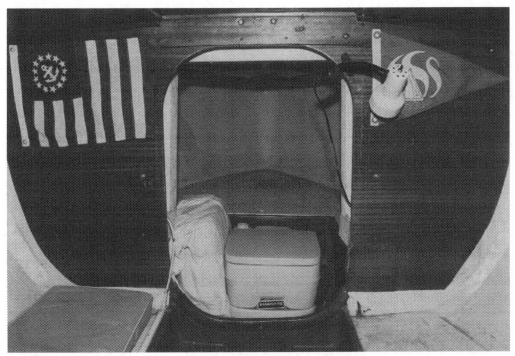

Prior to Electrical Panel Installation

Basic Electrical System Installation

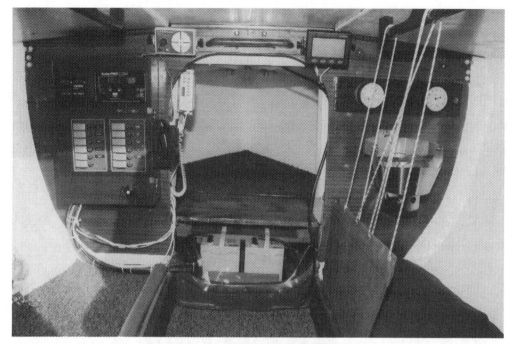

Completed Electrical System

Electrical Panel Interior

CIRCUIT BREAKER PANELS

The wires coming from the various electrical devices enter the electrical panel and are distributed among the 12 circuit breakers located on two water resistant 6-circuit panels. Although a couple of electrical devices share a circuit, most circuits control only one device. I can, therefore, be very specific as to which devices are using electrical power at any given time.

—◆—

ELECTRICAL MONITOR

It is wise to know what is going on within the electrical system of the boat and that is the function of the electrical monitor. To me, the important data it displays is:

1) Amps currently being used
2) Amp hours that have been drained from the batteries (and therefore the amp hours remaining)
3) Amps being returned to your batteries through recharging by the solar panel
4) Voltage of the batteries
5) The above should be specific for each battery (or battery bank)

Black Feathers used the Xantrex Link 20 Monitor. During the TransPac it worked well except when monitoring the amount of energy being returned to the batteries through the solar panel. It seems that the threshold for detecting returned charge was set incorrectly so although the solar panel continued to charge, the monitor did not fully detect it. After several consultations with the manufacturer, this significant problem still remains. In spite of this, I had no problems with the electrical system during the TransPac.

SOLAR PANEL AND ITS CHARGING REGULATOR

Without an engine to charge the batteries, *Black Feathers* relied on a 65-watt hard solar panel that had the potential of replacing 20 amp hours of energy to the batteries each day. The specific model, a Sunsei SE-4000, measured approximately 30" square. Since the amount of charge produced by this panel is significant, a solar panel regulator is required. I mounted the regulator in the electrical panel. The solar panel worked effectively even on overcast days. It also worked very well after the glass top cracked into thousands of pieces that somehow managed to stay intact. Later, after the race, I sealed clear plastic sheeting over the cracked glass to try to prevent water damage to the panel. Although the panel functioned well all those many months since the glass broke, in August 2009 I noticed the plastic cover beginning to discolor so I replaced it with a panel of 3/32" Lexan, sealing the edges with silicone. I do plan to replace the solar panel, but for now, this is a great temporary fix. It is fascinating to watch the panel pretend it's the Energizer Bunny—it's definitely "broken," but it just keeps on charging!

Solar Panel on Stern Pulpit

A concern with any solar panel is where it will be mounted and if that mounting can be adjusted to always face the sun. *Black Feathers* has a stern pulpit that provides a solid support across the transom and down each side for about 2 1/2'. I originally thought it would be ideal to have two panels; one mounted port and the other starboard near the stern, and have them angled to best pick up the sun. My concern being that if the panels stuck out over the boat very far they could easily get smacked by waves and be damaged or totally torn off, possibly along with portions of the stern pulpit. That issue would exist whether I used a single panel or dual panels. In considering a single panel, I realized I could not mount it in the transom area because it would interfere with the Monitor Windvane, or my access to the windvane. The remedy: To mount a single panel within the confines of the boat just at, and extending forward, of the transom. I placed a stainless steel crossbar about 2 1/2' forward of the transom crossbar on the stern pulpit to allow for a solid, nonadjustable connection to the stern pulpit. Although I received criticism for not making the panel adjustable, it functions very well. The panel, placed above the area where the engine goes into the engine well, provides adequate clearance to place and remove the engine. It presents only a slight inconvenience.

—◆—

WIRING

In general, all wiring of the electrical panel is now slightly oversized and of marine quality. The wiring that goes from the electrical panel to devices up the mast remains intact. By this I mean that I do not have an electrical connection on the foredeck in which to connect the mast wires. When taking down the mast, I must disconnect the appropriate wires from the panel and allow them to pass through the holes in the deck. My thought was that an electrical connection at the deck would be quite vulnerable to water damage and could be inadvertently stepped on. Instead, I had the wires from the mast exit the mast near its base, then enter a plastic junction box and go through the top of the deck into the V-berth area. I sealed the deck hole and entrance to the junction box on the deck with silicone to make them watertight. This seems to work well. Be mindful, however, that I keep *Black Feathers* in a slip and rarely take the mast down. Other techniques might work as well. The wires that run through the mast are for the VHF antenna, strobe/anchor light, and red/green navigation light. (You can see the junction box in the photo entitled "Deck Organization" in Chapter 26.) The wires from the mast exit the sides and enter the aft side of the junction box. A large single intact battery cable attached to the mast and also to a keel bolt, enters the top of the junction box. The intent of this large battery cable is to offer some protection from a lightning strike. It would hopefully allow the lightning bolt to run down the mast and out through the keel. I will only know if it works after I get struck by lightning!

—◆—

ELECTRONICS

Small boats never have the luxury of having enough space, electrical capacity, or guaranteed dryness to accommodate a large array of electrical devices. Special consideration must be given to where to mount such devices so that they are convenient but also safe from water damage. Electronics that can function independently are favored because they do not rely on other electrical equipment for support.

The electrical devices on *Black Feathers* were:

1) VHF radio: Most TransPac boats also have an SSB radio. For the first time, on the 2008 TransPac, a SAT phone could be used instead of the SSB. Several boats had both.

2) Handheld SAT phone

3) Two handheld GPS devices

4) CARD (Collision Avoidance Radar Detector)

5) AIS (Automatic Identification System) with a separate dedicated handheld GPS, with a power source that was hardwired to the boat.

6) Knot/depth meter combo

7) Autopilot

8) Various externally mounted antennas
   - VHF
   - SAT phone
   - GPS
   - CARD
   - AIS

—◆—

COMMUNICATIONS

For the TransPac, you are required to have a masthead-mounted VHF antenna and a second VHF antenna in case the mast comes down. *Black Feathers'* second antenna was mounted on the stern pulpit. It acted not only as an emergency VHF antenna, but also as the AIS antenna. The handheld SAT phone, an Iridium 9505A, has an antenna on the handheld unit, but it will not function well inside the boat. I wanted to use the SAT phone inside the boat, where it would be dry, more comfortable and possibly quiet, so I mounted a fixed external SAT phone antenna on the stern pulpit. The handheld phone would then connect to this. The SAT phone always lived in a waterproof box in the abandon ship bag when not in use. The SAT phone has proven to be an extremely effective mode of communication. As fond of SSB radios as many of the TransPac skippers are, these radios have demonstrated themselves to be worthless in the event of a dismasting.

—◆—

COLLISION AVOIDANCE

Two different devices were installed on *Black Feathers* for collision avoidance. The CARD detects the presence of radar and displays the direction from which it comes. When it detects radar, an alarm goes off. The antenna for the CARD is mounted on the stern pulpit. This device functions independently and doesn't need to be integrated into any other device (other then a power supply). The second device to detect ships is the AIS. This apparatus will pick up continuously transmitted information from most large commercial vessel transponders. It must be connected to a GPS so it can plot the target ship's position in relation to your own. It displays the ship's position, speed, course, and name. When it detects a target ship, an alarm goes off. I highly recommend both of these magical pieces of equipment.

On the TransPac, the CARD seemed to always pick up the presence of a ship sooner than the AIS. The AIS, however, shows the ship's path and proves much more valuable when dealing with low visibility situations. They cost about the same and install easily. On *Black Feathers* they are installed directly above the opening to the V-berth on the cabin-side of the bulkhead that is between the V-berth and cabin. Their placement keeps them fairly safe from water spray and convenient to use. The GPS for the AIS is mounted on the right side of the electrical panel. (For information about the manufacturers of these devices, see References and Resources.)

—◆—

KNOT METER/DEPTH SOUNDER COMBO

I used the Raymarine ST 40 Bidata System knot meter and depth sounder combo to meet the race requirements. The knot meter part of this gauge requires a transducer to be placed in a thru-hull. The thru-hull was located in the small compartment under the port side cabin berth. This location provides easy access. It is the only functioning thru-hull on *Black Feathers*. The thru-hulls for the head, originally located in the V-berth, have been capped.

The depth sounder portion of this gauge is designed to have the transducer placed in a thru-hull also. I have found that it works well by simply having the sensor placed against the hull in an enclosure filled with water. This is significant as it prevents having to place another thru-hull. The enclosure consists of a 4" tall plastic pipe fitting 4" in diameter that has been secured to the hull with silicone. The sensor lies within the partially water-filled fitting. This enclosure is located just under the cockpit area slightly aft and to the left of where the keel ends. Having it in this location makes it easy to check the water level and add more when needed, and keeps it out of the way of the various items stored under the cockpit.

— ♦ —

AUTOPILOT

The autopilot is an Autohelm ST 2000 that attaches to the tiller above deck near the stern. The electrical connection to the pilot comes from within a flexible PVC cowl vent located in the stern area of the cockpit. A wire runs within the boat from the electrical panel to the cowl vent. The autopilot plugs into this line, therefore, allowing the actual connecting receptacle to be within the cowl vent, somewhat protected from the weather. This has worked well. (See Chapter 26 for more discussion of autopilot self-steering.)

— ♦ —

ANTENNAS

There are five different antennas on *Black Feathers*:

1) VHF for radio—located at the masthead
2) VHF for radio (emergency) and also used with the AIS—located on the stern pulpit
3) GPS, CARD and SAT phone—all three of these antennas are located on the stern pulpit and resemble white mushrooms of various shapes and sizes.

— ♦ —

NAVIGATION LIGHTS

The TransPac requires a masthead strobe with a xenon bulb. Xenon is the name of the gas within the strobe bulb. Cal 20s generally have a small masthead with only a mounted Windex wind indicator. To this, I added a VHF antenna and a combination strobe/anchor light. It would be ideal to mount a full tri-color light with strobe, but I could not find one small or lightweight enough. Pyramid Technologies (see References and Resources) makes a combination strobe (with xenon bulb)/anchor light that uses very little energy. Much more compact than most such lights, it has proven reliable. I kept the strobe light on throughout the night when sailing in the open ocean.

I mounted a stern light on the stern pulpit. Aside from its function as a navigation light, it also acts to light up the Monitor Windvane if you need to check it at night. Each of the navigation lights has its own circuit on the electrical panel so only the ones you want showing need to be on. I would generally only have the strobe on at night, but if I made contact with another vessel, I would turn on the other navigation lights.

The red/green navigation lights create a particular problem for a Cal 20. The most common location for them is on each side of the hull slightly forward of the window and about at that level. This places them about 2 1/2' - 3' off the water and, therefore, not adequately visible. For the TransPac, I installed a red/green bi-color light on the bow pulpit. This did two things: 1) It raised the light a little, and 2) It made two lights out of one bulb thereby saving energy. Unfortunately, this light, probably never very visible, only served to make me feel better. After the TransPac, I was determined to install a bi-color light up the mast somewhere. It had to be somewhat lower than the masthead as it was already full. A Cal 20 is a 7/8 fractional rig, and therefore, has about 3' of mast from the masthead down to where the forestay is attached. This means that a light placed in this area will not be blanketed by the jib or spinnaker and, therefore, remains visible. I installed an Attwood 3500 series LED bi-color navigation light with two-mile visibility 25' up the mast about 1 1/2' shy of the masthead. This LED light uses very little energy (0.15 amps/hour) and can be seen nearly as well as if it were located at the masthead. I believe this is a good solution to an otherwise sticky problem. The original red and green navigation lights located near deck level are maintained as spare lights and have their own circuit on the electrical panel.

Masthead

Chapter 25

Meeting TransPac Requirements

As we begin using our boats for different purposes, we often realize there are new demands placed on them requiring certain changes and/or the need to acquire additional equipment. When we sail our boats on protected waters, the Coast Guard sets what it sees as basic safety requirements. When we sail a singlehanded race with the SSS, they too have a list of required items that extends beyond that of the Coast Guard. A singlehanded race extending into coastal waters expands the list again, and a race offshore to Hawaii expands the list even further. Many of these requirements present no particular challenge in achieving compliance. Some, however, present problems for small boats and these are the concerns addressed here.

—◆—

LIFELINES

For coastal and offshore racing, lifelines are required. With the SSS, a boat less than 28' must have, as a minimum, a multi-stranded stainless steel wire fitted continuously around the working deck with a minimum height of 18". It may be a single wire lifeline. The stanchions supporting the lifelines must be no more than 7' apart. Cal 20s did not come with lifelines. Adding them is not that difficult although there are some concerns. Having the mainsheet attach to the boom at the boom's end near the stern constitutes traditional rigging for a Cal 20. The mainsheet would then be led forward to a convenient location for the helmsman. Cal 20s were not equipped with travelers. Lifelines, or a stern pulpit, would create a problem for the mainsheet lines when the main is let out as in running downwind. Since this was not the way *Black Feathers'* main was sheeted, I did not have to deal with that particular problem.

In placing lifelines on *Black Feathers* I had two concerns:

1) Since I had added a traveler and rigged the mainsheet at mid-boom, the mainsheet would rub across the lifelines at mid-boat when going downwind with the boom extended far out. To remedy this, the lifelines had a reduction in their height at mid-boat.

2) I knew I wanted to have a solar panel mounted in the stern area, so I created a stern pulpit of stainless steel tubing and attached the lifelines to it. Check out the lifelines in the various photos throughout this book.

—◆—

RADAR REFLECTOR

For the TransPac, a radar reflector must be mounted at least 13' off the water. On a Cal 20 this means that it can be mounted just under the spreader, but no lower. It would be nice to have it higher, but small boats are adversely affected by weight and windage aloft. The race requirements were very specific concerning the radar reflector's overall size and radar cross-section measurements. This meant I had to use the large octahedral type, so I chose a Deluxe Echomaster by Davis. The possibility of having the mainsail chafe on the edges of the reflector when going downwind concerned me. To prevent this, I lined all the edges of the reflector with white vinyl snap-on, 3/32" diameter cable covers. The aluminum edges of the reflector slipped into the slit in the vinyl covers. A bead of epoxy held them in position. A wire cable that was attached at the base of the spreader at the mast and the wire shroud on the outboard side supported the radar reflector so there would be no weight on the spreader itself.

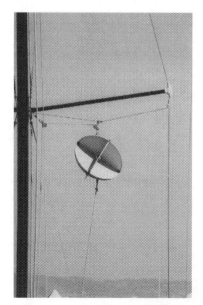

Radar Reflector

GALLEY

As I had no need or desire to cook, I tried to get the Race Committee to waive the galley requirement for such a small boat, but they would not. I, therefore, mounted a Seacook gimbaled propane stove by Force 10 inside the cabin on the right side of the bulkhead between the V-berth and cabin. Installed on a quick disconnect mount, it does not have to remain mounted and fits easily in a storage case. I never used it on the race but I understand it has a fine reputation. It is installed in the area of my berth on the right bulkhead in the cabin, but after the boat inspection, it rode to Hawaii in its storage case.

—◆—

WATER CONTAINERS

The SSS requires 21 gallons of fresh water. This water must be distributed in at least two containers with no container holding more than half the required amount. Twenty-one gallons of water weighs 170 pounds, so spreading out the weight is beneficial. I installed a flexible 28" square Plastimo water tank directly under the central portion of the cockpit adjacent to the cockpit lazarette. I placed a 32" square piece of indoor/outdoor carpet under the flexible 13-gallon tank to protect it from chafe and tied the tank in place with small lines. Also used were two storage crates by West Marine, each holding four one-gallon plastic milk bottles filled with water. Individual juice drinks like Kern drinks can also count as water. Eleven 12 oz. Kern drinks are equivalent to one gallon. I had 50 Kern drinks (about 4 1/2 gallons). During the TransPac I only drank 8 gallons of water plus about 4 gallons of Kern drinks. I never used water from the flexible tank. A reverse osmosis hand pump watermaker (Survivor 06) by Katadyn was available in case of an emergency. The watermaker was kept in the abandon ship bag.

—◆—

BATTERIES

The requirements call for a minimum of two batteries with a combined capacity of at least 120 amp hours. I installed two 73 amp hour Group 24 gel batteries by West Marine. They weighed 54 pounds each and were mounted in the compartment just inside the area of the V-berth. (Refer to photos entitled "Basic Electrical System Installation" and "Completed Electrical System" in Chapter 24.) The batteries were securely held in place by a teak support. By placing the batteries just inside the V-berth area, they are protected from possible water spray and easily accessible. Being low and centered, and only slightly forward of the keel, I felt their weight helped maintain the boat's balance. Clear flexible plastic sheeting covered the housing area of the batteries to further protect them from spray.

—◆—

CHARGING

As a Cal 20 does not have an inboard engine, the possibility of charging your batteries with the engine does not exist. Some small boat racers take generators but I had no interest in doing so because of the weight and noise. Having an effective solar panel gave me a suitable charging system. The Sunsei 4000 is rated at 65 watts and can restore 20 amp hours to your batteries each day, which more than supplied my demands so I was satisfied. This panel requires a solar panel regulator, which I incorporated into the electrical panel. The solar panel works best in direct sunlight but it does not need it to charge. It was overcast during most of the TransPac but the panel always charged effectively.

During the emergency of the broken rudder that occurred just past the halfway point, I lost my balance while carrying the spare rudder and fell against the solar panel. My elbow pressed on the top of the panel and the glass broke into thousands of pieces. The pieces stayed in place, however. I felt the panel would quickly become disabled but it did not, and even today, over a year later, it is still charging. After a couple of months, I sealed clear plastic sheeting over the panel to help keep water out. This sheeting was later replaced by clear Lexan, a more sun-resistant product. This panel has now become an experiment to see how long, in its broken state, it will provide an effective charge! (See photo entitled "Solar Panel on Stern Pulpit" in Chapter 24.)

—◆—

BILGE PUMP

The SSS requires an installed manual bilge pump operable from above deck with hatches and companionway closed. The pump shall be capable of pumping at least 10 gallons per minute. I found a convenient location for this within the cabin on the starboard side bulkhead between the cockpit area and cabin. I mounted an Amazon Universal by Jabsco that can pump at a rate of 22 gallons per minute and installed it in the interior cabin up high just under the cabin top. It can be operated from inside or outside the cabin. The water exits out a port located slightly below the cabin top deck.

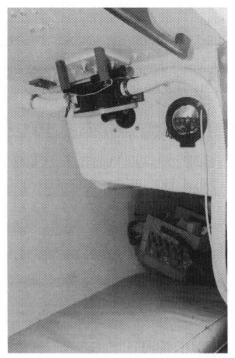

Bilge Pump

—◆—

EMERGENCY TILLER

I used the original Cal 20 tiller as a spare. Ideally this tiller should have the attachment devices mounted on it to allow for the use of your self-steering. Mine did not, but the self-steering attachments could have been added at sea without much trouble.

—◆—

EMERGENCY STEERING

That you can take a full-sized spare rudder as your backup is a great benefit of the transom-hung rudder of a Cal 20. With *Black Feathers*, her original 1961 solid mahogany rudder acted as her spare rudder. It was stored in the V-berth under a great many other things.

Another backup form of steering can be accomplished by using the Monitor Windvane in a particular manner. Some TransPac skippers view this particular windvane as their only backup. It is discussed in the next chapter under Self-steering.

Chapter 26
Addressing Additional Boat Prep Items

SELF-STEERING

To sail the TransPac effectively some efficient form of self-steering is needed although not required. Skippers talk about using the sails to steer the boat as in sheet-to-tiller steering, but I doubt many really try it. Most boats can hold a reasonable course to windward by merely holding firm the tiller's position, but this has limited effectiveness. Also, when going downwind the use of twin jibs (especially with no main) is rather self-correcting. But you wouldn't want to depend on these alone if you didn't have to. From my experience, there is simply nothing as gratifying in a race like the TransPac as solid, reliable, and dependable self-steering. To accomplish this, our choices are: An electrical autopilot, a mechanical windvane, or both.

Autopilots, set to a compass course, prove very dependable when they work. For small boats like a Cal 20, the autopilot will be located above deck, and therefore, subject to the weather. This can be a problem and many skippers who prefer autopilots with their small boats overcome this concern by having two or three extras. Because they require constant energy, they eat up battery power so the ability to have or generate enough energy becomes more of an issue. *Black Feathers* has an autopilot. I use it mostly when flying the spinnaker in light air and have found it to be ideal when used in this fashion.

Some form of windvane represents the other available self-steering option. These fascinating mechanical contraptions, once set to the desired course, hold the boat, not to that course, but to the boat's relationship to the wind. If the wind direction changes, the boat's course will also change. Although this seems like it would pose a concern, in reality on the open ocean it does not because the wind maintains a fairly constant direction.

Two things about windvanes make them particularly desirable: 1) They use no electrical energy, and 2) They tend to perform their steering tasks better as the winds increase in strength. There are downsides to windvanes, of course. For a Cal 20, the most obvious downside being that they can be bulky and heavy, and the transom-hung rudder may get in the way of the windvane.

When I did the TransPac in 1994 on an Ericson 32, I had a Monitor Windvane and it functioned beautifully. When considering a windvane for *Black Feathers*, I of course remembered the Monitor, but I wanted to look at other options because the Monitor is a bit bulky for a small boat. I considered a Navik because it was originally designed for small boats. As the Navik was no longer being manufactured, I became concerned about replacement parts so I opted against it.

About a year and a half before the 2008 TransPac, I became friends with a 1980 TransPac veteran. An experienced sailor, he had owned several sailboats, on each of which he had constructed and fit his own windvane. His style of windvane, common to the 1970s, had proven successful for him in several Pacific crossings including his 1980 TransPac. This sailor, John Hill, represents that "I can do anything" attitude that becomes so helpful when you are working on a complicated project. John proved particularly valuable in putting together the electrical plan for *Black Feathers*, and I was hopeful we could expand on that success in our quest for a windvane.

John and I applied many of his tried and true concepts of self-steering. All his boats had been significantly larger and heavier than a Cal 20. The liveliness of the Cal 20, and the way it could be knocked around by seas, made it difficult for his windvane concepts to work reliably. After a number of experimental trials, with great reluctance, we decided to look elsewhere.

Ultimately I chose to go with what I had experience with and confidence in, that being the Monitor Windvane. The basic Monitor structure is the same for all boats, whether 20' or 60'. The only difference is the way the basic unit is supported on the stern of the boat. The project of mounting the Monitor to the boat took one weekend, and I did it by myself. John joined me at the very end to help hold a wrench while we did the final tightening of all the fasteners. Although it wasn't of his design, the Monitor's sturdiness and solid engineering impressed John.

The Monitor Windvane can be adapted to function as an emergency rudder. I have not used it in this manner, but I can certainly see how it would work. When used as an emergency rudder, it cannot function as a self-steering device. With *Black Feathers*, it was comforting to realize that if her regular rudder as well as her spare rudder failed, I could fall back on the use of the Monitor to steer the boat.

Monitor Windvane Accompanied by John Hill

A final word about self-steering seems in order whether it be a windvane or an autopilot. For either to work well and continue to do so, the helmsman must do all that can be done to balance the boat with the sails. If the sails are unbalanced causing much stress on the tiller (e.g. weather helm), any self-steering will struggle to hold a desired course.

— ◆ —

DECK ORGANIZATION

It is a thing of beauty to see how some singlehanders manage their boats. Usually what makes it fascinating is that it seems effortless. Generally, at least in a significant part, this is due to good equipment and a well-organized deck layout. You need enough control lines to manage your sails and they need to be located where they will function well and can be easily reached. Below is the current deck layout for *Black Feathers*. I say "current" because if I can think of something more efficient, I won't hesitate to make changes.

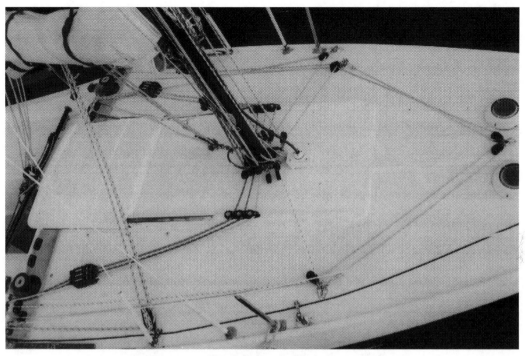

Deck Organization

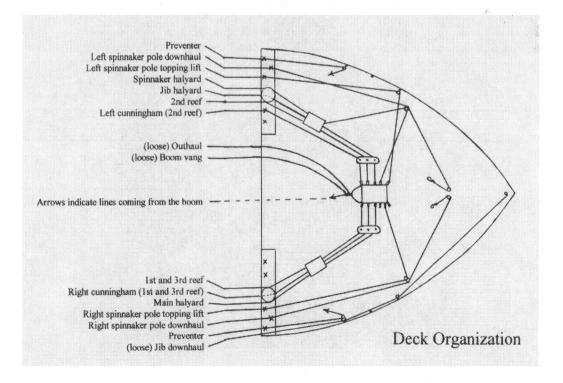

Preventer
Left spinnaker pole downhaul
Left spinnaker pole topping lift
Spinnaker halyard
Jib halyard
2nd reef
Left cunningham (2nd reef)

(loose) Outhaul
(loose) Boom vang

Arrows indicate lines coming from the boom

1st and 3rd reef
Right cunningham (1st and 3rd reef)
Main halyard
Right spinnaker pole topping lift
Right spinnaker pole downhaul
Preventer
(loose) Jib downhaul

Deck Organization

DOME

I made a new hatch cover to replace the original Cal 20 cover and incorporated a clear Plexiglas observation dome measuring 18" in diameter and 9" in height. The objectives for this dome were to allow for visual checks without having to open the hatch and also to allow additional light to enter the small cabin. By placing a lightweight plastic folding chair below the dome, I can comfortably sit on the chair and see out and about. Since the dome is deep (tall) enough, it allows sufficient headroom to even see over the weather side of the boat when the boat is heeling. At times, condensation builds up on the interior of the dome but this does not present a significant issue.

Dome

I was concerned as to how a badly damaged dome could be managed so as to prevent water from entering the cabin. When I cut the 18" hole out of the 3/4" plywood hatch (this hatch was a newly-fabricated one which was flat to replace the original Cal 20 hatch which was arched), I saved the circular piece. I then drilled holes to accommodate the placement of four large screws that would secure large fender washers, which in turn would support the circular insert. In the event the dome became badly broken, the emergency 18" insert could easily be secured in place from inside the cabin. This repair would take very little time due to the predrilled screw holes.

A soft overlay covers the dome when not under sail. Then, the entire hatch is covered with a Sumbrella canvas cover. The dome hatch can easily be replaced with the original hatch if ever desired.

—◆—

COCKPIT CONCERNS

The Cal 20 has a very large cockpit making it a fun and roomy daysailer with crew, but the cockpit poses a significant liability when considering the Cal 20 as an offshore racer. During the TransPac I had no problem with the cockpit taking on anything but spray, but I constantly worried about possible flooding. Prior to the TransPac I improved the cockpit drainage, but I did not address reducing the cockpit size. Sadly, sometimes when dealing with boat prep, there are things that fail to become a priority, even when they should.

Cal 20 cockpits have an engine well. While sailing, the engine is usually removed from the well and stored in the lazarette area. The well is then covered on the outer side of the hull with a fiberglass form-fitted portion and on the cockpit topside with a wood cover. These two portions are connected together with adjustable lines to keep them firmly in place. The boat's speed would be seriously compromised if the hull-fitted portion were lost, so on the TransPac I took a spare. The well will accommodate only a small engine. Many Cal 20 owners no longer use engines in their well because they prefer a transom-mounted engine. The transom-mounted option was no longer possible with *Black Feathers* as the Monitor resided on the transom, thus allowing no room for an engine mount.

Normally a 1" drain hole exists for cockpit water to drain into the well in order to exit the boat. On *Black Feathers* I enlarged this hole to almost 3" and raised the top well cover 2" by attaching supports along its forward and aft edges. This created openings along the engine well sides of 2" X 11". Although water would begin to drain immediately into the well from the single 3" hole, it would not begin to spill into the well from the 2" X 11" openings until the depth of water in the cockpit reached about 4".

If the cockpit became truly flooded and the engine well drained too slowly, the 22-gallon/minute bilge pump could aid in the drainage. I installed the intake for the pump on a sufficiently long flexible tube to allow it to reach the cockpit floor from its usual position, which is just inside the cabin, beneath the forward part of the cockpit.

After the TransPac, I addressed the dilemma of the cockpit's size. To help reduce the volume of the cockpit, I simply moved the life raft into the cockpit from where it had been stowed within the cabin. (See the Life Raft discussion later in this chapter). I placed the life raft in a waterproof bag and installed tie-downs to keep it in place. The forward part of the cockpit adjacent to the hatch afforded a more convenient storage location. Trial sails demonstrated that this location creates no inconvenience.

A more meaningful reduction of cockpit volume could be achieved when considering changes to the aft portion of the cockpit. This area involves the well, as well as the area located under the swing of the tiller. Because of the tiller's swing, a skipper or crewmember sitting in this portion of the cockpit has limited mobility. Once the engine is removed from the well, and the well covers secured, the portion of the cockpit extending all the way to the forward end of the tiller becomes unnecessary as a cockpit. If you should decide to place your engine on a stern mount, you no longer will need the engine well to house your engine, so you can use this aft portion of the cockpit to install a permanent locker. You would still have ample cockpit area to sail even with crew.

Since I DO use my engine well, I had to find a way to fill this rear cockpit area with something relatively easy to secure—AND easy to remove. The remedy could not be a permanent installation. The solution: To construct a solid contoured Styrofoam block to occupy that space. The top and forward surfaces were covered with a 3/8" teak veneered plywood and coated with a protective polyurethane. The Styrofoam block was constructed by cutting sections from a 2" thick sheet of 4' X 8' Styrofoam available at home improvement stores, such as Lowe's. The sections were glued together to form a solid block. Significant areas of relief were cut into the bottom surface to allow water to gain access to the various drainage areas in the well. The result: A structure that fit into the cockpit snugly held in place with straps, but could be readily removed. Such a structure would only be necessary when sailing offshore.

One Solution to Reduce Cockpit Volume

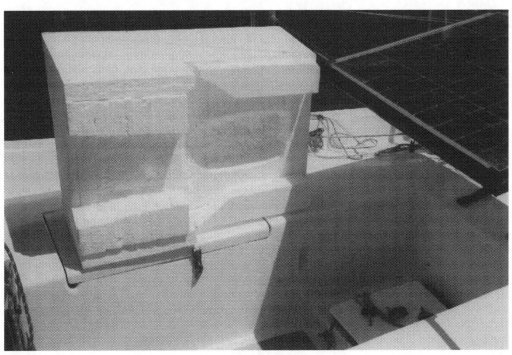

Bottom View of Styrofoam Structure

Drain Area of Finished Styrofoam Structure

Here is how it affected the cockpit:

	Regular Cal 20 Cockpit	Cockpit after reduction (life raft and foam structure in place)
Overall Volume	15.3 cubic ft.	5.6 cubic feet
Gallon Capacity	119 gallons	44 gallons
Sea Water Weight	979 lbs	358 lbs
Floatation Ability	0 lbs	248 lbs of floatation

Modifying the cockpit proved extremely beneficial. The above statistics show that the cockpit volume has been reduced by almost 2/3. It can no longer be considered "too large" and, if the cockpit were to flood, the Styrofoam would provide some floatation.

Relevant Facts:	Seawater weighs	64.0 lbs/cubic foot
	Seawater weighs	8.23 lbs/gallon
	Styrofoam provides	55.0 lbs of floatation/cubic foot

— ◆ —

SAILS

Black Feathers does not have an extensive sail inventory. The sails taken on the TransPac were:

- 6 1/2 oz Cal 20 class main with three reef points
- Two 6 1/2 oz Cal 20 class jibs (equivalent to #3 approx. 115%)
- 3/4 oz radial spinnaker
- 7.0 oz storm jib (85%)
- Extra (older) class main with two reef points

The sails, all constructed for offshore sailing, have reinforced corners and headboards with triple stitched seams. Ideally, I would like to have had a couple of larger jibs (e.g. 135%) for times of light wind, but then I would have had to face the huge challenge of finding someplace to store them.

—◆—

RIGGING

The standing rigging for the Cal 20 class is:

- Headstay   1/8" 1 X 19 stainless steel
- Upper shrouds   "
- Aft lower shrouds   "
- Forward lower shrouds   "
  (*Black Feathers* has no forward lowers)
- Backstay   3/32" 1 X 19 stainless steel
- Jumpers   "

Black Feathers has standard-sized rigging. Some suggest these dimensions be increased by one size for offshore use, but I have not done that. It is something to consider.

A traveler with the boom sheeting located slightly aft of mid-boom replaced the original mainsheet running rigging. The traveler car, a Harken Small Boat Windward Sheet car, is unique in that the car stays in place during tacking. Also, when the car is pulled to windward, the leeward control line automatically releases. These are both very convenient features when sailing singlehanded.

—◆—

ENGINE

When I bought *Black Feathers*, she had an old 2 h.p. engine that fit in the engine well. As stated previously, Cal 20s have an engine well at the aft-end of their cockpits. When not in use, a cover is placed over the cavity. In addition, a fiberglass cover fits in from beneath the hull to give the hull surface a smooth contour. If this lower cover is not in place, or if the boat is sailed leaving the engine within the well, water sloshes around, not only slowing the boat but also allowing water to splash into the cockpit.

The old 2 h.p. engine seemed too weak to be efficient against any significant tides at the Gate so I bought a new 8 h.p./4 stroke Honda engine that lived on an engine mount on the transom. The heavy (90 pounds, including the mount) 8 h.p. engine didn't seem to adversely affect the boat that much, and it did prove efficient in motoring the boat through the Golden Gate during an unfavorable tide.

Cal 20s that are set up to do one-design buoy racing would never have such a heavy engine or one that would have to remain on the transom. Instead they would have an engine like the 2 h.p. engine I replaced. During a race, this 2 h.p. engine would be taken from the transom mount, or removed from the engine well, and stowed in a secure place, which would provide a favorable weight balance for the boat.

Each year the SSS sponsors a race to Half Moon Bay. You exit the Gate and head south for about 25 miles. This race is fun for a couple of reasons. It allows you to sail down the coast staying rather close to shore so you can appreciate the beautiful coastline, and you find yourself enjoying a long spinnaker run. (In 2001, *Black Feathers* and I had the honor of winning First In Division in this race!) The return the following day often falls short in the fun department. The morning wind generally takes awhile to fill in, so much of the time you find yourself motoring. Once during such a return I realized two things about my engine being placed on the transom. If I encountered waves of much significance, the boat would tip fore and aft enough that the prop would come out of the water and cause the engine to race alarmingly. Also, a wave hitting the engine sideways would often cause the engine to rotate, necessitating the helmsman to sit far aft in order to keep the engine straight. After a few hours of this, I began thinking of alternative engine set-ups.

I used the 8 h.p. engine for a few more years, but while making plans for the windvane steering that would be used on the 2008 TransPac, it became clear that there would be no room for an engine mount on the transom once the windvane was in place. The solution, as with most things, turned out to be a compromise. I opted to go back to an engine in the well. This had the advantage of perfect placement performance-wise as waves did not hit the engine and the prop never rose out of the water. The disadvantage: The engine had to be small enough to physically fit into the well. I chose a 2 h.p./4 stroke air-cooled Honda, which has proven very effective in moving the boat 4 1/2 - 5 knots through calm water. It has its limits in going against a tide and needs to be removed from the well during sailing. When sailing, the engine lives in a storage bin just within, and slightly aft, of the opening to the cockpit lazarette. Although inconvenient to remove the engine from the well, place it in the lazarette and position the well covers, the inconvenience proves less than critical. When encountering a strong adverse tide, I must simply deal with it by sailing until the tides change or anchor in a safe place to wait out the tides. Potential tribulations, definitely, but then—that's part of sailing and working with nature's elements.

— ◆ —

EMERGENCY CONTINGENCIES

The following outlines how I prepared for a variety of emergency contingencies for the 2008 TransPac. Each skipper should address these contingencies given their particular boat and offshore situation.

1) **Rigging:** I carried a spare set of upper shrouds, aft lower shrouds and a headstay from the most recently replaced rigging.

2) **Mast Repair:** It is difficult to know what to do when considering the possible loss of your mast. Hopefully we will never have to know, but we still have to develop a plan. The plan can be to simply create a new (smaller) mast out of the broken parts available, knowing there will be plenty of extra lines or emergency rigging to work with, but with a small boat, we can aim for an even "higher" resolution. One advantage of a small boat is there is at least the possibility of a reasonably effective mast repair should the need arise. Larger boats have huge, heavy spars and to try to get much mast back up seems an improbable task. Small boats often have a tabernacle with smaller and lighter spars that make an effective mast repair much more plausible. So with these thoughts in mind, I tried to come up with an internal splint repair that MIGHT allow a broken mast to be repaired and restepped. My preparations to make a mast repair consisted of a series of plastic pipes that would telescope into each other, and could be tapped into place within the broken mast segments once the ends were cleaned up by removing any crushed portions. I fashioned a hardwood 1 1/2" dowel to fit snuggly within the

length of the pipe. The repair pipes and dowel were 4' long, which meant they would extend 2' into each side of the broken mast segments. Although this repair idea is untested, I feel it was reasonably conceived.

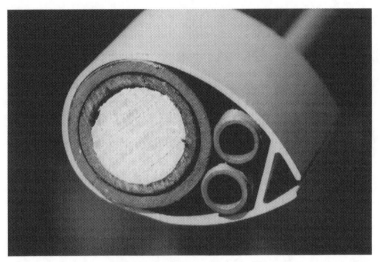

Close-up of Mast Repair Kit

Full View of Mast Repair Kit

3) **Gooseneck:** A spare gooseneck was among my emergency items. It would have been attached to the mast with rivets. I had plenty of rivets onboard.

4) **Halyards:** Three spare halyards were available to use in just about any capacity, their lengths sufficiently long enough to serve as any halyard. A block was secured

to the masthead to allow for a spare main halyard. A messenger line of 1/8" nylon ran through this block and down to the deck. If a spare main halyard was ever needed, the messenger line could be used to thread any of the spare halyards.

5) **Emergency Tools:** The toolkit on the boat has quite a complete generalized array of tools, given the space and weight limitations. For emergencies, I also included a rivet gun, cable cutters, a 2-pound sledgehammer and a hacksaw with many spare blades.

6) **Lifting Sling:** Many, if not most Cal 20s live on their trailers and are regularly lifted into the water using a lifting sling. *Black Feathers* resides in the water, but I made sure I had a lifting sling onboard in case I had to discontinue the TransPac and head for a safe haven where the only way to remove her from the water might have required the use of a sling. Also, if I needed to remove her from the water in Kauai, using a sling with a crane may have been my only option as there are no travel lifts available on the island.

7) **Emergency Navigation:** *Black Feathers* has two handheld GPS devices plus another handheld that is hardwired into the boat's power supply and integrated with the AIS. If these GPS devices failed, I had a sextant onboard, but no sight reduction tables. The idea being to use the sextant to find the latitude by using local noon sightings, then follow the latitude until I hit the islands. Following the TransPac, I read George Sigler's book, *Experiment In Survival*, detailing his survival experiment done before he organized the SSS. During this trans Pacific survival crossing, he used a nomogram that he called a "Solargram" to determine his latitude. One had to know the exact time of sunrise and sunset to determine the exact length of a given day. From the length of said day, his Solargram will give you the latitude. Knowing these sunrise and sunset times allow you to calculate the exact local noontime. Using this local noontime, you determine your longitude by the time difference between your local noontime and Greenwich Mean Time. I haven't tried this procedure yet, but it is worth investigation. All one needs is an accurate watch adjusted to GMT and Sigler's Solargram. Many other techniques exist for emergency navigation that may be useful to you. Always interesting to learn, it's best to be competent in at least one of them. During the 1994 TransPac crossing I relied on celestial sightings to "confirm" my GPS readings and received the Navigation Award.

8) **Life Raft:** The smaller the boat, the more critical is the weight of the life raft. Rental life rafts generally weigh about 66 pounds and are rather bulky. I chose a four-man Winslow Superlight Offshore Racing life raft, weighing 39 pounds and measuring

9" X 16" X 21" prior to inflation, which meets all offshore racing requirements. Vacuum-sealed, it has been placed in a valise-style exterior cover. A raft in a valise alone is generally not considered waterproof, but because mine has been vacuum-sealed, it IS waterproof. Winslow vacuum-sealed life rafts come with a three-year, rather than the typical annual, certification. For the TransPac, *Black Feathers'* life raft was stored just to the left as you entered the cabin. The abandon ship (ditch) bag was attached to the raft. The life raft was always in the way. I believe a better place for it would be out in the forward part of the cockpit just below the companionway hatch. Winslow said the vacuum-sealed valise covered raft would do fine in the cockpit, but I feel it would be safer if it were first placed in a waterproof soft bag. This would also provide chafe protection. Some strap tie-downs would need to be installed in the cockpit. The advantages of placing it within the cockpit:

- It would be more readily available for use
- It would reduce the volume of the rather large Cal 20 cockpit
- It would save valuable space within the cabin

9) **Abandon Ship Bag (Ditch Bag):** As you acquire all the required emergency gear, and then add a few optional items, you quickly realize just how bulky and heavy a ditch bag can become. Because of this, I had two ditch bags—one with truly critical items, the other with more optional items. If time did not allow me to get both, I would simply work with the critical bag. What is considered critical could be argued forever, so you need to make that judgment for yourself. Below is how I divided things up for the TransPac: (* = required by SSS)

A. Items often packed within the life raft
   1. Raft repair kit and emergency inflation pump *
   2. Small sea anchor *
   3. Bailer *
   4. Knife *
   5. Waterproof flashlight *

B. Items in the critical ditch bag
   1. Solas flares (red parachute and red handhelds) *
   2. VHF radio (waterproof)
   3. EPIRB (Emergency Position Indicating Radio Beacon)*
   4. GPS
   5. SAT phone in waterproof box

      6. Mirror signaling device

      7. Watermaker (Survivor 06)

      8. Water and some emergency rations *

      9. Fishing kit

    10. Extra knife

    11. Extra waterproof flashlight

    12. First-aid kit

    13. Collapsible water storage bottle

    14. Survival manual

    15. Log and pencils

C. Items in the optional ditch bag

      1. Extra flares (e.g. Solas orange smoke)*

      2. Extra water and food rations

Chapter 27
Everyday Essentials

Packing the Boat

One of the most challenging tasks that must be done is to organize and pack the boat. This is particularly challenging when packing a Cal 20! We did not wait until the last minute to begin this task. As equipment accumulated, we organized it in clear plastic boxes when possible, weighing it after labeling all sides. Gear not placed in clear plastic boxes with tops, found a home in an open-topped plastic case or durable gear bag. We weighed everything not permanently installed on the boat. Total weight equaled almost 900 lbs. To a boat that weighs slightly less than 2,000 lbs we were now adding 900 lbs!

For descriptive purposes we can divide the boat into three sections.

V-berth area	(total weight added to this area = 260 lbs)
Mid-cabin area	(total weight added to this area = 270 lbs)
Aft areas under cockpit	
and cockpit seats	(total weight added to this area = 338 lbs)

Some areas were more easily accessible than others, so we stored things depending on their weight and frequency of use. The extra sails resided on top of boxes in the V-berth. They consisted of a twin jib, storm jib, extra main and the spinnaker.

In the mid-cabin area we have the port and starboard berths. I used the starboard berth to sleep so any items stored there had to be moved in order for me to retire. I always kept a space clear where I could sit. Each berth had a lee cloth that prevented things from shifting. I chose the starboard berth as a sleeping area because it is usually on the weather side, making my weight helpful in balancing the boat.

A few of the items I brought proved to be unnecessary. The propane stove, a race required item, was never used. I only used half the water requirement. Now, when I go through the list, I see only about 35 - 40 lbs I would eliminate.

—◆—

FOOD

The race requires enough food for 30 days. We packed all the food and canned drinks into four bags that were exactly the same and weighed 30 lbs each. I vowed to eat everything in the bag before going to the next, and I generally stuck to that. Pudding cups were my only downfall. When I sail, I want my diet to be simple and easy to eat. I did not want to have an open flame in the boat, not only for safety but also because of the inconvenience. All cans had pop-tops, but we did our best to find plastic or pouch containers to eliminate bulk for storage and disposal purposes. There was lots of Dinty Moore Stew onboard. Everything I ate, I ate cold and out of its container. The only exception was the breakfast of instant oatmeal mixed with applesauce that I mixed in a small stainless steel bowl. A typical day's menu:

1) Breakfast
   - Two packages of Quaker Maple & Brown Sugar Instant Oatmeal mixed with one Dole applesauce snack cup
   - One coffee candy
   - One Kern drink
2) Lunch
   - One can of Campbell's chunky soup or one can of spaghetti & meatballs (all cans had pop-tops)
   - One Dole fruit cup
   - One Kern drink
   - One coffee candy
3) Dinner
   - One packaged meat entrée (e.g. Bumble Bee Chicken Breast)
   - One Dole fruit cup
   - One Hunt's Snack Pack pudding cup
   - One Kern drink

4) Typical Snacks
   - Saltine crackers
   - Hunt's Snack Pack pudding cup
   - Dole fruit cup
   - Coffee candy
5) Daily Vitamin Supplements
   - Two 225 mg Kelp
   - One Acidophilus (highest strength available in non-refrigerated form)
   - One Multi-vitamin
   - One 1500 mg Vitamin B12
   - One 1000 mg Vitamin C
   - One 400 mg Vitamin E
   - One 81 mg Aspirin
   - One 900 mg Calcium plus Vitamin D
   - One or two Stool Softeners

The prevention of leg cramps became my most important physical concern. I find it strenuous to be confined on and within a small boat. During weekends when I would stay on the boat to work, I was often plagued by leg cramps. This vitamin regime was derived by my wife to prevent the cramps and keep me healthy. She says the Calcium plus vitamin D will eliminate leg cramps. For me, it works!

—◆—

FUN

No matter how small the boat, you need to make room for some things that will provide entertainment. For me, the best thing is a musical instrument. I play a 30-button Anglo concertina. Sometimes referred to as a "squeeze box," an instrument you would commonly find in an Irish pub—and great fun to play. I was a bit reckless by taking it because it is a nice one, and I took the chance of incurring water damage to the outside as well as to the reeds on the inside. But, all went fine and it provided endless entertainment.

I also took some books as well as some audio CDs. A few of the CDs were musical, but most were educational. Being alone on the open ocean provides a great environment for educational topics that are of personal interest. As 2008 was an important election year, and as our country's economy was drastically changing, I found the TransPac to be a perfect place and time to catch up on the latest thoughts concerning these topics.

Photography, black and white, as well as color, is another of my interests that I hoped would blend well with the TransPac. They are so important to me that even with limited space I took two full camera bags of photo equipment. Even though prepared for the wetness problem, I hadn't counted on the persistent overcast conditions. With very few clear days, nature was unable to flaunt the beauty of the Pacific so I found it difficult to make use of much of what I brought. Next time I will consider bringing only one camera bag!

— ◆ —

CLOTHING

If you sail much in San Francisco Bay on a small boat, you know about getting wet and cold. It doesn't take long to work up an apparel selection to prevent these things. The key to success: Stay dry and wear enough of the right insulation to keep warm. There is one other key, however, that being you must don these items BEFORE they are needed. Too often we wait until we take that first wave in our face before we even zip up our foul weather gear. Once wet, if you are heading for your harbor slip there is no problem, but if you have 10 hours of ocean racing before you can return, you may be in for a miserable, bone-chilling day.

My typical summer attire on San Francisco Bay consists of several layers. Some are for dryness and some for warmth. The most inner layer, thin and breathable, must wick moisture away from the body. The second layer, usually fleece, provides insulation and needs to be thick enough to be effective. For the third layer, the lower portion consists of your foul weather pants and on the top, a thin, breathable waterproof shell. A wet suit hood with shoulder extensions goes on next. (See photo entitled "Robert and Jonathan" in Chapter 20.) The upper foul weather jacket goes on last. (See photo entitled "Ready to Sail" in Chapter 20.) With this combination, I can take continual water splashes in the face without having water penetrate the inner layers. The water goes between the wet suit hood and the foul weather jacket. As the water continues downward, it travels between the foul weather jacket and the waterproof lightweight jacket under the wet suit hood and then exits the clothing at the tail of the two jackets. This works very well. You must make sure the second layer is thick enough to keep you warm, however.

For boots I use Sperry Top-Sider's Fathom boots, purchased from West Marine. These waterproof leather boots have all kinds of features to keep you comfortable. I wear them with thick, wicking, breathable, high top socks usually used in snow camping available online from Cabela's. This may sound like overkill to some, but for me it works. I hate being cold!

On the TransPac, it takes about a week of sailing before things warm up. From then on, clothing lightens as you near Hawaii. I always wear some form of shoe on the boat to protect my feet. When days become warm, tabis make great footwear. These are also known as reef walkers. They have a dense felt-like sole and a sock-like top. The heel and toe are rubberized and provide protection. Tabis are cool, slip resistant, and don't develop odor if washed every couple of days. They are easy to find in Hawaii where they are intended to be used as reef walkers. Finding them elsewhere may require a bit of searching, but I feel they are worth the effort. The Internet?

—◆—

Toilet Talk

Originally Cal 20s came with a head installed in the V-berth area. Over the years, most Cal 20 owners removed these for a wide variety of reasons. The head had been removed from *Black Feathers* and replaced with a Port-a-potty. I felt the Port-a-potty took up too much space so I rather quickly replaced it with a square bucket.

The SSS requires all racers to have a 2-gallon bucket with a lanyard attached. Upon this bucket, I would temporarily place the lightweight toilet seat from the Port-a-potty and, "voila," I had a comfortable, rather stable and very functional toilet. It worked fantastic, but I would advise you to never try washing it out overboard without attaching the lanyard to something secure (like a winch). While going only 5 knots, one miscalculation and the water pressure can pull the bucket right out of your hand, or worse yet, your arm out of its socket. I also took a spare bucket with lanyard. The buckets I selected were square in shape making them more efficient if ever needed for bailing out the boat.

—◆—

Keeping Watch

My greatest concern in the TransPac: Getting run over by another vessel, so I wanted to develop an effective as possible, workable plan. For the boat's part, this involved using a masthead strobe at night, keeping the CARD and AIS on with their alarms activated at all times; and at night, once visual contact had been made with another vessel, to turn on the other navigation lights.

Singlehanders have devised many plans over the years to try to keep an effective watch. When I am within 250 miles or so of the coast (mainland or Hawaii) I try to look around the horizon every 15 minutes. It takes about that long for a ship to come over the horizon and cross your path. Therefore, when trying to sleep, I use a small electronic timer set for 15 minutes. When the alarm goes off, I get up, carefully look around, and then reset the timer for another 15 minutes, and go back to sleep. It sounds horrific, but it's really not that bad. If I can, I try to do most of my sleeping during the day, but that doesn't seem to work well for me. As I get further offshore, I lengthen my sleep intervals, as I am less likely to encounter traffic.

During the 1994 TransPac, I chose to sleep as much and as long as I could. Fate was to determine the outcome! It worked, but I now feel that plan was unnecessarily reckless. During the 40 days I was at sea in 1994 (16 days to Hawaii and 24 days to return), I saw only three vessels. In the 2008 TransPac I must have seen at least 30! Were there fewer vessels in 1994, or did I sleep while we passed? Probably both.

The important thing is to come up with a reasonable plan. You must find that balance between being an alert observer and a rested skipper who can function effectively with a clear (or nearly clear) mind.

Chapter 28
Sail Handling

REEFING

Black Feathers has three reef points in the main. Generally, when sailing alone and in a 15-knot wind, I put in the first reef. It is important to be able to put in your reefs when on either port or starboard tack as well as when going upwind or downwind. When sailing, I always have a cunningham hook in the next reef point on the luff so I can quickly put in another reef if it becomes necessary.

To most easily visualize what I am about to discuss, you may want to refer to the diagram: Deck Organization in Chapter 26.

There are two reefing lines involved in placing a reef in *Black Feathers'* main. One line controls the luff and the other controls the leech. Some boats have one line to control both. To put in a reef, I ease out the main halyard as I pull down on the cunningham. When fully lowered, the cunningham is locked in place. Then I pull in the respective reef number (e.g. 1st reef) to lower the leech portion of the mainsail. With this completed, I raise the main halyard to tension the luff. Lastly, I make sure the next cunningham hook is in place so I am ready to put in another reef. I do not tie up the reefed portion of the sail because it doesn't seem to be necessary, however, if the reefed portion were flapping around I would not hesitate to do so. If I tied it up, I would be afraid I might forget to untie it when letting the reef out, possibly causing the sail to rip.

The deck organization is set up so both the 1st reef line, plus the cunningham line with its hook in the 1st reef point, are on the starboard side. And likewise, the 2nd reef line, plus the 2nd cunningham line with its hook in the 2nd reef point, are on the port side. With this set-up I can easily go from none, to 1st reef, then to 2nd reef and back—all lines are ready to go.

If I feel a 3rd reef might be necessary, I will have to reroute the 1st reef line into the 3rd reef point on the leech. I will also need to move the 1st reef luff hook up to the 3rd reef luff hole. This rerouting would not be that difficult because the main would already have a 2nd reef in place so the distance to the 3rd reef hole could be reached fairly easily. I have never put in a 3rd reef on *Black Feathers* while sailing, but I use the 1st and 2nd reefs quite often.

— ◆ —

Using Twin Jibs

When sailing fairly dead downwind, you have the option of sailing wing-on-wing with your main out to leeward and your jib poled out to windward, sailing with your main and spinnaker (or just your spinnaker), or using twin jibs each poled out with or without your main. There could be other options as well, but these are the sail configurations used the most.

Sailing with twin jibs, especially without using the main, provides for a very stable ride. The twins themselves act to self-steer the boat making it very easy on your windvane or autopilot. You give up a little speed for not using the spinnaker, but your boat will be better balanced and your course may be straighter. With twins flying, squalls can pass over without causing broaches that, although exciting, may break gear or destroy sails. At night and during times of frequent squalls or strong winds, I am not inclined to use the spinnaker. If sailing on a broad reach, I will go wing-on-wing. As the wind moves more aft, the option of using twin jibs becomes available.

Black Feathers uses two class-size jibs that hank onto a single headstay. The jib halyard attaches to both jibs and raises them together. Their hanks are staggered and do not interfere with each other. Single jib sheets are attached to each jib, and then poled out. A topping lift and downhaul (foreguy) is attached to each spinnaker/whisker pole. The mast has a track on it that holds two adjustable rings. It is recommended that the rings be positioned 8" - 12" apart to spread out the compressive forces on the mast created by the twins. Twins can be depowered by raising the topping lifts or by allowing the poles to move more forward. The two spinnaker/whisker poles on *Black Feathers* are identical Forespar's Twist-Lock Whisker Poles, #406300 HD 6-12 DL designed for boats up to 25' and adjusted to a distance of 7' 4" between the center of the jaws. A large bolt, placed through the pole, holds the adjustment. An upper and lower bridle was made for the topping lift and foreguy. The deck organization has one topping lift and one foreguy on the port side of the boat and one of each on the starboard side.

— ◆ —

Spinnaker Handling

Setting the spinnaker singlehanded is always exhilarating for me, and I am constantly amazed when it goes up without a hitch! There are plenty of things that can go wrong and oft-times do, however, any problems on a small boat can usually be dealt with rather easily. My general procedure in putting up the spinnaker begins with having the autopilot steer if in light wind, or the windvane steer if there is ample wind. Sometimes I take the jib down before I set up the spinnaker, but not always. It seems easier to run the various lines if the jib is up because the deck is less cluttered. The spinnaker turtle snaps onto rings on the leeward side of the bow pulpit. The spinnaker pole is one of the poles used with the twins. For me, the technique for setting up the spinnaker and its hoist mimics what is done with a full crew, except you do it yourself while the autopilot or windvane steers. It takes longer than you feel it should and for that reason I often tend to hurry and may get some lines connected wrong. Since I only use a spinnaker when I can keep it up for a fair amount of time, I have not developed speed in the set-up. I respect the many singlehanders who are most efficient with their spinnaker handling.

I am too conservative to be considered an aggressive competitor, but that is by choice. Because of this nature, I do two things when flying a spinnaker which help with its control that others may not like or see as necessary.

1) I use an escape line which allows me to "blow (release) the guy" when things start getting ugly. The escape line, a red colored 1/4" line, goes from the cockpit to the shackle at the end of the spinnaker guy. A clip on one end affixes to the end of a wire fishing leader that has been attached through the quick release shackle on the spinnaker guy line. When the escape line is pulled, the fishing leader squeezes the quick release portion of the shackle on the guy and the shackle opens to release the spinnaker. The spinnaker will flag to leeward where it can then be pulled into the cockpit after releasing the spinnaker halyard. The spinnaker on a Cal 20 is about 290 square feet, which converts to about six armfuls, so the drop is pretty quick. For me, just knowing I have a reliable method to instantly depower the spinnaker gives me increased confidence to use it. The 60 lb wire leader, commonly used on a sturgeon rig, can be found at fishing stores. The quick release shackle is by Wichard (#2673).

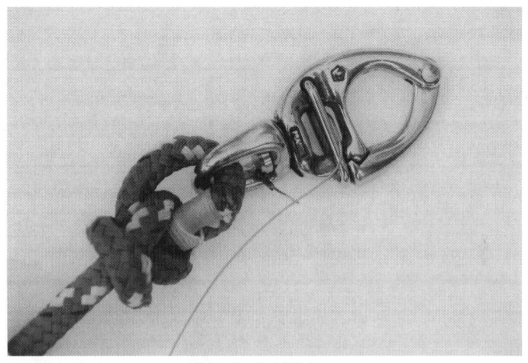

Spinnaker Quick Release

2) The spinnaker sheet and guy do not go all the way to the back of the boat. Instead, I lead them to blocks slightly aft of the midpoint of the boat. This means the spinnaker is always somewhat choked and, therefore, easier to control. To truly choke a spinnaker you would:

- Move the spinnaker sheet lead forward
- Have the pole positioned more forward
- Have the pole positioned more down
- Over-trim the spinnaker sheet

In my set-up of the spinnaker, I have done the first of these. Like I have said, this conservative style isn't for everyone, but I am comfortable with it.

—◆—

PREVENTERS

Preventers are lines that extend from the boom to a point forward of the boom, and then back to the cockpit, where you maintain control. There is a preventer line on both the port and starboard side. Preventers, used when sailing downwind, serve to keep the boom from doing an accidental gybe. Their use can be a bit controversial.

The advantage of using preventers: When all goes well they can prevent damage to the boat or someone's body by keeping the boom from slamming across the cockpit during that accidental gybe. The disadvantage: They can sometimes cause the boom to break or possibly even cause a dismasting due to too much stress being placed on the boom or mast. When activated, the point where the preventer attaches to the boom is under great stress. Locating the preventers about mid-point on the boom can be particularly stressful. If the preventers attach to the boom at the end near the sail's clew, it is less stressful but the preventer lines will be quite long. A dismasting can occur when the boom dips into the water because of a roundup or broach. The stress created by the water can either break the boom or cause a compression break of the mast where the boom attaches to the mast.

My 1994 TransPac boat, *Now or Never,* had preventers, and they attached to the boom about mid-point. I used them religiously going downwind with and without a spinnaker. I also used them to accomplish an intentional gybe. I would set the preventer and turn the boat to the point the mainsail backwinded. The preventer kept the mainsail from slamming across the cockpit. Then I would slowly release the preventer to allow the main to cross the cockpit in a controlled manner.

During the buildup to the '94 TransPac, the concerns other skippers had about preventers caused me to consider their use with more caution. As an alternative way to use them, I and several other skippers, placed about three wrappings of 1/8" nylon parachute line on the fitting of the preventer to the boom so that if too much force were created, the 1/8" nylon wrapping would break before the boom or mast. Hopefully this time delay would give the skipper a chance to duck before the gybe occurred. When I left on the 1994 TransPac, the preventers were set up this way.

The 1994 TransPac was a particularly windy race that ultimately allowed for some outstanding sailing performances, particularly by Peter Hogg, Stan Honey and Reed Overshiner. With increased wind most skippers find things tend to break and things were definitely breaking in '94. Before I began using the nylon line breakaways on the preventers, I had never had any breakage problems, but after the breakaways broke three times causing damage to some blocks on the traveler, I abandoned the use of the breakaways but still used the preventers. I had no further problems and this gave me a favorable opinion of preventers in spite of the cautions I had heard.

When *Black Feathers* came my way, I decided I would equip her with preventers. I attached them to the boom slightly forward of the mid-boom area. For three years I used them in the same manner I did with *Now or Never* and had no problems, but then came the day I learned my lesson.

It was during an SSS Farallones Race. The day was windy with lumpy seas. Fairly early in the race after I had gone out the Gate, but only about a fourth of the way to the Farallones, it became apparent the race was developing into a "no-fun" day. The 8 h.p. outboard on the transom bounced around on the mount because it had not been secured well with bungees and I was already double reefed. Thoughts of the wet and cold ride before me were not pleasant, so I decided to turn around, return to the berth and pursue other interests. For some reason, I opted to gybe rather than tack around. This gybe would be similar to the gybe I would have made as I rounded the Farallones to head for home. I guess I felt I might as well do this one gybe even though I was dropping out of the race. So that's what I did, and as I neared the point where the boom would begin to swing to the other side of the boat, I put on the preventer to allow for a very controlled release of the boom. As the wind filled to backwind the main, the boom folded over like a piece of paper at the point where the preventers attached to the boom. It was so anticlimactic that I felt a somewhat bizarre sense of disappointment. At least if I broke a boom, it should go out in a crash or something noteworthy! Fortunately the breaking of the boom did not result in a tearing of the mainsail. As I returned to San Francisco and passed under the Gate, I realized how lucky I was that this incident hadn't occurred out on the far side of the Farallones.

The lessons learned with this episode are important and must be kept in perspective. Lesson one: To gybe using your preventers is a BAD IDEA and UNNECESSARY because the stress on your rig during a properly executed intentional gybe is not that great. Lesson two: Preventers that attach to the mid-section of a boom will be particularly stressful to the boom and should be avoided, or at least treated with abundant respect. When I had *Black Feathers'* new boom constructed, I again placed the preventers on the boom—AND in the same position, but I vowed never again to use them in that risky fashion. The preventers, and this vow, have done me well.

I did not want the preventers extending all the way out to the end of the boom because their lines would be awkwardly long and interfere with the lifelines and stern pulpit. I already had extensive lines within the cockpit and I didn't want to amplify the situation. Other skippers would disagree with me, and I would not argue the point too aggressively. It's a matter of preference.

There are two other times when preventers are very convenient, but these don't involve sailing. Preventers can hold the boom out of the way to provide for a boom-free cockpit, and during times of no wind when the boat just sits there rocking back and forth, the preventers can be used to stabilize the boom to minimize the slapping of the sails.

SAILING WITH THE MONITOR WINDVANE

It is fascinating to watch this mechanical marvel do its thing! Each element of the contraption has its own task and the various elements all work together to take you where you want to go, but you MUST assist. You do this by:

1) Reducing friction on all lines as much as you can
2) Balancing your sails so the boat has as neutral a helm as possible

Friction can be reduced by making sure the lines are not rubbing against anything, by having the lines lead fairly (straight) through blocks and making sure there is some, but not too much, tension on the control lines.

Trimming your sails to balance the boat is the key to effective windvane steering. There are some tricks to be aware of when sailing and the manual that comes with your windvane will hopefully cover these. The manual for the Monitor is well worth devouring for it provides a wealth of useful information. The windvane may require subtle adjustments when sailing under varied conditions. Light air conditions require the use of the large air vane in order to detect the more subtle wind angle changes. Light air sailing may not provide enough wind to activate the air vane if the pendulum lines are too tight.

There are tricks to employ to achieve the most effective steering with the windvane for each of the points of sailing. Two general concepts to remember with using a windvane: Avoid carrying too much sail and sheet the sails a little looser than you might otherwise. If your windvane does not have a very helpful manual, you may find the manual for the Monitor quite beneficial even though you have a different style of windvane. The general concepts are similar. You can order a Monitor manual from the manufacturer, Scanmar International. (See References and Resources)

Chapter 29

Emergencies: When, not if, they happen—

It is fair to say that some degree of emergency will occur with every TransPac skipper. Often a problem ignored will evolve into a full-blown emergency. The general philosophy is simple: Keep all your senses alert to anything that seems different. A daily visual inspection of as many parts of the boat as you can get to will be rewarded with finding early, easily resolved problems. All sounds that seem different should be investigated until you can pinpoint their cause. When *Black Feathers* broke her fiberglass rudder, my clue to a problem was not a change in course, but instead the scratchy sound of torn fiberglass rubbing on the hull.

In our TransPac preparation, we try to plan for those emergencies that have most commonly occurred in the past with our boats, or have been known to occur with others. These were previously discussed in Chapter 26 under Emergency Contingencies. Hopefully the tools and spare parts that have been selected will be versatile enough to allow you to make a reasonable repair under a wide variety of circumstances.

During the TransPac when the rudder broke, I found I was trying too hard to complete my repair and return to racing. I DID take time to think out my plan, but I still found myself rushing unnecessarily. My haste caused me to lose my balance while positioning the rudder, and I leaned on the solar panel. The sound of glass cracking into thousands of small pieces was horrifying. I had gone from a broken rudder to now a broken rudder and a damaged solar panel. This is not how one wants to manage emergencies.

Continuing with the concept that during an emergency we must remain cautious to keep things from becoming worse—when I took the spare rudder aft I attempted to seat its pintles into the gudgeons located on the transom. This turned out to be difficult because the pintles were the same length and both the upper and lower pintles had to enter the gudgeons at the exact same time. As the sea created a great deal of movement, the rudder was nearly pulled from my hands. I had not taken the time to tie a safety line on the rudder, therefore, it could have easily been lost overboard thereby creating a REAL emergency. I realized the recklessness of my haste and stopped to secure a safety line to the replacement rudder. As a side note, because the pintles had to enter simultaneously, it took me about 30 minutes struggling with the tossing rudder before the pintles finally seated. Later that evening I realized I could have simply sawed off 3/8" of the upper pintle allowing the pintles to align easier, thus avoiding frustration and exhaustion. I did so after the TransPac. (For further information on the rudder incident, see Chapter 8.)

Lastly I should mention that during the stress of what we perceive as an emergency, we sometimes fail to treat our bodies with respect. Injuries can easily occur and be overlooked until all has calmed down. These injuries may create critical situations given time.

I learned a good lesson with the broken rudder incident. The lesson is not that the lower pintle should be slightly longer than the upper pintle so that the lower can be engaged first and then the upper. This fact is true, but I knew that before the TransPac. The lesson is that if you know something is incorrect, fix it in a timely manner. Do not assume the issue will never come up in an emergency situation, or possibly create its own emergency.

— ◆ —

HEAVY WEATHER TACTICS

Any skipper sailing offshore needs to have a plan of how they will deal with heavy weather. Since weather affects smaller boats sooner than larger ones, smaller boat skippers should definitely have a plan. Many books have been written about this topic and it is time well spent when reviewing them. (See References and Resources for information regarding two of my favorites: *Storm Tactics Handbook* and *The Drag Device Database*.)

Although I did not have to deal with any alarming heavy weather in the 2008 TransPac, thoughts about it were never far from my mind. At one point the weather had picked up to the degree that I felt it best to alter course so as to lessen the effects of the wind by sailing with it. At this time I had already reduced sail by putting two reefs in the main and considered a third. This "active" tactic kept me moving in somewhat the direction I wanted, and proved much more comfortable and easy on the gear than to sail against it. Since my self-steering functioned well and accomplished all the work, this plan was sustainable. At some point active tactics may no longer be sustainable or effective and you may need to resort to a "passive" tactic. These include hoving-to, laying ahull and employing the use of a sea anchor. In truly bad weather my best option would be to try to ride it out with a sea anchor. I had a 9' parachute-style sea anchor and two sets of ground tackle, with 150' of 3/8" three-stranded nylon rode and 15' of 3/16" P.C. chain each. Had I used the sea anchor, I would have assembled the system as follows:

Sea anchor—150' rode—15' chain—15' chain—150' rode—Boat

Whenever using any anchoring system (at sea or near shore) chafe becomes a real concern so I had plenty of chafe protection, mostly in the form of old fire hose lengths.

As with all the safety equipment you take along on a race or cruise, you really don't think you will need it. It is, however, comforting to know you have it, are able to readily locate it on the boat and have the knowledge to use it.

Chapter 30

Elapsed Time, Corrected Time and Boat Handicap Ratings

The actual time it takes a boat to sail the race is the elapsed time, a necessary indicator for determining First To Finish and any record-setting performance, but it does little to truly compare the various skipper performances. In order to accomplish that comparison, there needs to be some way to alter or "correct" the elapsed time in order to negate some of the inherent advantages of the boat itself.

In a boat race, the result comes from the blending of two variables: 1) How well the boat performed, and 2) How well the skipper performed. A handicap tries to equalize the variables of the boats. IF that can be done effectively, then the race becomes a test of the competing skippers' abilities.

The subject of "corrected time" very quickly gets to be a sticky issue in any discussion. There can be endless arguments about the fairness, or lack of, in determining a boat's handicap. No one seems satisfied with any handicapping process. Although certainly not an exact science, experts in the sailing community do their best to assign boats an appropriate handicap so we, as participants, can compare "apples" with "oranges" in a given race.

Most boats are given a Performance Handicap Racing Fleet (PHRF) rating, which considers a boat's ability to sail on all points of sailing. The handicap rating used for the TransPac, the Pacific Cup Rating (PCR), modifies the PHRF rating to compensate for a race that has a primary downwind component.

I believe the attempt to handicap boats adds a meaningful element of interest to the races even though it has innate and unavoidable inaccuracies. I have heard it said that the larger boats resent the high handicaps of the small boats. In reality, all boats, except the very largest and fastest benefit by the handicap system, which provides for some level of fairness in the competition. Your perspective all depends on where you land in the food chain.

Perhaps the time has come to point out that if there were no handicaps, there could be no meaningful races for unlike boats—unlike in size, technology, class, etc. Otherwise, every race would come down to only one factor—the fastest boat.

As a small boat skipper, I do recognize, however, that a small boat may have a built-in advantage with its rating. The handicap rating is based on the boat being sailed by her skipper to the boat's full potential. Some people would argue it is easier for a lone skipper to sail a smaller boat to its potential than a larger one. That seems reasonable to me. I can see how a Cal 20 could be more easily sailed to its potential by one person than a large Cal 40. And likewise, one person may be able to sail a Cal 40 to its potential more easily than an Open 60. (See Chapter 22 for a discussion of the advantages and disadvantages of a small boat.)

There may never be a perfect solution when trying to compare the performances of different types of boats. We should remember though that most TransPac racers do this race to measure themselves; therefore, their handicap is far from their primary concern.

Chapter 31

Planning the Race and Return

THE RACE

TransPac races, both singlehanded and fully crewed, have been sailing regularly from San Francisco to Hawaii for some 30 years. With each race, we increase our knowledge of how to best sail the course. My intent here is to cover some basic principles with the hope you will seek out more detailed information.

The Pacific High pressure area forms in the Northeastern Pacific and in the summer hovers generally some 800 miles off the coast of Northern California. It moves around, as it has no permanent home. The center of the High is dead calm. Leaving the center, the winds circle the High in a clockwise manner. The basic strategy of the race entails sailing a course that may not be the shortest route, but one that provides the best wind for your boat without requiring you to travel too many extra miles. Easier said than done! Without getting too picky about things, let's agree that a straight line drawn from San Francisco to Hanalei Bay is about the shortest and most direct route, and we will call this route our rhumb line course. (See diagram entitled "Rhumb Line and Projected Course" in Chapter 6.)

The Pacific High will generally be positioned above the rhumb line, but may move down into or below it. If you check out the routes of boats over the years, you will see that some sailed the rhumb line and did well, but most sailed a more southerly course during the first third of the race. The fastest large boats may go significantly south but you don't want to do that in a small, slower boat. My plan (projected course) was to sail a bit south of the rhumb line, but not much.

The coastal winds out of San Francisco are generally from the northwest, so you will usually be heading into these for the first few days, which often proves to be rough and cold. It is tempting to fall off the wind by sailing more southerly but you want to avoid doing this too much. If it didn't become too rough and uncomfortable, I would try to sail as much of a rhumb line course as possible the first couple of days. You should check the weather charts showing the High and the associated isobars just before you start such a race so you will know what you are heading into. Most larger boats will be able to get these weather fax charts while sailing, but small, potentially wet boats may not have the necessary electronics onboard.

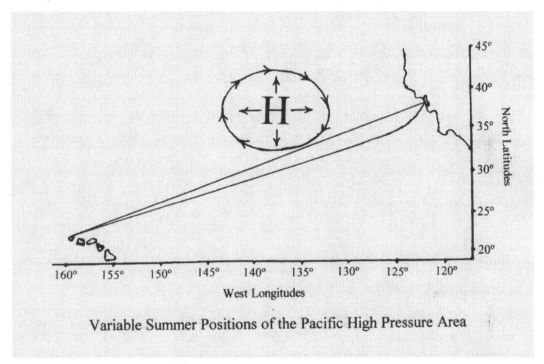

Variable Summer Positions of the Pacific High Pressure Area

I think it fair to say that most small boats (unless they are ultralights) will do best if they try to stay close to, or a bit south of, the rhumb line.

The race has been divided into three broad sections:

1) The Windy Reach off the coast
2) The Ridge or Light Run area, sometimes referred to as Slotcars, which marks the transition between the coastal Northwesterlies and the Northeast Trades
3) The Northeast Trades, which involves the last half of the race (See diagram entitled "Sections of the Race" in Chapter 7.)

The Ridge area presents the most confusing part of the race because you are not really sure if you are there yet. During this part of the race the wind direction and strength change. You hear a great deal of discussion about where you should cross The Ridge as this crossing dictates how you will be able to sail the last half of the race. I often felt that much of the more sophisticated race strategies applied to large, fast boats equipped with the necessary weather information. These boats have enough speed to respond to weather changes. Such information may not be very applicable to the slower small boats, but you will no doubt benefit by learning all you can about TransPac race strategies. Check the Singlehanded Sailing Society and the Pacific Cup websites for more information.

—◆—

THE RETURN

The TransPac is, of course, all about doing the race. But what about the return? Serious thought has to be given as to how you will get your boat back home. There are several options. Some racers sell their boats in Hawaii. Although this is not common, it also is not all that unusual. In fact, after the 2008 TransPac, three boats changed owners in Hawaii. Most skippers sail their boats home by themselves or, more commonly, with a friend or two. For some of the larger boats, a crew may be hired to deliver the boat home. Other options could be to have the TransPac serve as the first leg of a more extensive cruise, or to plan on leaving the boat in Hawaii for a period of time in order to sail the islands at a later date before sailing the return.

Although becoming quite expensive, many of the smaller boats are shipped home. At this time you still cannot ship your boat from Kauai because of a lack of facilities to haul it out, but with time that may change. At the present time, if you choose to ship your boat back, you will first need to sail it to Honolulu, not an easy feat, and prepare it for shipping.

In 1994, I sailed my Ericson 32 home by myself—a trip that took 24 days and was quite enjoyable. The return sail, like the race itself, is controlled by the Pacific High. For the race, we generally sail south of the High and use its clockwise wind rotation to blow us to Hawaii. For the return, we sail due north from Kauai for several hundred miles in order to get above the High. Then we can turn right and have the High's clockwise rotation blow us back to California. It works very well on paper, but is often not so clear-cut in practice. If you don't get north of the High, you will find yourself sailing into it. Since a High is an area of calm, you run out of wind and must wait for the High to move, or start motoring. Many skippers enjoy the two to four days they end up motoring for it is quite peaceful (except for the noise of the engine.) When considering boats with little or no motoring capabilities, things get a little more critical. You need to sail further north to avoid the High, and to do this you would benefit greatly by having more accurate weather information available (e.g. receiving weather fax). On my return in '94, I sailed north to latitude 41 (level with the border of California and Oregon) and still hit the High. I motored on and off for almost four days. I must admit that the calmness of the sea was fascinating. For a small boat, the skipper should expect to spend 30 days or so on the return.

Black Feathers was shipped home after the 2008 TransPac. I sailed her to Oahu where she was loaded aboard a truck trailer designed for transporting boats and then shipped to the mainland. Often the skipper will need to supply a cradle or boat trailer for a boat that is being shipped. What a relief not to have to do that. The company I used, Load-A-Boat, provides their own trailers which are adaptable to the various-sized boats. Once on the mainland, *Black Feathers* was trucked to San Francisco. The sail to Honolulu, all upwind in the Trades, was rough and wet. It took 34 hours to cover the 120 miles—not a lot of fun, but still an adventure. Be sure to get a chart showing Oahu in detail. Such a chart is not one of the four required for the TransPac.

Final Thoughts

The Singlehanded TransPac Race has been the highlight of many lives. It can be a wonderfully challenging and adventuresome event for all participants as well as their families. It makes winners out of all who participate because it is the doing of it that is of greatest importance. And if you win—all the better!

The purpose of sharing my boat preparation thoughts and experience with you is to give some guidance and encouragement so that all skippers who may strive to do the TransPac, no matter what the size of their boats, will take those first steps to get their journey underway. Once started, the excitement of the journey will be self-sustaining. Getting to the starting line is the greatest challenge—the rest is pure fun!

—◆—

Comments are always appreciated, as well as accounts of any adventures you might wish to share. Please send them to Robert and Jeanne Crawford, P.O. Box 675, Mi Wuk Village, CA 95346.

The majority of our readers have come to the end of the reading of this book, but some will wonder about *Cherish*, the halfway gift Jeanne presented to Robert. So we offer it here for those of you who wish to continue the journey—this part being a blend of fantasy and reality.

Halfway Gift *Cherish*

Written just for you by Jeanne

I. THE IRON MONSTER

She sat on her very own cool, flat rock at the edge of the sand watching the waves break and then slowly glide up onto the beach of her little cove. The water raging and then mellowing into a gentle kiss against the shore was tranquil indeed. Her hand rested on the rock and the water tickled her long, slender fingers as the water danced over the sand before flowing back to the sea to rage again. Water diamonds glistened on the surface of a nearby pool. A soft spring breeze drifted through the opening to her secret inlet, ever so gently touching her long, flowing hair. Perfection described her day.

Suddenly a horrible clanging sound interrupted her peaceful bliss. It startled her and she dove off her perch and quickly swam out of the cove, tucking herself behind a large somewhat distant boulder so she could see what was coming her way. It was a monster—a tall, metal monster with the sun glistening off its surface. The size of a man, but it lumbered like a bear, squeaking and screeching as it moved across the sand toward the sea.

A man accompanied the creature. Dressed all in white, the man carried a large, handled basket and wore a hat that held no particular form or style, but did serve the purpose of protecting his head and face from the sun. Although small of stature, the man did not appear frightened by the enormous metal being.

"Sir, you must be tired after such a long battle."

The metal hulk replied to his manservant, "Yes, Tatum, I am. I need some rest and relaxation."

She was intrigued. The metal entity could speak. His voice was weary, but masculine and gentle.

Tatum and his companion walked directly into her cove! She always thought the cove to be known only to her, but obviously both of these intruders were familiar with her special treasured place.

Tatum set the basket beside her flat rock, removed his hat and placed it on a little pedestal rock nearby.

"Sir, let me assist you," he said as he turned and began to dismantle the creature.

First, off came the head, then Tatum unhinged the chest portion and then the metal leggings.

It wasn't a creature at all. On the sand stood a most handsome, slender man no longer encompassed in shiny steel.

Tatum approached his task with reverence and precision, standing each piece of discarded metal carefully against a boulder next to the opening of the tiny inlet. The creature-turned-human wore a white shirt with billowing sleeves and forest green fitted leggings, and now stood in his stocking feet as Tatum helped him remove his heavy boots—which also had been encased in metal. The master sat down on a rock and pulled his stockings off, then dug his toes into the cool, wet sand. He appeared to be extremely weary.

Tatum's mission accomplished, he left the newly-revealed man sitting on the rock and turned to his next assignment. Tatum knelt on the sand, opened the basket, removed a beautiful tapestry and spread it over the flat rock—her flat rock. Then he laid out a feast of wine, cheese, fruit and some coarse brown bread. From the bottom of the basket he retrieved a woven mat and carefully placed it on the ground. Then he lifted a large soft blanket from the basket and laid it over top. Back into his treasure trove he went and brought out a small tray and an array of tiny bottles, which he positioned next to the pallet he had just made.

So intent on watching the scenario unfolding before her, she hardly remembered to breathe. Although she did not wish to be discovered, she had become too mesmerized to take her leave.

"All is ready, Sir." He knelt at the head of the resting place he had prepared for his master.

The tall man removed his shirt and stepped over to the pallet, went down on his knees and slowly sank facedown onto the blanket. Once reclined, he turned his face to one side and closed his eyes.

Tatum reached for one of the bottles, opened it and poured a small amount of scented oil into his left hand. He rubbed his hands together and then placed one steady hand on the upper back of the reclining man. With his other hand he began to apply the oil. Then he moved both his hands to Sir's shoulders. She could see Sir's face. His eyes were closed and a look of relaxation and peace began to overtake him. Tatum began a soft, soothing chant as he continued Sir's massage. She could smell the fragrance of the potions. Breathing deeply now and no longer fearful, all her anxieties evaporated.

After a few minutes Tatum stood up, still chanting softly, went to the place where the water danced over the rocks and washed his hands, drying them on a small white linen cloth.

"Your meal is prepared and waiting, Sir," his only comment as he took his leave of the cove. The chanting became a hum and then only the sound of the waves kissing the rocks lingered, the prone man on the mat remaining silent. She thought he had fallen asleep, but in a few minutes, he rolled over on his back, and sat up. He sat serenely watching the sea raging and mellowing, raging and mellowing, then rose up and went to sit on the rock next to his supper.

She watched him sipping wine and eating grapes.

She leaned forward to peek around the rock to garner a better view. Suddenly her hand slipped off the wet rock and she gave a little gasp. He immediately turned in the direction of the splash—her direction. She feared she would be discovered. She quickly slipped under the surface of the sea and disappeared.

II. THE SHELL

He was weary. It had been a long day, a long year—a long life. Battles had been fought, some won, some lost, some—who knew, but now a time for peace had come, if only for himself. His life to this point had been doing what was asked of him, but now he grew tired and longed for his own adventures, his own accomplishments judged by his own scale.

His friend and manservant, Tatum, met him at the gate, dressed in his usual white attire. Today Tatum had donned his favorite battered hat and carried a large handled basket.

"Welcome home, Sir. Come, you have earned a respite." No argument—the master obeyed.

He followed, his armor clanking as they went along the path that wound down to the sea. The cool breeze made the tall grass dance as they passed, but he was too tired to notice. Only because of his trust of Tatum did he have the strength to go these last few steps.

Walking on the sandy beach in his heavy boots and metal attire made his body even more aware of his need for rest.

As they reached the cove, he felt a rush of relief. Cherish Cove had always been a place of great rejuvenation for him—tranquility beyond compare. He had not been to the cove for a number of years due to his commitment to duty. Now he would bask in the peaceful solitude of his beloved special place.

He stood on the sand within the confines of the tiny cove as if in a trance, doing little more than absorbing his surroundings, letting the place wash over him like the affection of a beautiful woman.

Little was said. Little needed to be said. Their mutual goal: Rest for the weary soldier.

Tatum skillfully removed the heavy armor and stood it at attention in the sand against a nearby boulder.

He laid the meal out on the flat rock at the edge of the water and prepared a place of rest in the warm sand.

"All is ready, Sir."

He gratefully sank to his knees on the soft pallet and then slowly fell forward. His angry muscles rejoiced at the touch and fragrance of the experience provided by Tatum. Tatum's soft chanting in his native tongue was soothing to his soul.

Tatum continued to chant as he left the cove simply saying, "Your meal is prepared and waiting, Sir."

He felt completely relaxed for the first time in months. He began to drift off, but knowing Tatum would have provided only his favorite tidbits, accompanied by the fact he hadn't eaten in a good many hours, he roused himself with thoughts of the tasty morsels.

He sat beside the large, flat rock sipping his wine, gazing out to sea, and meandering through the feast Tatum had left for him. He noticed the fare was spread out on a tapestry that had belonged to his grandmother.

Suddenly he heard a splash followed by what sounded like a gasp. He turned toward the direction of the sound, but observed only ripples in the water.

He finished his meal and sat looking out to sea for a bit before he let himself be lured back to the comfort of his pallet.

He awoke the next morning to find Tatum had removed last night's supper remnants, replacing it with a hardy breakfast. Fresh clothes and a large thick towel waited for him on the rock near the dancing waters. And next to the towel, rested a bar of rough oatmeal soap in a beautiful translucent shell.

He bathed, dressed and ate his breakfast, then spent the rest of the morning languishing on the beach. Alone for the first time in months, he dreaded the trek back up the path to deal with his homecoming responsibilities, but as the sun rose high to its mid-day position, he made his way back to civilization.

Later that evening Tatum came to his master's chambers to turn down his bed.

"Here is the shell you found today, Sir. It is exceptionally beautiful so I thought you would like to place it where you might enjoy it."

"The shell I found? I'm happy to have it, but I didn't find it. You put the soap in it."

"No, Sir. I put the soap on the rock beside your towel. I did not place it in the shell. I only saw the shell when I went to retrieve your belongings."

III. INTRODUCTIONS

Some weeks passed. Much to do. Business to tend to, old friends to see, demands he had not thought of when he dreamt of coming home. Tatum had taken fine care of things as best he could, but some things had to be dealt with in person by the landowner, far more things than he felt prepared to address, but address them he must, so he did.

"Sir, you have taken your leave of the drudgery of knighthood, perhaps the time has come for you to take your leave of the drudgery of everyday tasks."

"Right you are, Tatum. Pack me a lunch. I'm going to spend the day at Cherish Cove."

Less than an hour later he was enjoying the rush of the sea breeze on his face as he hurried down the ridge path, eager to revisit his place of contentment and revitalization.

When he entered the cove, he admonished himself for staying away so long. No place brought him such contentment.

He set the lunch basket on the flat rock and quickly removed his boots and stockings, rolled up his pant legs and eased his feet into the chilly ocean water. He turned to pick up a sock that had floated in behind him and was caught off guard by a wave that smacked him from behind. He laughed, but then he realized he was not laughing alone.

He looked around the inlet and there just beyond a far rock, peeking out from behind, gazed a lovely creature with long reddish tresses.

"Hello, Sir."

"Hello, m'lady. Are you enjoying this fine surf today?"

"I enjoy it everyday. Why do you come to my special place again?"

"Your special place? I've always thought of it as my special place, but if it has become your special place, I do so hope you find yourself willing to share it with me."

"Well, you don't come often, so I suppose I could grant your request. You do find the same peace I do when here."

Her comments took him aback. The only time he had been to the cove in years was the day of his homecoming a month ago. How did she know he found peace here in Cherish Cove?

"Would you like to share my meal with me?"

"Yes, the grapes please, the big ones like you had last time."

The splash, the gasp—it must have been her.

She swam around out beyond the big rock for a while and then slowly made her way to shore. As she came closer he realized she was nude, but she seemed quite comfortable with her state of undress, so he accepted her as presented. What man would complain of such a treat?

She perched herself on the edge of the flat rock and from time to time would reach for another grape as they conversed. She did not partake of the other fare or accept wine when offered.

The main topic of conversation: The sea and its inhabitants. She knew the sea as no one he had ever known before, although he felt unsure where fact and her imagination merged. She spoke of fish of many colors that shone like diamonds, fish you could actually see through and sea creatures that look like filmy pink pulsating pillows with ribbons streaming behind them as they swim.

He told her of his travels to faraway lands and how he would leave soon on an adventure of his own choosing in a small sailboat with no armor to encumber him. He would sail free with no battles to fight, except those against the elements.

"Sir, why were you so weary when you were here last time? Was it because of all the metal you were wearing?"

"I had been in battle for many days." He explained, adding that he was a knight and wore armor when he fought.

She didn't seem to understand the concept of war, or so he thought.

"Sir, is war like the plague?"

He was quiet for a moment. "Yes, I guess it is. I never thought of it that way, but there are many similarities. People suffer and are gone for no reason we can understand." Perhaps she understood war far better than most.

Their sharing returned to more gentle topics. Tranquil and at ease with each other, their time slipped by quickly. The day was ebbing, but neither appeared anxious to take their leave.

"Sir, will you come to the cove again soon?"

"Yes," was his quick response. "You may call me Robert."

"Isn't Sir your name?"

"No, my full title and name is Sir Robert Crawford, but those close to me call me Robert. I would like it if you called me Robert. What is your full title and name, m'lady?"

"I am called Nixisipish."

He tried several times to repeat it with her help, but to no avail. She told him he could give her a name of his choosing if he wished.

"My mother's name was Marion, but that name doesn't seem to suit you." He thought for a moment. "Because I didn't know this cove belonged to you, I named it Cherish Cove. May I call you Cherish?"

"What is meant by Cherish?"

"To hold dear, to treasure as precious as any find."

So it was decided, the lady would henceforth be called Cherish.

The sun began to set.

"Cherish, I must go."

Suddenly without any forethought, he reached out and put his hands in her hair, running it through his fingers. The sun glistened on the strands, bringing highlights of many colors to the shiny locks. She caught her breath. Had he offended her? No. Their eyes met and he had no doubt she felt happy to be near him. He realized he didn't want her to leave. He wanted the day in the cove to last and never end.

She touched his hand and smiled up at him.

"Cherish, the shell under the soap—did you leave it for me?"

She nodded.

Then she slipped from the flat rock and swam out to sea.

IV. A Fine Lady

The next morning Robert awoke much earlier than usual. He called out to Tatum, asking him to pack a basket for him.

"Be sure to put in some grapes, the large ones."

Tatum smiled at the thought of Sir Robert returning to the cove so soon. It obviously was good for him.

When Robert arrived at the cove, Cherish was nowhere to be seen. His heart sank, but within a few moments of his arrival, he saw her swimming toward him and watched as her glistening body came up out of the surf to greet him. He held out his hand to her.

"M'lady, it is indeed a pleasure to see you this fine morning."

She smiled up at him. "And you, Sir. And you, dear Robert."

They spent about an hour chatting and munching on the lunch Tatum had packed, even though it was far too early to truly call it lunch.

He played his concertina for her. She loved the happy tunes. He showed her where to place her fingers and she played a few notes. They both laughed at her attempt to make music on the instrument that was so foreign to her. They agreed she would never be a great musician.

They frolicked in the surf and sunk their toes into the wet sand. She had a fascination with toes, especially her own.

"When is your birthday, Cherish? When were you born?"

"I'm not sure," was her response.

He stared at her and then threw his head back and laughed. "My dear, you are of far too few years to have to hide your age from me."

Suddenly hurt appeared in her face and tears in her eyes. "Robert, I hide nothing from you. I tell you only the truth—always."

He gathered her in his arms and held her close, stroking the curve of her face. After a while, she gently moved away from him and settled herself on the moist sand.

"My parents loved me very much, but the plague came and took them away. I was very small. I remember celebrations for me, but I don't remember the exact dates or purpose. I do remember my mother would take me to the sea almost everyday, to a cove much like this one—she would play with my hair and tickle my toes and we would run in the surf."

"I'm sorry I hurt you, Cherish. Now I understand."

He encircled her with his arms again and they sat on the beach in peaceful silence.

When the time came for him to journey back up the path, she started packing the basket. Under the food, Robert had spread a lovely piece of silk cloth Tatum had provided. With all the food items tucked away in the basket, Cherish jumped up whipping their table covering from the flat-surfaced rock. She held the corners in her hands and reached high above her head, dancing around on the tiny beach and into the surf with the lovely forest greens and vibrant rusts billowing in the wind above her head. She ran back to Robert and stopped directly in front of him.

"Help me." It was the first time she had ever demanded anything of him and it was quite clear she expected him to comply.

He stood at attention, waiting for further direction as to nature of his task.

She handed him one corner of the brightly colored cloth, and then wound herself up in the fabric until she came back to face him. Then she took the corner from his hand and tucked it into her cleavage.

"Now I am a fine lady. I have a dress of silk," she stated proudly.

"Cherish, you ARE a fine lady and it has nothing to do with a piece of silk."

Her excitement evaporated and in its place, a glow consumed her entire face. Her eyes brimmed with tears.

"Now I understand my name. Please always cherish me as you do today."

"I will do my best."

He gently lifted her chin and bowed his head, kissing her cheek and then her lips. The magic had begun.

V. DISCOVERY

Each day they would meet at the cove. They never set a time, but when he appeared, she appeared. He never asked where she came from. For some reason he decided it best he did not know.

She would bring him shells and other treasures of the sea. He, having a deep affection for birds and feathers, especially black ones, would often surprise her with a newfound feather, but —he always brought her grapes, the big ones.

Their time was spent embracing the tender side of life and reaching for the stars.

Almost every time he came she would fashion for herself some flowing frock from the fabric Tatum sent along to spread under the food.

"Would you like me to buy you a dress?"

"No thank you, Robert. I have no need for dresses, but I enjoy the color and flow of these fantasy pieces. I can pretend I am a princess from a faraway land."

"You are my princess."

"Yes, I know, so as you can see the clothing I make from these pieces suits my needs exactly."

One day as they were sitting enjoying lunch, a noise startled her. She suspected an intruder, but he assured her it was only a falling rock finding a new resting place. He explained to her that no others would be coming to the cove. The property belonged to his estate and all of his staff knew they were never to come to his private place without permission.

She seemed quite relieved to hear their cove would remain only theirs, although she didn't seem to comprehend ownership of land, much less anyone having sole rights to the sea and its inlets.

Later that day they were cavorting on the beach.

"Cherish, catch me if you can," he yelled as he suddenly darted away from her heading out beyond the surf.

She giggled and watched him for a bit, enjoying his playfulness, but not terribly eager to catch him just yet.

He dove into a wave and she waited for him to bob up on the other side, but he didn't. Her eyes explored the horizon, but saw no Robert. Suddenly fear gripped her heart. She ran into the surf and dove down through a huge incoming wave, searching for him. Then she saw his legs dangling down from the surface above her. She swam quickly upward and was greeted by his laughter.

"I never told you. I can hold my breath for a very long time." He grinned at her, but she was not amused. She turned away from him and swam back toward the inlet.

He knew he had worried her needlessly and headed back to apologize.

As he stepped onto the shore, she turned to him, and to his surprise, he received a big smile.

"You can hold your breath for a long time?"

"Yes."

"A really, really, really long time?"

"Yes."

"Then come with me." She held out her hand and led him back into the surf. They went through the waves and started down—they swam side-by-side but she was the obvious navigator. He followed her lead. They suddenly took a sharp right downward turn and there directly in front of them appeared a dazzling light. The light seemed to be radiating from the fish—the fish of many colors, the fish that shone like diamonds, fish he could actually see through. And gently pulsating, floating ever so slowly just ahead were the translucent pink pillows with the ribbon streamers. Her imagination was reality.

When they came back to the surface, she stepped onto the beach and turned to him.

"Now you understand my world."

She was beaming, she was radiant, her skin glistened from the water droplets from the ocean, but her eyes glistened with tears of happiness.

His prank had become their blessing.

VI. DEPARTURE

His tiny seafaring vessel, *Black Feathers*, underwent many hours of intensive preparation in order to be ready for his upcoming solo sailing adventure.

He told her he needed to do this journey alone. This voyage would help him define the rest of his life. Having anyone, even her, along would prevent him from accomplishing his goal.

As the time drew near for his departure, it became clear to each of them that their parting would be most difficult.

The night before he left, Tatum prepared a very special repast for them with a generous helping of large grapes. They met at the cove at dusk and spent the night together lovingly intertwined in their secluded shelter from the world.

As he prepared to leave the cove, Cherish presented him with a soft leather bag. Inside—a handful of the tiniest shells of every color and shape one could imagine.

"There is one for each day you will be at sea. Each day select one and study it. You will feel my presence and love surrounding you. They tell of the sea—they tell of me."

Then she handed him a small wooden box.

"Open this one when you reach your halfway mark and are ready to return home to me."

He held her close.

"Cherish, please come to the dock to see me off."

"Robert, don't ask that of me. I can't bear to say goodbye to you in the presence of others."

He did not insist, but as he sailed out to sea, he hoped he would see her in the distance waving to him. No Cherish appeared.

VII. THE VOYAGE

A small vessel, *Black Feathers* took his full attention to stay on course. He navigated by the stars and the winds were kind to him, affording him good progress each day. He thought of Cherish and sometimes felt her presence, even though he knew she was miles away.

Tatum had prepared simple fare for the voyage. At first because the sea's motion made him ill, Robert ate bits of bread washed down with a few sips of water and nibbled on ginger root. The next couple of days his meals consisted of hard-boiled eggs and fruit—the large green grapes reminding him of his precious moments with Cherish. Soon he had been out to sea too long for fresh food to be safe—time to turn to preserved foods. He really missed the tasty meals Tatum usually prepared for him, but very much appreciated the hours Tatum had spent drying fruit and overseeing the cook's preparation of hard tack and jerky.

Tatum was his manservant, but also his friend. Because of the difference in their status, their relationship remained formal on the exterior, but both men were well aware of the value and trust each placed in the other. Tatum, the only person who knew of the existence of Cherish, knew she only ate grapes, was always sans clothing and that Robert had no idea where she lived or her status in life. Tatum was as accepting of her as Robert, telling his master and friend, "The value of a woman is not in her public status, but in her ability to love."

Sir Robert continued on with his solo adventure knowing there were two people in his world in total support of his quest.

Each day he retrieved a tiny shell from the soft drawstring bag Cherish had given him. He would hold the shell up to the light, view its kaleidoscope of color, carefully inspecting each facet. Each one shared a dimension unlike any of the others, but somehow each one seemed to bring Cherish closer to his heart. He missed her, but treasured this time to explore the sea and himself, appreciating that she understood his need to take this self-exploring journey.

The days passed. He ran with the dolphins, he reached with the winds, he read his books, played his concertina and navigated by the stars. The days passed, each one sharing a dimension unlike any of the days before. Days and shells—all were precious.

The seas were becalmed. Lazing on the deck he waited and waited AND waited for wind. He thought he heard a splash and a little giggle, but realized it was only his wishful thinking. He rolled over on his stomach and rested his head on his crossed arms, thinking back to that first day in the cove when he heard the little gasp and splash, but was unaware of her presence. Who would have known such a miniscule incident would be the start of such a loving relationship.

The winds picked up and he again set sail for his destination, but the essence of Cherish wafted over him like the gentle breeze of Cherish Cove. She seemed to be granting him peace and rejuvenation from far, far away. Thoughts of her tugged at his heart, but also brought smiles to his face.

He had been at sea for two weeks. He awoke to a plop-plop sound. Up on deck he saw shiny flying fish bombarding the deck from all directions. Scurrying around, he scooped them up, returning them to the sea—a lighthearted start to his day.

As the days progressed, he felt good with his venture, but longed to hold Cherish close and tell her of his love for her. Even though lonely without her, he felt jubilant because the trek was giving him the resolve and direction he needed to seek the simple life he knew held true value for him. He had wealth, he was a notable knight, honored in his country as a gentleman, but what he wanted most—simplicity, peace and love.

He woke up one night not understanding why. The boat was behaving normally; the seas were acceptable. What woke him? He went up top and spotted a bright light shining down on the port side of the boat. The clouds extinguished the moonlight. Where was the light coming from and what was it pointing to? He looked where the beacon pointed and observed a shroud that was about to come undone. He went below, retrieved his implements and quickly averted the impending failure. The beacon had disappeared. He must have dreamt it. He proceeded on his way.

Robert felt euphoric when he arrived at his halfway point. He had accomplished his goal. Rewarding for sure, plus it had served its purpose. He proved he could do it; he had spent time alone with his thoughts and now knew the course he wanted to set for the rest of his life.

Ready to head home, he retrieved the small wooden box Cherish had presented to him that last night in the cove.

He sat on his bunk and unwrapped her gift. Inside the box lay a smattering of tiny shells and in the center rested a figurine—a bronze mermaid with a swooping green tail. Her hair had a reddish cast. He smiled. The mermaid reminded him of Cherish. Everything reminded him of Cherish. He turned *Black Feathers* toward home. Home was Cherish.

As he drew close enough to see land, he searched the shore for her, but he was too far away to distinguish people. He hoped she would be waiting on the dock for him.

Suddenly he heard a splash and a giggle. In the water off the port side swam his Cherish.

"Hello, Kind Sir. Do you need to do the rest of your voyage solo or may I come aboard?"

"You, Sweet Lady, are most welcome aboard."

He helped her onboard and they headed directly for the cove. He anchored and they swam ashore together.

He was home!

VIII. THINGS OF THE PAST

"Tatum, please bring me the trunk containing my mother's things."

"Yes Sir." Tatum hurried away and returned a short time later placing the trunk at Robert's feet. Tatum opened the trunk, then left the room, closing the door behind him.

Robert carefully lifted the various treasured items from the trunk until he came to what he sought, a dress fashioned from the finest Chinese silk. The color of gemstones, the swirled pattern resembled the sea. The dress, fitted at the waist, had a high neck. A pair of burgundy high-button shoes, shoes made of the softest kid leather, nestled beneath the dress. Tucked neatly inside one shoe—a pair of black silk stockings.

He placed the shoes and stockings in the bottom of a basket he found in the pantry, then carefully folded the dress and laid it on top.

He sat for a moment staring at the basket. His mother, like Cherish, had been a woman of small stature. Would Cherish treasure these items as much as he did? Somehow in his heart he knew she would and he wanted her to have them.

He went to the chest under the window and opened the drawer, removing a small black velvet pouch. He poured the contents of the pouch into his hand—a lovely polished, slightly curved, wooden hair clip he had spent hours crafting. He had created a woven nautical knot to adorn the surface of the clip. The clip would be perfect in her hair—her hair that he loved so much.

He placed the clip back in its pouch and slipped it under the dress in the basket. He covered the contents of the basket with his grandmother's tapestry. Picking up the basket, he headed for the cove. He forgot the lunch Tatum had prepared for them. A ways down the path, Tatum came on the run.

"Sir, your lady will be hungry."

Robert smiled, accepted the lunch basket and continued on down the trail, a basket in each hand.

"Hello, Sweet Lady."

"Hello, Kind Sir."

The day was warm, the breeze relaxing, lunch refreshing and conversation easy. Toes were tickled and stuck in the cool sand.

"I have something for you, something I hope you will enjoy."

"Did you bring me a feather?"

"No, not today."

He stood up and reached for her hand. She took his hand and rose to her feet, standing in front of him. He placed the basket of gifts on the flat rock and removed the tapestry covering.

He had a planned speech, telling her how important the items in the basket were to him, but somehow the words would not come.

He lifted the dress from the basket and heard a little gasp. He held the dress up in front of Cherish. She wrapped her arms around the dress, holding it close to her body and danced around the beach as if at the finest ballroom in the land.

She was obviously elated with the gown.

Next came the shoes and stockings.

He handed them to her. She took them with a puzzled look on her face. She sat them down on the flat rock next to the basket and, still holding the dress close to her, stooped down to inspect the shoes—from a distance. Finally she stood up and turned to Robert.

"They will do fine. I like them. They are very pretty. Thank you for these lovely gifts."

"They belonged to my mother."

"I know," was her quiet reply.

They were both silent for a moment.

"I have something else for you. Something I made for you."

"You made me something? When did you have time to make me something?" She knew between the demands of his household and property, plus the time he spent with her at the cove, he had little time left even for sleeping.

"I made time."

He reached into the basket once more and brought out the small velvet pouch. He laid it in her hand. She looked up at him and smiled. She gently opened the drawstring on the pouch and removed the hair clasp. She became very quiet as she drew the outline of the woven knot with her fingers. She handed it to him and turned her back to him so he could put the adornment in her hair.

After the clip was secured in her shiny locks, she turned back to him.

"I love it. I love you."

They stood for a few moments on the beach. Then she picked up the shoes and took them with her dress behind the boulder at the edge of the cove. After a few minutes, she came back into view. The dress fit perfectly, as did the shoes. She curtsied and said, "May I have this dance, Kind Sir?" He reached for her and they waltzed on the sand to music provided by the sea.

IX. THE PARTY

Days became weeks, time brought them closer and their love grew. He still had no idea where she lived or how she came to appear each time he came to the cove. He only knew he ached for her when they were apart. Their time at the cove brought him to the realization that he wanted to spend the rest of his life with this woman.

"Cherish, there is a party being given in my honor. I want you there by my side. Will you come?"

"Yes, I will come."

"I will go to the city and bring back some silks from China. You may choose the one you like best and I will have a fine gown made for you. One of your very own in any style you choose."

"I have a dress. I want to wear my dress, the dress you gave me that belonged to your mother. Is it not appropriate?"

"Yes, it would be perfect for the occasion, but wouldn't you rather have a new dress?"

"No, I like my dress. It makes me feel cherished."

"YOU are cherished."

"Then it is obviously the right dress for me to wear. Will you fetch me here?"

"Is that what you want?"

"Yes, please."

The day of the party arrived. Robert dressed early, donning his best clan kilt, cut-away jacket with the hammered silver buttons and Crawford tartan—and then began pacing. Tatum smiled, but remained silent. He knew he would have occasion to finally meet the lady who brought his master such happiness. He would be nearby all evening in case Sir Robert needed him.

Robert told Tatum to proceed to the banquet; he would be along shortly.

The sun was waning. He must hurry. He wanted to bring Cherish back up the path before it got dark. This evening he would insist on returning her to her home. It was only proper.

As he approached the entrance to the cove, Cherish appeared. She looked radiant. The dress suited her fair skin perfectly. She had her hair done up with ringlets wisping down from her hairclip. She held her shoes and stockings in her hand.

She gently kissed his lips, turned him around and around exclaiming how handsome he looked, and then led him up out of the sand to a rock beside the path. Taking her place on the rock, she lifted her skirt, dusted the sand particles off her feet, taking a moment to smile at her toes. She pulled a stocking onto each foot. As she reached for a shoe, Robert gingerly whisked it out of her reach.

"May I do the honors, m'lady?"

"But of course, Kind Sir."

After the shoes were in place, she stood in front of him for inspection.

"Hmmmm, something is missing."

"What?" came her startled reply. What had she forgotten?

He took her by the shoulders and turned her around with her back to him. He reached in his pocket and took out a strand of creamy pearls and draped them around her neck. Her fingers came up and stroked the smoothness of the pearls and she smiled. He connected the clasp, turned her around to face him, kissed her on the cheek, and offering his arm they headed up the path to the carriage waiting at the top of the hill.

As they reached the crest of the hill, he felt her stiffen. He looked down at her. He thought he saw fear in her eyes, but then she looked up at him, smiled and stepped up into the waiting carriage appearing not to have a care in the world.

When they arrived at the party, the other guests were perceptibly taken aback to see Sir Robert with a lady on his arm, but even more evident was their supportive acceptance of the situation.

Many high-ranking officials and their ladies attended the large, formal party. If Robert had any concerns as to how Cherish would present herself in a social situation of this magnitude, his fears were quickly laid to rest. If uncomfortable, she certainly didn't appear so. The men loved her, going out of their way to charm her, but it seemed THEY were the ones who fell under her spell. The women were curious, but polite, and kept their inquiries to trivial things. Cherish provided vague but appropriate and polite answers.

Tatum stood at attention off to one side most of the evening. At one point, Sir Robert made a point of finding time to introduce him to Cherish.

When introduced, Cherish exclaimed, "I am very happy to meet you. Thank you for providing me such a generous supply of the delicious grapes—the big, green ones."

Robert was a bit startled she would make such a revealing statement. Tatum was disarmed. Truth was the way of Cherish.

Cherish partook of the delicious cuisine as if it were her norm. She sipped a glass of wine and joined in the various toasts. She conversed and laughed with the other guests. She and Robert danced together. No one could have recognized this as a social milestone for this elegant lady.

After settling themselves in the carriage for the ride home, Robert asked Cherish if she had enjoyed the evening.

"I loved dancing with you. I pretended we were dancing on the sand in the cove under the stars."

She took his hand and pressed it to her cheek. Nothing more was said about the party.

As they rode through the countryside the moon shone brightly, creating a silhouette of the trees, which made for a lovely late-night romantic scenario.

"Where do you live, Cherish? I want to drop you at home this evening. It is the proper thing to do and it is very late."

"My home is with you."

"Please, Cherish."

"The moon is perfect and I want to go to the cove to say goodnight."

Obviously she was not going to give him a destination other than the cove. The carriage driver dropped them off at the crest of the hill and they walked down the moonlit path arm-in-arm. When they reached the edge of the sand, Cherish plopped down on a rock and extended her right foot, pulling up her skirt.

"Do your duty, Kind Sir."

Robert dropped to one knee and removed her shoe and stocking. Then she extended her left foot. With both shoes removed, she took him by the hand and they entered the cove. She had him remove the necklace and put it back in his pocket. Then she began to undress him. She slipped out of her dress and they made love on the beach.

Toward daylight, she woke him and told him he had to go home. She handed him his clothes. He dressed and left the cove with her sitting on the sand smiling at him.

He still had no idea where she lived.

X. REVELATIONS

Robert entered the cove carrying the lunch basket provided by Tatum, complete with a most generous serving of grapes.

Robert was surprised to see Cherish sitting on the flat rock. Never before had she been the first to arrive.

"Are you eager to see me?" he asked laughingly.

"Always."

"Are you hungry?"

"ALWAYS!"

He ate cheese, dark brown bread and cold roasted chicken while he sipped his wine. She nibbled on her grapes.

She sat dipping her toes in and out of the water, intently watching the movement, as if she were a long way away.

"I believe my mother may have been a mermaid," she announced calmly.

"Of course she was. My mother was an angel and yours a mermaid."

"I'm serious."

"Cherish, what would make you think your mother was a mermaid?"

"Because I am a mermaid."

Robert stared at her in silence.

Cherish remained quiet for a long time. Then she let out a long breath and began her saga.

"As you know my mother took me to the beach every day. When my parents died, I was left alone. Many of the townspeople became very sick. Many died. There was no one to take care of me. I was hungry and dirty. The house was empty. I walked down to the sea, to the cove where my mother took me everyday. I had no one to love me—no one who cared about me remained. I sat by the sea and put my feet in the water, then the sea came up over my legs—." Her voice trailed off.

Robert waited.

Cherish wiggled herself further into the water. "Look," she commanded.

As the water lapped up onto her legs, their shape began to change. Her toes began to disappear, her legs joined and little feather-like things began to flutter under the water. She was growing a tail and fins. Robert was stunned. He couldn't move; he couldn't speak.

"I'm sorry, Robert, I didn't know how to tell you. I didn't want to lose you."

She continued—

"When I was little and alone, I went to the sea and the sea became my home. I had no one onshore I could trust or love, no one who was kind or cared for me. I stayed in the sea living with the sea creatures until the day I saw you and Tatum in the cove. You were kind to me so I was able to come to shore in human form. Because of you, I can interact with other human beings."

"Cherish, I love you, I want you to be my wife—I can't live in the sea with a mermaid."

Robert stood up and strode from the cove, up the path into his house, straight to his chambers and closed the door, throwing the bolt behind him.

He lay in the dark staring at the ceiling. He loves this woman and now this woman turns out to be a mermaid. He would wake up soon and it would all be a dream, except he didn't want it all to be a dream, just the mermaid part.

Sleep would not come. He stared at the ceiling some more.

XI. Acceptance

"Sir, I made you a basket meal to take to the beach. And of course, I put in a goodly portion of grapes."

"I won't be going to the beach today."

Tatum could tell it best not to ask why, but he didn't like the sound of his master's voice.

Weeks went by and Sir Robert did not go back to the cove.

"Sir, you have to eat something. You are losing weight. You need sleep. You can't pace all night and remain healthy."

"I'll be fine."

The door sprang open and Tatum rushed into the room.

"Sir, come quickly. Cherish is ill."

"What are you talking about?"

"I was worried about you, Sir. I know I didn't have the right to go, but I went to the cove with the hope of talking to Cherish to see if she would come to see you. When I got there I found her lying on the sand. I think she is dying."

Robert jumped to his feet and rushed out the door, and down the path to the cove. There on the flat rock, half in and half out of the water, lay Cherish—Mermaid Cherish, her face gaunt, her eyes sunken, her body lifeless.

Robert knelt beside her and picked her up in his arms, holding her close to his chest.

"Cherish, I love you, I love you so much."

"But not as a mermaid," came her faint response.

"Actually, my Sweet Lady, I love you anyway you are!"

Tatum was standing beside Robert holding Robert's grandmother's tapestry.

Robert said, "She's a mermaid."

Tatum replied, "Yes Sir, and a fine one she is. Now we just need to give her some care and love—and grapes, and she will be well soon. Let's wrap her up and take her home where she can rest."

XII. PLANS

"How are you feeling this fine morning, my Sweet Lady?"

"Fine. How are you feeling, my Kind Sir?"

"Very fit, thank you."

In the days since Tatum had discovered Cherish suffering on the beach, the focus had been on getting her well, both of them regaining their strength and well-being, and simply loving each other.

"Cherish, I need to know how this works."

"It's really quite simple Robert. As I said, I believe my mother was a mermaid, but only because after I was left with no one to love me, I emerged as a mermaid and went to live in the sea where I felt safe. I never saw my mother in a mermaid state. My father loved her dearly. My mother lived a very happy life. I believe she was a mermaid, but her need to be a mermaid never equaled her need to be with my father and me.

I felt safe as a resident of the sea, but now I find the sea lonely because you are not there. I love the sea, but I love you more. I can be an appropriate land person because of you. I will always hope we can go to the sea and live near the sea, but my place is with you. I love being by your side. I love touching you. I love looking at you. I love being with you. I love you."

"And I love you. My voyage was to help me decide the life I want for the rest of my life. I no longer want the prestige of knighthood—the social obligations, the big estate, the large staff. I want a simple life.

What would you say to our building a small cottage here near the cove? The land I own will support us well. Tatum can have the big house and the staff and the stature. He has earned it. He can oversee the stock and the planting of the land—all we will need is a small stipend. We can do what we enjoy—we can enjoy each other. We can play music and eat grapes and make love on a pallet on the beach."

"Sounds delicious."

"I do need to tell you one more thing though—because you should know," she said.

"Oh no—" He staved himself for what was to come.

"Remember when you were on your voyage? I know you wanted to be alone, but the day you heard the splash and the giggle, I confess, I didn't respect your wishes. And when those flying fish jumped onboard. They didn't jump. I tossed them on the deck because I thought you needed a smile. I didn't mean to intrude; I just needed to see you. I made a mistake. Please forgive me."

"So you made the light shine on the shroud."

"The shroud?"

"So I would know to fix it. I woke up for no reason and went up top and the shroud was coming undone—I saw a light."

"No, Robert, I had nothing to do with the light or the shroud. I felt I should leave you be to accomplish your journey the way you needed to, so I turned back. Whatever happened with the shroud was due to your own instincts. I had nothing to do with it, unless hoping and praying you would be safe is a factor. Do you forgive me?"

"Yes, I forgive you. You didn't interfere and you did bring me a smile, but you brought me smiles long after you took your leave. You were not physically onboard, but you were my constant companion—and you will be for the rest of my life."

"I love you, Kind Sir."

"And I love you, my Sweet Mermaid."

Tatum packed them a lunch, complete with grapes, the large green ones, and they walked down the path to Cherish Cove.

> Your true halfway present
> sits at home
> Awaiting your return—
> As I do.
> I love you, Kind Sir.

Photo Credits

The following photos are courtesy of:

Latitude 38 Magazine/LaDonna Bubak
- Front Cover Photo
- Out The Gate

www.norcalsailing.com

Christine Weaver/Jonathan Gutoff
- Robert and *Black Feathers* After Anchoring
- *Sparky* Finishes The TransPac

Winston Crawford
- Back Cover Photo
- *Black Feathers* Fully Loaded
- Sailing from The Corinthian Yacht Club
- Winston, Jeanne, Robert, Kendra and Sarah
- Tree Time
- TransPac Skippers Cheer *Sparky's* Anticipated Arrival
- Ruben Aboard *Sparky* in Hanalei Bay
- Robert and Jonathan
- Ready to Sail
- Goodbye Embrace
- Jeanne on The Bluffs
- Coming Ashore
- A Warm Embrace
- Hanalei Bay from The Princeville Bluffs
- Author Photo: Jeanne and Robert

Photos by Authors: Robert Crawford/Jeanne Crawford
- Smooth Sailing
- Glassy Smooth Sea
- Early Morning
- *Black Feathers'* Spinnaker

Diagrams by Robert Crawford

References and Resources

BOOKS

1) <u>Cal 20 Association Owners Manual</u> 1989 (available free online) www.ewind.com/user/sfca1120/

2) <u>D.D.D.B.—Drag Device Data Base—Using Parachutes, Sea Anchors and Drogues to Cope with Heavy Weather</u> 1990 by Victor Shane, Para-Anchors International (publisher)

3) <u>Emergency Navigation</u> 1986 by David Burch, International Marine Publishing

4) <u>Experiment in Survival</u> 2001 by George Sigler, Vero Technical Support (Publishers)

5) <u>Monitor Windvane Manual</u> by Scanmar International, www.selfsteer.com 432 South 1st Street, Point Richmond, CA 94804

6) <u>One Hand for Yourself, One for the Ship</u> 1982 by Tristan Jones, Sheridan House Publishers

7) <u>Pacific Cup Handbook—A Guide to Preparing for the West Marine Pacific Cup</u> 1992 by Jim and Sue Coreman, Available through www.pacificcup.org

8) <u>Storm Tactics Handbook</u> 1996 by Lin and Larry Pardey, Pardey Books

9) <u>Twenty Small Sailboats to Take You Anywhere</u> 1999 by John Vigor

10) <u>Trekka Round the World</u> 1999 (1963) by John Guzzwell, Fine Edge Productions

EQUIPMENT

1) Automatic Identification System (AIS), Nasa Marine AIS Radar by Nasa Marine Instruments, marketed by Si-Tex Marine Electronics www.si-tex.com

2) Collision Avoidance Radar Detector (CARD) by Survival Safety Engineering, Inc., www.survivalsafety.com P.O. Box 581, Oak Grove, MO 64075 1-888-475-5364

3) Cal 20 (and other classic plastic small boats) hardware, spares and rigging, Steve Seal's Spars and Rigging www.sealsspar.com

4) Dome (18" diameter X 9" high) clear acrylic by Global Plastics Services International, www.domes.bz 150 Route 1, St. Stephen, New Brunswick E3L3X4, 1-877-433-4568

5) Masthead strobe/anchor light (Model #314A) Pyramid Technologies Industrial, LLC, www.pyramidtech.com 48 Elm Street, Meriden, CT 06450 1-877-453-8669

OTHER RESOURCES

1) Boat Shipping: Load-A-Boat (Worldwide Boat Transport) www.loadaboat.com 1-877-277-2628

2) Singlehanded TransPac Seminars—held annually in the San Francisco Bay area beginning approximately eight months prior to the TransPac start. www.sfbaysss.org

WEBSITES

1) Cal 20 Association (for Cal 20 news and forum discussions) www.cal20.com

2) Pacific Cup www.pacificcup.org

3) Singlehanded Sailing Society (Home page updating events, race archives of past TransPacs, TransPac race requirements, rules, etc., plus discussion forums) www.sfbaysss.org

4) Weather Fax Information (To find weather fax information from the National Weather Service Radiofax Charts for the North Pacific from Pt. Reyes Station) www.weather.noaa.gov/fax/ptreyes.shtml

From the above site, consider these charts in particular:

- **Wind/Wave charts (shows wind strengths)**

48 hour Wind/Wave Forecast VT00Z 20N-70N 115W-135E (GIF)

- **Surface charts (shows highs and lows plus isobars)**

48 hour Surface Forecast VT00Z 30N-70N 115W-135E (GIF)

About The Authors

Robert Crawford has been a member of the Singlehanded Sailing Society since 1991. That year he purchased an Ericson 32 and began sailing singlehanded events. In 1994 Robert participated in the Singlehanded TransPac and became enchanted with the race. Alarmed by the increasing complexity and cost of the TransPac boats over the last several years, he felt it would be worthwhile to prepare one of the most common of small boats for the race to ensure the TransPac is a race still open to the common man with a dream. He found, indeed, it is!

Robert, a retired dentist, from the San Francisco Bay area now resides with his wife, Jeanne, in the mountains near Yosemite. *Black Feathers,* berthed in San Francisco, is always anxious for her next adventure.

Jeanne and Robert

—◆—

Jeanne Crawford is NOT a sailor and never will be. She experienced the TransPac adventure from the support person's perspective—on dry land. In addition, she gained a new family due to her involvement with the planning and events portion of the race. Always an avid writer, she enjoyed the composition of this book and weaving the various aspects of the story together.

Jeanne retired from Intel Corporation in Folsom, CA in December 2005 after a varied career that included being an event coordinator for the Towe Auto Museum, as well as the owner-operator of Navlet's Flower Shop, both in Sacramento, CA.

Now she writes. In addition to co-authoring *Black Feathers—A Pocket Racer Sails The Singlehanded TransPac*, she also wrote *The Kindness of Strangers*.